CONTENTS

ACKNOWLEDGEMENTS

The research reported in this book was conducted as part of a project entitled 'Changing sites of education: educational media and the domestic market', funded by the Economic and Social Research Council (grant no: R000238218). We would like to thank the following people for their guidance and support: Pam Dix from Islington Education Library Services, Julian Sefton-Green from Weekend Arts College, Jacquie Disney from Parents Information Network and Claire Drinkwater from the Institute of Education. We would also like to thank Wendy Allison for giving us access to archive materials.

Special thanks are due to the four London schools which distributed the questionnaires on our behalf and to the families who took part in the research, either by completing questionnaires or participating in interviews. We are particularly grateful to Steve Archer for his help in organizing the survey of parents. We are also indebted to all the publishers, software producers and retailers who took part in interviews.

CHANGING SITES OF LEARNING

The home, the school and the marketplace

'The parent is the child's first teacher.' This familiar platitude both expresses a truth and registers a problem. Parents clearly do teach their children, both implicitly and explicitly – and probably to a much greater degree than they might overtly recognize. As children enter school, the primary responsibility for education shifts to the state; yet parents are still increasingly urged to join a 'partnership' with teachers. Parental involvement in supporting children's learning is widely seen as a pre-requisite for educational success.

However, a parent is not the same thing as a teacher, just as a home is not the same thing as a school. Children are (as another platitude would have it) 'learning all the time'. Yet this is not to say that they are always students or pupils – that is, subjects of a specifically educational process. And learning is not coterminous with teaching: you can learn without being taught – just as you can be taught without necessarily learning anything. So where do we draw the line here?

This book is about learning in the home – and, more specifically, about the role that 'educational' media such as books, magazines and software can play in that process. The inverted commas we use here are not simply a result of academic caution. Considering how such media are produced, designed and used necessarily invokes fundamental questions about what *counts* as education. In a sense, this book is about the boundaries between different sites and forms of learning – between the home and the school, between work and play, between education and entertainment, between teaching and parenting, and between the public and the private spheres. These are boundaries that are increasingly being crossed and blurred, with consequences that are both productive and problematic.

In some respects, the phenomena we describe are nothing new. Informational and educational texts for children have existed at least since the Renaissance; and such texts have always been designed for use in the home as well as in schools. As Carmen Luke (1989) and others have pointed out, the modern 'invention' of childhood was accompanied by a whole range of pedagogic initiatives aimed at parents and children, including primers, advice manuals, instructional books and playthings. Ellen Seiter (1993) and Stephen Kline (1993) have traced the growth of the toy market in the early twentieth century, which was partly founded on beliefs about the developmental and educational value of play. More recently, we can both remember being bought encyclopaedias, information books and educational magazines by our parents; and, of course, a subsector of the publishing and media industries has always subsisted on appealing to parents' educational aspirations for their children. Yet as the sets of encyclopaedias countless children were bought in previous decades have now been largely superseded by their online versions, there has also been a significant expansion in the market for home education in various forms.

In order to understand the reasons for this, we need to trace the emerging connections between government policy on education and the changing operations of the commercial market. It is these connections and their consequences that are central to the phenomena we analyse in this book. We therefore need to begin with a brief – and perhaps necessarily contentious – sketch of the big picture.

Education, education, education

Tony Blair's now familiar declaration of his three main priorities in the run-up to the general election in 1997 serves as an index of what has become a growing preoccupation within contemporary British culture. Education, Blair asserted, 'will be the passion of my government'. 'Levering up standards and achievement' in schools and banishing 'the deadening culture of low expectations' would, he argued, be the key to reversing Britain's economic and social decline. And through a variety of policies, including the reintroduction of grouping by 'ability', the extension of 'parental choice' and the use of new technology, Labour promised to 'open up opportunities for all children', regardless of their background (Blair 1997: 159–76).

Whether or not one believes that Labour has delivered on these promises – and indeed, whether or not it ever could – it is important to see this new emphasis on education within a broader context. In an era in which state welfare provision is increasingly seen to be problematic, education remains one of the more obviously legitimate areas for government intervention. Educational initiatives may be affordable and visible in a way that other attempts to address longer-term structural issues such as poverty and inequality are not. Meanwhile, education has also been one of the key areas in which central government has sought to limit the autonomy of local government, and thereby to centralize power.

More broadly – and despite the evidence of decades of sociological research – education is still seen in Britain in fundamentally meritocratic terms. It offers the promise of upward mobility in a time where inequalities of income have in fact continued to grow. In the international arena, it is charged with producing a well-trained workforce, and thereby with advancing Britain's competitive position as a nation. And in more local terms, it is increasingly seen to be responsible for the moral regulation of children – for keeping idle hands busy, and thereby preventing delinquency and crime. Both pragmatically and philosophically, therefore, education appears to provide solutions to many of the perceived problems of contemporary Britain.

The current preoccupation with education is most obviously manifested in the emphasis on 'standards and achievement' that Labour inherited more or less unchanged from the Conservatives. National testing and the publication of league tables of schools' examination results have generated a growing culture of competition, both among children and among parents. The government's renewed emphasis on homework – which we discuss in more detail in Chapter 2 – reflects an educational 'work ethic' that is not expected to let up once children walk out of the classroom door. Indeed, early in 2000, the government was proposing to lengthen the school day by an hour and half: children were to work an eight-hour day, as compared with the average five and half hours of their European peers.

In this context, learning and leisure have become increasingly difficult to separate. For adults, 'lifelong learning' and the growing emphasis on qualifications and educational credentials are turning both the workplace and the home into new sites for education (Edwards 1997). Meanwhile, leisure providers – sports centres, museums, youth clubs, community arts projects – are also increasingly charged with educational responsibilities, and required to justify themselves in these terms. The government's controversial Millennium Dome in London is perhaps the most emblematic example of this penetration of education into the sphere of leisure (Buckingham 2000a). In the process, the boundaries between education and entertainment – between 'learning' and 'fun' – have become increasingly problematic.

Money, money, money

Many of the developments identified above are driven by – or at least inextricably connected with – the work of commercial corporations.

Private companies have increasingly taken over areas of leisure and cultural provision that were previously the responsibility of national or local government; and many public organizations (not least in the field of education) have reorganized themselves on commercial principles. In the process, the boundaries between the public and the private have become ever more blurred – a tendency that is now actively promoted by a government whose solution to most social problems lies in the development of so-called 'public–private partnerships'.

This growing colonization of the public sphere by commercial forces is, of course, a function of the global expansion of capitalism in the post-war era, particularly following the demise of the USSR. Right across the developed world, the state has effectively retreated, leaving the provision and management of many key services to the market. Deregulation, both nationally and in terms of international trade, has been seen as essential to economic growth and prosperity; and nation-states themselves are increasingly unable or unwilling to control the activities of global corporations.

In this context, the provision of public services has increasingly been left to market forces. State-provided welfare is regarded not as an entitlement for all but merely as a 'safety net' for those most at risk; while cultural institutions such as museums and public libraries have either been forced into decline or required to levy charges which themselves result in falling attendance. While Labour has begun to reverse some of these developments, it has vigorously pursued others; and one of its earliest demonstrations of its commitment to education was its abolition of grants for university students – a process whose consequences in terms of reducing access to education for disadvantaged groups are now beginning to emerge.

These developments impact on schools in several ways. Most obviously, we are now seeing a gradual privatization of schooling – a trend that is much further advanced in the USA (Bridges and McLaughlin 1994; Buckingham 1997; Kenway and Bullen 2001). This is most spectacularly the case in the growing number of schools and local education authorities whose management has been handed over to commercial companies; yet it is also apparent in other government initiatives such as Education Action Zones and specialist schools, which are required to attract commercial sponsorship. Corporations are increasingly keen to be seen as 'sponsors' of schools, and to provide 'free' equipment, curriculum materials and e-mail accounts. Meanwhile, the devolution of school funding from local authorities to individual schools – the so-called Local Management of Schools – means that schools are now much more independent consumers of commercial goods and services than they were in the past.

In this situation, private corporations large and small have become increasingly interested in the education market. This development is most apparent in the area of information and communication technologies, where Microsoft, Apple, ICL and others compete to be seen as sponsors of the latest educational initiatives. Yet even in more traditional areas such as book publishing, there is intense competition to corner the market: the publisher Heinemann, for example, enjoys a monopoly on providing resources for one of the main English syllabuses, while other publishers are competing to make textbook deals with examination boards (which are, of course, profitable private companies in their own right).

Meanwhile, companies with interests in very different areas, such as supermarkets, are increasingly keen to promote themselves as sponsors of education. As we shall see in more detail in Chapter 4, Tesco's highly successful Computers in Schools scheme is a key aspect of its promotional strategy in what has become a highly competitive sector of retailing; while Rupert Murdoch's News International has a parallel Books in Schools scheme in association with Walkers potato crisps. These initiatives reflect the general ascendancy of 'promotional culture' (Wernick, 1991); and in this context, education has a strong 'feel-good factor' that renders it particularly valuable as a means of defining and promoting a given brand. Here again, resources from the private sphere – in this case, the parents who actually shop at Tesco and buy Walkers crisps – are increasingly being used to supplement shortfalls in public provision.

Bringing learning home

For several reasons, the home has been a key target for these new educational initiatives. Government policy has increasingly sought to harness 'parent power' – employing a consumerist rhetoric which has again been taken over wholesale from the Conservatives. For both the main political parties, 'parent power' has been seen as a means of wresting control of education from an 'education establishment' that is still considered dangerously radical, if not merely recalcitrant and resistant to change. Thus, there has been a growing emphasis on parental choice and involvement in schooling (David *et al.* 1993); while national testing and school league tables have purported to provide parents with the information they need to identify the 'best' school for their children. 'Home–school agreements' have attempted to place the 'partnership' between parents and schools on a quasi-legal basis, by specifying parents' responsibility for supporting the practices of the school. New institutions and organizational structures have emerged which reconfigure the boundaries between home and school, such as 'homework clubs' and 'breakfast clubs' (which are aimed at both parents and children); and there is a growing movement for home schooling. In New Labour's first term, this new emphasis was reflected in a series of papers and publications from the Department for Education and Employment (DfEE), such as the white paper *Excellence in Schools* (1997), the green paper *The Learning Age* (1998b), the

DfEE consultation paper *Meeting the Childcare Challenge* (1998c) and the Home Office document *Supporting Families* (1998).

Meanwhile, there is growing interest in what is termed 'family learning' – that is, 'planned activity in which parents and children come together, to work and learn collaboratively' (Office for Standards in Education (Ofsted) 2000: 5). To date, much of the work in this field has been in the area of early literacy, for example via projects such as Bookstart and Books for Babies, which aim to provide books for families in disadvantaged communities (Millard and Marsh 2001). One practical guide to such work is symptomatically entitled *Baby Power: Give Your Child Real Learning Power* (Wade and Moore 2000). The family learning movement has been strongly promoted by influential think-tanks such as Demos (Alexander 1997) and the Campaign for Learning (2000), and by charities such as Education Extra and Parentline; and it is supported by a whole range of new sources of government funding. For advocates of family learning, the influence of 'good parenting' is seen to override that of material deprivation and social inequality; and family learning is thus held out as the solution to crime, community decay, family breakdown and a whole range of other social ills (Alexander 1997). Nevertheless, it is clear that parents are not always to be trusted in this respect. Parents are, in Alexander's (1997: 13) terms, 'lead agents in the care and education of children'; but many will be in need of remedial 'parenting education' if they are to fulfil these responsibilities adequately.

As we shall indicate in more detail in Chapter 2, these interventions have been decidedly double-edged. On the one hand, they are motivated by a genuine desire to bridge the gap between the 'education rich' and the 'education poor'. As Alexander (1997) points out, the greatest inequalities in education spending are not between private and state schools, but between different home backgrounds. In so far as they equalize access and opportunity (for example, through specifically targeting disadvantaged groups), such initiatives can only prove beneficial – although evidence as to their effectiveness in this respect is rather limited (Ofsted, 2000). Yet, on the other hand, such initiatives also seem to be motivated by a kind of puritanism – and even authoritarianism – that commentators have seen as characteristic of much of New Labour's social policy. This new emphasis on education in the home could be regarded as symptomatic of a 'curricularization' of family life – that is, a way of transforming children's leisure and everyday interactions into a form of educational 'work' (Walkerdine and Lucey 1989). Such initiatives frequently rest on normative assumptions about 'good parenting' or 'healthy family life', against which many parents and families are implicitly found lacking. They offer ideals that the majority of parents – and particularly the disadvantaged – may find impossible to achieve; and in this respect, they may result merely in feelings of guilt and inadequacy (cf. Urwin 1985; Duxbury 1987).

However, government is far from being the major player here. Commercial companies have increasingly come to regard the home as the 'new frontier' in the selling of educational goods and services. The marketing of home computers is the most obvious manifestation of this move. Households with children are significantly more likely to possess a PC than those without (Livingstone and Bovill 1999); and 'good parenting' – like 'good teaching' – is widely seen to require this form of technological investment (see Nixon 1998). Yet there are many other dimensions to this commercialization of out-of-school learning. There has been a steady growth in private home tutoring, and at an ever younger age; and there are now several commercial companies franchising private supplementary classes, not just in 'extras' such as the arts and computer literacy, but also in core curriculum subjects.

Media of various kinds are particularly crucial here, which is why they form our central concern in this book. As we shall indicate in Chapters 3 and 4, there is an increasingly competitive market for broadly 'educational' toys, software, books and magazines targeted at the domestic consumer. Thus, there has been a proliferation of educational magazines, particularly aimed at pre-school children and their parents; the market for popular information books has become crowded with increasingly glossy and attractive new products; and, building on the faltering home software business, we are now seeing the emergence of a significant new market in interactive 'e-learning', led by well-established television companies. These developments are considered via the series of case studies that make up Chapters 5–8.

As we have indicated, this commercial involvement in home learning is not a new phenomenon, although it has grown considerably in scale over the past ten years. Of course, it would be possible to condemn it all as merely a matter of exploitation. It is tempting to conclude that such companies are doing little more than capitalizing on parents' genuine (and growing) anxieties about their children's educational achievement. Yet such views are unduly pessimistic – not to mention unduly sanguine about the alternative merits of state provision. Aside from anything else, these views tend to underestimate the degree of risk and insecurity in the business: there are, after all, quicker ways to make a buck than producing educational materials. More fundamentally, there is a danger of ignoring what the market can in fact provide – and indeed, that the market may offer certain kinds of access to education for those who might otherwise not be able to achieve it.

Nevertheless, commercial corporations are clearly governed by imperatives other than those of universal social – or educational – good. What is available in the educational marketplace is determined primarily by the logic of the global media industries. As we shall indicate in Chapters 3 and 4, these industries are rapidly converging: traditional book publishers are merging with television, new media and toy companies, hoping to exploit their copyrights across a range of platforms, and in markets across the globe. Maximizing profit and minimizing risk are the order of the day. 'Old' and 'new' media, as well as production and distribution, have become more and more integrated. In the age of AOL Time Warner, cultural production is increasingly characterized by '360 degree marketing', and driven by merchandising and commodification (Kinder 1991).

Meanwhile, as parents and children come to be redefined as 'educational consumers', definitions of education themselves may begin to blur and change. Unlike school textbooks, which are purchased by teachers and used in compulsory settings, the material we discuss in this book needs to target a dual market. It has to satisfy parents' expectations about what counts as valid education, and hence as a worthwhile way for their children to spend their time; and yet, if children are to be persuaded to use it in their leisure time, it also has to qualify as pleasurable and entertaining. To some extent, this accounts for the emergence of 'edutainment', a hybrid mix of education and entertainment that relies heavily on visual material, on narrative or game-like formats, and on more informal, less didactic styles of address. At least on the face of it, this material embodies a form of 'popular' pedagogic discourse that is much less authoritarian – and much more 'interactive' – than that of formal schooling (cf. Bernstein 1990). As we shall see, the sales pitches for such material rely on an obsessive insistence that learning is inevitably 'fun'. These new forms of 'edutainment' are therefore offered both as an acceptable leisure-time pursuit and as an attractive alternative to the apparent tedium of much school work. Children, it is typically argued, will gain a competitive edge on their peers – and yet they will not even know that they are learning.

For their most enthusiastic advocates, these developments offer the potential for new 'learning cultures' that transcend the limitations of established institutions such as schools. New computer software, in particular, is seen to foster an 'interactive', creative style of learning that is more in tune with children's natural modes of thinking (Papert 1996). On the other hand, of course, there are those who see these developments as further evidence of the 'dumbing down' of education. The popularization and trivialization of academic knowledge, the replacement of the rigours of print with the easy pleasures of images, the association of learning with the superficiality of popular culture – these are all developments that have been seen with alarm, not just by the more traditionally minded but also by the self-professed modernizers of New Labour. Yet in our view, both responses are at least premature. We need to begin – as we do in Part Two of this book – by considering whether these changes are in fact any more than superficial. Does 'edutainment' represent a fundamental shift in definitions of knowledge and learning, or merely an exercise in marketing?

Facing the consequences

So what are the consequences of these developments? Will they necessarily result in the 'levering up of standards and achievement', let alone
'open up opportunities for all', as Tony Blair might wish? Will they
effectively mobilize private resources for more general public benefit?
And will they close the gap between the 'education rich' and the 'education poor'?

Our response in this book is frankly sceptical. There are several inter-
connected reasons for this, which will surface at different points in our
analysis. In general, we would argue that the market is an inherently
unequal mechanism, whose ultimate effect is to bolster the privilege of
professional and middle-class parents (cf. Gewirtz *et al.* 1995). Educational commodities of the kind we analyse here are much more likely
to be available in middle-class homes; and the characteristic ways in
which they address and position parents and children are likely to
be more in keeping with the cultural styles of middle-class families.
Ultimately, this is the logic of the market: companies obviously want
to sell their products to those who are most likely to buy them, and
new markets will only become attractive once established markets
have become saturated. As such, the market in educational media is
likely to widen, rather than close, the gap between the 'education rich'
and the 'education poor': those who already possess what Bourdieu
and Passeron (1977) call 'educational capital' will use these means to
acquire more, while those who possess less in the first place will be left
further behind.

A second reason for our scepticism is to do with what counts as learning. As we have suggested, children's everyday lives are suffused with
'informal' learning of many kinds. Yet there is a significant difference
between this everyday learning and the learning that arises from explicit
instruction – which necessarily entails different kinds of relationships
between 'teachers' and 'taught', as well as the application of technologies of assessment and surveillance. The risk here is of a kind of
colonization – a 'curricularization' – of domestic space and family
relationships by the imperatives of the school. In the process, certain
kinds of learning and certain pedagogic relationships come to be valid-
ated and legitimated, while others are not. It is the school that dictates
what will count as teaching and learning, and how knowledge is to be
acquired and defined. For many working-class children, in particular, the
home and the school frequently become almost hermetically sealed
worlds: learning at home and learning at school are seen as separate
and unrelated. This in turn establishes an opposition between 'work'
and 'play' – or between 'learning' and 'fun' – that 'edutainment' must
then set out to overcome. The alternative – that learning in school
might become more like learning in the home, and that schools might

take more account of the cultural resources children develop outside school – is one that educational policy-makers have steadily (and in fact increasingly) resisted.

However, this is to present the terms of our analysis in rather blunt ways. Inevitably, it is all rather more complicated than that. Thus, the polarization between 'middle class' and 'working class' is much too easy, not least because it fails to take account of individuals' *trajectories*. In our view, class is not something given: it is a relationship rather than a fixed position, and a matter of historical movement (or possible movement) rather than stasis. It is about where you have come from, where you have passed through and where you think you are going (Reay 1998). As we shall indicate in our case studies of families (Chapters 9 and 10), education is of course a key focus of parents' aspirations and fears about social mobility. In metropolitan London, where we undertook our research, inequalities of income and resources are everywhere apparent; and education seems to many to offer the promise of moving a few rungs upwards on the ladder, or at least a guarantee against the risk of slipping further down. This is precisely why investing in education – not least in educational commodities of the kind we consider here – seems to possess such symbolic power. Yet whether or not parents actually achieve advantage in this way – whether they get what they pay for – is a rather more open question.

Likewise, there are tensions and contradictions in the texts we analyse here, and in the ways they are used. For want of a better label, our analysis here is broadly 'post-structuralist'. From this perspective, texts are seen to offer 'positions' from which they can be read and understood; but those positions are not necessarily coercive. A text that purports to be both 'educational' and 'entertaining' need not necessarily be read as both or either. Likewise, parents may be positioned as teachers, and children as pupils, by the pedagogic texts they encounter; but they may refuse to occupy those positions, or ignore or resist them in various ways. Thus, what counts as education or as learning is not something fixed: it is something that the texts we analyse here must struggle to define, in the light of what their producers perceive to be the interests and motivations of their readers (or users). On the one hand, they must not be too 'worthy' or 'didactic'; on the other, they must avoid 'triviality' and 'dumbing down'. Learning must be 'fun'; but it cannot afford to be *too much* fun. Likewise, as we shall see, parents do not have absolute power to determine how their children will spend their time, or to ensure that the activities they engage in are appropriately 'educational'. At a certain age, children may accede to their parents' pedagogic interventions; but most of them quickly learn how to manipulate the rules of the game. Both in 'educational' texts themselves, and in the everyday interactions of family life, drawing the line between 'education' and 'entertainment' is very much a matter for negotiation.

The shape of the book

Our central concern here, therefore, is with the *production*, *design* and *circulation* of 'educational' media aimed primarily at the domestic market (although, of course, we recognize that there are often significant overlaps between home and school in this respect). Our main emphasis is on books, magazines and software. In Part One of the book, we trace the political and commercial context of the market in these 'educational' commodities. We look in turn at government initiatives in this field; at the production of educational media by publishers; and at distribution, retail and marketing. In these three chapters, we attempt to outline a 'political economy' of educational media, tracing the complex and uncertain operation of market forces in this field, and their relationships with government policy.

In Part Two, we focus on texts, via a series of case studies selected to illustrate a range of media and subject areas. Chapter 5 looks at the market in pre-school 'edutainment' magazines; Chapter 6 examines information books aimed at older children, specifically focusing on books about history; Chapter 7 considers the nature of 'interactivity' as it occurs in educational software; while Chapter 8 analyses the relationships between 'education' and 'entertainment' in a range of media, with a particular focus on texts about dinosaurs. Our analysis in these chapters therefore focuses on the textual characteristics of this more 'popular' style of pedagogy, and the ways in which it positions parents and children.

Part Three presents some data from our research into the users of these media. This includes the findings of a substantial survey, conducted in four London schools, and a series of family interviews. Our analysis here focuses on two broad themes. First, we consider how parents and children conceive of the nature of learning in the home, both in the specific form of homework and more broadly. Here we look at parents' sense of their own responsibilities as educators, and their feelings about this role. Second, we consider parents' and children's responses to specific educational texts. These include texts selected by us in the light of our case studies, as well as texts selected by our respondents. Here, we consider how parents and children perceive and respond to the positions that such texts mark out for them.

Our account seeks to bring insights and approaches from media and cultural studies to the analysis of education. Readers familiar with media studies will certainly recognize the kind of three-stage analysis we have undertaken (cf. Buckingham 2000b). What informs it is a broad view of cultural processes, which sees them in terms of the dynamic relationships between *producers*, *texts* and *audiences*. At the same time, our account should be seen in relation to ongoing debates in the study of education, particularly those that focus on the role of education markets, connections between parents and schools, and the broader relationships between schooling and social class. We hope that our analysis of what counts as education in the texts and processes we consider here will make a useful contribution to discussions in both areas, and to future debates about educational policy and practice.

PART ONE

CHAPTER 2

NARROWING THE GAP?

Parental involvement, homework
and the 'Learning Journey'

In September 2000, the Department for Education and Employment (DfEE) launched a significant new initiative to promote parental involvement in education. 'Learning Journey' involves a parents' website, a free termly magazine, a set of booklets outlining the National Curriculum for various stages of schooling and a collection of leaflets covering key curriculum topics. The launch was backed by extensive television advertising and strongly promoted in the national press. Writing in *The Guardian*, Secretary of State David Blunkett (2000: 6) proclaimed that the Learning Journey would 'fill the gap' in parents' understanding about 'what is actually being taught to youngsters' in schools. Opinion polls had apparently found that parents lacked confidence in talking to teachers and in supporting their children's homework, but that they wanted to play a more important role. Blunkett was keen to forestall the criticism that the initiative was 'preaching' to or 'nannying' parents. The guides were described as 'only advisory' and 'not orders' (Ahmed 2000), and the initiative as a whole was presented as an extension of 'parent power'. Speaking at an Institute for Public Policy Research conference in September 2000, schools minister Jacqui Smith even went so far as to claim that it was 'putting the National Curriculum into the hands of parents' (see DfEE 2000). At the same time, the Learning Journey was also seen as part of the government's broader policy agenda on 'social exclusion'. As Blunkett wrote:

> Arming parents with the facts about what's happening in their children's school not only gives them the chance to play a part at home, it empowers them to play a supportive role at school with

teachers, too; and it narrows the gap between 'those in the know' and those unfamiliar with the complexities of the education system.

(Blunkett 2000: 6)

We will be analysing some aspects of the Learning Journey initiative – particularly the curriculum topic leaflets – in more detail later in this chapter. Yet it is important to begin by considering the rhetoric that surrounds the initiative, and the claims that it makes. How are parents *positioned* here in relation to other potential participants in education?

On the one hand, Blunkett is keen to proclaim (using the very same platitude with which our book began) that parents are 'a child's first educator' – and indeed 'essential partners in their children's education'. Yet, on the other hand, parents are implicitly defined as in some way lacking the knowledge and skills they require to perform this role. To be sure, Blunkett implicitly places much of the blame for this situation on schools rather than on parents themselves: his article begins by condemning the view of education as a 'secret garden', and concludes by claiming that this initiative will finally 'open' schools to parents. Yet ultimately, parents are seen to be failing to play their part in a drama whose script is essentially written by the school – and indeed, by the government in the form of the National Curriculum. They need to be 'armed with facts', given 'the right tips' and provided with 'practical support' from government if they are properly to fulfil their function as educators. In this 'partnership', the balance of power is clear: parents are expected to perform an appropriately 'supportive role', but what *counts* as education or as learning is not something that is up to them to define.

Like many such attempts to promote parental involvement in education, the Learning Journey initiative therefore raises some difficult questions. Who defines the terms of this 'partnership' – or, as it is often called, 'dialogue' – between parents and schools? To what extent do such initiatives 'narrow the gap' between parents who are 'in the know' and those who are not – and to what extent might they actually widen it? What models of parenting and of family life are offered here, and to what extent are they either realistic or desirable?

The limits of partnership

Research on parental involvement in education generally provides rather gloomy answers to such questions. Of course, this is not to say that home backgrounds make no difference. On the contrary, decades of research in the sociology of education have found that most of the variation in levels of educational achievement can be directly traced to the influence of family background – and particularly, of course, to the role of social class. Obviously, schools make a difference too; but despite decades of comprehensive schooling and intensive government reform of education, overall inequalities in achievement between social classes have remained more or less unchanged (Douglas 1967; Halsey *et al.* 1980; Jones and Hatcher 1996; Furlong and Cartmel 1997; Mortimore and Whitty 1997).

The growing emphasis on parental involvement in schooling over the past thirty years has arisen at least partly in response to this situation (David *et al.* 1993). The recognition of 'cycles of disadvantage' in children's home circumstances, and of the dissonance between working-class children's home cultures and the culture of schools, has led to a series of initiatives that have precisely sought (in Blunkett's terms) to 'narrow the gap'. In the 1960s, for example, the Plowden Report (Central Advisory Council for Education, 1967) proposed to compensate for these inequalities, not only by targeting resources towards disadvantaged areas (in what became Educational Priority Areas) but also by involving parents – or, more particularly, mothers – as 'partners' in education. In her evaluation of the effects of the report, Baroness Plowden recalled this as a revolutionary move, given the dominant view of education as a 'professional' activity; yet she feared that only middle-class parents would be interested (Plowden 1987). Nevertheless, by the 1980s, parental involvement had been almost universally accepted as a key aspect of education policy. A whole body of research undertaken at this time pointed to the importance of parental support for children's learning, not only in the pre-school years, but also once children had entered school (e.g. Wolfendale 1983; Tizard and Hughes 1984; Tizard *et al.* 1988; Jowett 1990). Meanwhile, the growth of parental involvement was also encouraged by the Conservatives' populist rhetoric of 'parent power', and the new educational markets that were emerging: parents were given greater 'political' powers on school governing bodies, while the publication of league tables and inspection reports supported the emergence of a kind of educational consumerism (Gewirtz *et al.* 1995).

The fundamental problem with such initiatives is one that is very familiar to the large majority of teachers. Parental involvement inevitably tends to favour 'enthusiastic' parents, who are confident in their relations with the school, and comfortable with seeing themselves as educators at home. In the process, it is bound to disadvantage others, and hence to increase the inequalities between them. Schools will unavoidably favour parents who share their own view of education, and who are willing to play the game by the school's rules – even if they may occasionally appear somewhat 'pushy'. Parents whose priorities and orientations – and indeed cultural styles – differ from those of the school will be ignored or marginalized.

Obviously, parenting styles can differ quite widely within particular social groups; but research and experience consistently confirm that working-class and middle-class parents generally have very different orientations towards teachers and schools. This is not to suggest that working-class parents are less 'interested' in education, or that they are less ambitious for their own children to achieve. Relative to their respective starting points, both groups of parents in fact seem to have equivalent aspirations: parents with degrees aspire for their children to gain higher degrees, while those who left school at 16 aspire for their children to go to university (David *et al.* 1993). Nevertheless, working-class parents generally feel less confident in their dealings with schools, and in their ability to support their children's school work, and as a result are less likely to benefit from initiatives that promote parental involvement.

This disparity is clearly confirmed by a broad range of research studies. Annette Lareau (1989), in an American study, found that working-class parents' relationships with the school were largely characterized by *separation*: they did not generally intervene in their children's schooling, gave relatively little support for homework, and tended to defer to the teachers' expertise. By contrast, middle-class parents' relations with the school were characterized by *interconnectedness*: they reinforced school work at home, hired home tutors and other professional support, and were generally better informed about – and occasionally more critical of – their children's schooling. Both groups wanted their children to succeed, but the middle-class parents were able to exert a greater influence on the school (particularly through social networks of other middle-class parents), and hence to ensure that their children were better served.

Following Bourdieu and Passeron (1977), Lareau argues that this inequality arises because of parents' differential access to 'cultural capital'. To some degree, this concept enables her to avoid a deterministic view of social class, and to account for variation within classes. From this perspective, social class is seen to provide access to cultural resources and dispositions – and, in particular, to forms of specialist language that may or may not be attuned to the professional language of the school. Nevertheless, these resources must be *activated* via particular social practices if they are to have any effect. Parents have to invest their cultural capital and use it wisely if they are to realize a social profit.

Similar arguments emerge from studies in Australia (e.g. Toomey 1989) and the UK (e.g. David *et al.* 1993; Reay 1998). In Diane Reay's study of two London schools, working-class parents' interventions in their children's education were less confident and assertive – and hence less effective – than those of middle-class parents. For Reay, this is not only a matter of cultural capital, but also of material and social capital. Middle-class parents had the money to buy houses in the catchment areas of 'better' schools, or cars to drive their children to such schools; they were able to employ home tutors and other educational specialists to offer support they were unable to provide themselves; and they could employ domestic labour in order to free their time to work with their children on school tasks. Meanwhile, as in Lareau's study, the middle-class parents belonged to social networks with other middle-class parents, and their children also socialized more extensively with others; and while this encouraged a degree of competition, it also enabled the parents to make powerful, well-informed, collective demands on the resources of the school.

However, it is important to reiterate that these differences do not arise because working-class parents are necessarily any less interested in, or committed to, schooling or education. On the contrary, as Lareau (1989) argues, such parents are positively *excluded* from participation: the way the school defines and positions them leads them to feel that they lack the necessary understanding and competence to respond to teachers' requests for support and involvement.

Defining what counts

So how and why does this exclusion occur? Broadly speaking, most initiatives in parental involvement have tended to operate in terms of the *school's* definitions of what counts as knowledge or learning (Merttens and Vass 1992). Schools have sought to control the terms of the parent–school relationship, and to define how parents should fulfil their responsibilities as educators – although that is not to suggest that parents necessarily accept this situation. Nevertheless, what is predominantly sought is parental *compliance* rather than parental *collaboration*. As Alexander (1997: 17) suggests:

Parents are often treated as instruments for the delivery, discipline and domestication of school children, not as the *primary* partner in education. Sometimes parents are told what they can do to help the school. More rarely are they actively involved in the child's learning or asked for their views. Communication about educational matters focuses almost entirely on the school's view of the child.

David *et al.* (1993) argue that schools' implicit definitions of 'good parenting', and hence the forms of parental involvement that are seen as legitimate, are precisely those that are characteristic of the educated middle classes. As they suggest:

The model for most of the various home–school strategies and provisions [that emerged in the 1970s and 1980s] remained that of the middle-class mother, who devoted her time and attention to the education and upbringing of her children exclusively rather than being involved in other activities. Moreover, it was assumed that her skills and interests were consonant with those of the school and the teachers.

(David *et al.* 1993: 44)

Walkerdine and Lucey (1989) offer a powerful critique of this view that 'good mothers' should necessarily be responsible for educating their children in the home. They focus particularly on the practice of using everyday domestic tasks – shopping or cooking, for example – as means of promoting children's learning. This practice is frequently recommended by child psychologists and educators: for example, books on early mathematics for parents describe how laying the dinner table or doing the washing can be used as an opportunity to teach basic concepts such as sorting, matching and comparing (Walkerdine and Lucey 1989: 66). The mother effectively assumes a didactic role here, drawing out the (school-defined) educational content of such activities. Yet according to Walkerdine and Lucey, this transformation of domestic tasks into a series of opportunities for pedagogy is particularly characteristic of middle-class homes. In the process, working-class mothers, who maintain clearer boundaries between 'work' and 'play', and who are under greater pressure to get the housework done, are implicitly seen as 'insensitive' to their children's needs.

Andrew Brown's (1993) analysis of a particular home schooling initiative – the IMPACT primary mathematics project – further illustrates these points (see also Brown and Dowling 1992). Brown argues that the IMPACT materials, which are sent home to parents, embody a 'normalising discourse' that implicitly defines what counts as good parenting. Parents are expected to work on the activities with their children, and provide feedback to the teacher on how they performed; and in this way, the project serves as a form of surveillance, in which parents are evaluated as well as children. Parents who refuse the terms of this participation – who will not play the game – are implicitly pathologized. According to Brown, the materials also seek to 'colonise domestic activity', by redefining or recontextualizing everyday experiences in the specialized terms of school mathematics. However, the principles of mathematical knowledge that are embedded within the activities are not made explicit. Parents are presented with all sorts of imperatives about what they should be doing, but they are not given access to any explanation as to *why* they should be doing it: the parent is simply to act as the agent of the teacher, carrying out activities according to instructions and delivering the results back to the school. In this respect, the materials embody a form of 'invisible pedagogy' (Bernstein 1977), whose informing concepts and evaluative criteria are not made available to – let alone subject to debate with – the parents and children themselves. Ultimately, while projects like IMPACT may set out to foster 'partnership' between parents and schools, Brown argues that they can end up simply maintaining the power of the teacher over the parent and reinforcing existing social inequalities (see also Brown 2000).

In addition to these broader social consequences, many of these researchers point to the more psychological one of stress, both on children and on parents. Lareau (1989) found that this arose particularly in her middle-class sample. These parents' 'educationalizing' of the home environment led to increasing levels of competitiveness, both between siblings and with other children, in a manifestation of what has been called the 'hurried child' syndrome (cf. Elkind 1981). However, as Reay (1998) suggests, stress of this kind may not be confined to middle-class homes: all the mothers in her study, regardless of class, spoke of the pressures that arose from the expectation that they should support their children's school work at home – although these pressures were most strongly felt by single parents and working mothers. In Reay's terms, assuming a teacherly role requires a degree of 'emotional capital' – an ability to persuade and support children, and to handle feelings of guilt and inadequacy. The line between concern and undue anxiety, or between understanding and over-identification with one's children, is a fine one.

As David *et al.* (1993) point out, these pressures are increasingly coming from both ends. The growing demand for parental involvement in education has arisen just at a time when mothers are increasingly working outside the home, and as the form of family life is changing (via the rise in divorce and single parenthood). For those in employment, working hours appear to be rising, and are well above the European average. There is accordingly a premium on 'quality time', although (as we have noted) middle-class parents are clearly in a better position to purchase it. And, despite the fashionable gender-neutrality of the term 'parents', it is essential to recognize that most of this burden continues to fall on *mothers*.

Whose homework is it anyway?

The growing significance of homework – particularly for primary school children – is perhaps the most visible manifestation of these developments. As we shall see in Chapter 9, many of the parents in our study felt that the amount of homework set had increased significantly since they were young; and this is effectively confirmed by a report from Ofsted (Weston 1999). As we noted in Chapter 1, homework has recently become a key aspect of government education policy. The white paper *Excellence in Schools* (DfEE 1977) was probably the first government publication to raise the issue explicitly. This was soon followed by *Extending Opportunity: A National Framework for Study Support* (DfEE 1998a), which provided for so-called 'homework clubs' to be run in after–school hours; and by the publication in 1999 of national guidelines on the amount and nature of homework tasks. Parental responsibilities regarding homework are now written in to most home–school agreements; and, as we shall also see in Chapter 9, schools appear to be under growing pressure from some parents to set more homework, and to do so at an ever younger age.

Yet evidence about the value of homework in terms of raising achievement is, to say the least, equivocal, particularly in respect of younger children (Cooper 1989; Hallam and Cowan 1998). The problem here is partly methodological: as Ofsted also acknowledge (Weston 1999), it is hard to identify a specific 'homework effect' independent of the other factors in play – not least the nature and aims of the work itself. Yet as Cowan and Hallam (1999) suggest, the potential benefits of homework – in terms of promoting learning, fostering independence, developing self-discipline and so on – need to be set against the potential disadvantages – such as the additional pressure on parents and children, and the disruption of family life. Perhaps most significant in terms of our concerns here is the tendency of homework to increase the gap between low achievers and high achievers, and hence to reduce the motivation of the former. Particular types of homework may also favour those who have access to facilities and resources, and thereby disadvantage those who do not – however strenuously schools may attempt to avoid this.

Etta Kralovec and John Buell (2000) argue that homework places additional pressure on working parents, and on already disadvantaged children; and that, like streaming (or tracking), it accentuates educational inequalities. They challenge the idea that homework leads to increases in educational attainment, or that it strengthens home–school relations, and argue that both children and parents need more unstructured 'downtime' together. Significantly, they suggest that the growing emphasis on homework in the US context derives from the global pressure towards economic competition; and that increasing homework appears to offer a political solution to educational problems that are in fact much harder to solve. Homework, they argue, represents an unwarranted intrusion of the state into the private world of the home; and it can lead to conflicts between parents' educational agendas and those of schools.

Of course, homework is an activity that is by definition dictated and evaluated by the school; and, as such, it is not our primary concern here. The potential of home learning is obviously much broader than homework. Yet even where activities in the home appear similar to those undertaken in school, it is important to acknowledge the differences between them. Reading, for example, is an activity parents are frequently urged to undertake with their children; and most schools operate reading schemes (such as PACT) that provide for 'dialogue' between parents and teachers, in the manner of the mathematics programme Brown (1993) describes. Yet reading at home is likely to differ from reading in school in many ways – for instance, in terms of its length, its context, the relationships between the reader and the listener, the purpose of reading, the degree of control on the part of the child, and so on. Here again, the evident danger is that the school will come to 'colonize' the home – that home literacy practices will only be seen as valid in so far as they conform to school literacy practices, or are subject to evaluation in school terms. In the process, the literacy practices of working-class homes may either be ignored or invalidated (Heath 1983; Wells 1987; Weinberger 1996; Millard and Marsh 2001).

Taken together, therefore, these studies suggest that the promotion of learning in the home is by no means a socially neutral or unproblematic issue. This is the case whether such learning is primarily in the form of homework or structured programmes such as IMPACT, or whether it is apparently more integrated within domestic routines (as in the practices described by Walkerdine and Lucey 1989). Prescriptions for learning in the home need to be assessed in terms of what is seen to *count* as learning, and how this is defined; and in terms of the positions that are thereby marked out for teachers, parents and children themselves.

A national curriculum for parents?

Against this background, how might we interpret the government's Learning Journey initiative? As we have noted, there are several elements to the initiative, but the one that is most relevant to our concerns here is the collection of curriculum leaflets. At the time of writing (mid-2001), there have been 23 such leaflets, covering a range of curriculum areas (geography, history, music, science, religious education, and so on). Each leaflet takes a specific topic – so in the case of science, for example, there are currently leaflets on electricity, light and sound, materials and plants. All the leaflets are aimed at parents of primary school children, in some instances across the whole range (5–11-year-olds), in others for each key stage (5–7 or 7–11). Each leaflet is four A4 pages in length, and is headed 'Help Your Child Discover . . .'. At present, the leaflets are only available via the parents' website of the Department for Education and Skills (DfES), where they can be downloaded, either as complete laid-out documents or as files which can be edited by teachers and then distributed to parents (www.dfes.gov.uk/parents/discover).

As in the other Learning Journey publications, parents are addressed here as 'partners' – in this instance via a headline and a simple graphic on the front page of each leaflet. Parents are then informed about the purpose of the leaflet, as in the following example:

PARENTS AS PARTNERS
Your child is going to learn about religious buildings. This leaflet gives ideas on how you can help them to find out more about the topic. It suggests things to do when you're out with your child, activities you could carry out at home, and where to go for more information on religious buildings.

By trying some of the activities in this leaflet, you will help your child to understand and remember what they learn in school.

The front page of each leaflet also contains a bullet-point summary of what and why the child is learning about the topic (as specified by the National Curriculum); and the leaflet itself then contains a series of suggested activities, covering things to do 'out and about' and 'at home', and a final section on 'finding out more' (for instance, from libraries, bookshops or websites). The leaflet is illustrated with cartoon-style images of parents and children engaged in the activities described.

In their analyses of the IMPACT materials, Brown and Dowling (1992) discuss how particular 'voices' are arrayed or structured in the text. In our more post-structuralist terms, we would describe this in terms of the marking out of 'subject positions'. How are the various participants in the educational process – government, teachers, parents and children – addressed and positioned here? The text quoted above provides some initial indications. The child is very much on the receiving end. The child is 'going to learn' about the topics the government dictates (whether it likes it or not); and this learning will happen primarily in school, even if 'understanding' and 'remembering' might be promoted at home. The parent – to whom the text is addressed – is also on the receiving end, but in this case of 'ideas' and 'suggestions' rather than instructions: there are things you 'could' do, and you might decide to 'try' just *some* of the activities. Nevertheless, the consequences of doing so are clear: 'you *will* help your child' – an offer no self-respecting parent could reasonably be seen to refuse.

As in the IMPACT materials, the dominant mode in the descriptions of the activities is the imperative:

> *Be* a vegetable detective!
> With your child, *look* at a collection of different vegetables. *Try* to find clues to help you decide which part of the plant the vegetable comes from. *Encourage* your child to use all of their senses . . .
> (Emphasis added)

However, this imperative voice is leavened by modal verbs, such as 'could' – 'alternatively, you could use', 'you could ask your child'. There is also a good deal of 'trying' here: parents and children together 'try' visiting websites or making things, 'try to guess' and 'try to find out more'. Only when it comes to the safety instructions that appear, for example, on some of the science leaflets, are these imperatives strongly reinforced via words such as 'never' and 'always'.

At the same time, as the above extract suggests, the role of the parent in relation to the child is that of a facilitator rather than an instructor: the parent 'encourages', 'asks', 'helps' – and only occasionally 'gets' – the child to do the activities. The parent is repeatedly urged to 'talk to your child' and to 'explain' what is happening. Questions are also significant here: many of the activities contain questions which the parent and child are encouraged to 'talk about' together, or at least for the parent to ask the child. Answers are generally not provided, although in some instances the text provides information which the parent is implicitly assumed not to know (or at least to need reminding about), which they are then urged to 'explain' to their child.

Keeping active

As all this implies, learning is seen here very much as a consequence of *activity*. To some extent, the activities suggested are similar to those that would be undertaken in most primary classrooms: reading and drawing, filling in charts, making picture dictionaries and scrapbooks, doing musical counting, sorting and classifying objects, studying maps and pictures, and making lists and posters. Likewise, parents are encouraged to create their own water cycles with bowls of water and plastic bags; take their children on neighbourhood walks to examine settlement patterns; grow cress in cardboard boxes and study the effects of exposure to the sun; and read religious stories to help children understand about festivals and celebrations. These are all activities that most primary school teachers would be likely to undertake with their classes at some stage.

However, other activities suggested in the leaflets make use of the specific opportunities available in and around the home. Thus, there are tasks that involve extending or adapting familiar everyday activities, in the manner Walkerdine and Lucey (1989) describe. Parents are encouraged to experiment with everyday objects, or to ask questions about them. For instance, the leaflet on light and sound contains a section on mirrors: parents are asked to 'go around the house with your child' comparing different mirrors; to 'talk with your child' about where else they see mirrors; and to 'explain' that reflections in mirrors are reversed. A second type of activity is of the 'make and do' variety familiar from British children's television programmes like *Blue Peter*. Thus, in this case, the leaflet contains instructions about how to make a kaleidoscope with your child using mirrors and card, and how to make percussion instruments or drums from household objects. Several other leaflets contain recipes (for Victorian or Roman food, for example) or craft activities (such as making greetings cards or collages). A third type of activity involves taking specialist knowledge and reinforcing it by transforming it into 'fun'. For example, the leaflet on electricity contains instructions for a 'Snap!' card game using symbols for the common parts of electrical circuits; while the one on religious symbols involves a matching game. Finally, there are activities that might involve special journeys outside the house, to libraries or museums, or to talk to people 'in the community'; or things to do on journeys or when 'out and about'.

In general, therefore, the emphasis is on activities that involve 'discovery' and 'fun' rather than explicit instruction. Yet in Bernstein's (1977) terms – and as in the IMPACT materials analysed by Brown (1993) – much of the pedagogy here is 'invisible', in the sense that the concepts and principles that underlie the activities are rarely made explicit. To return to the earlier example, the booklet on light and sound contains several activities that entail an understanding of wave forms. For instance, there are instructions about how to make whistles out of waxed-paper drinking straws, through which children are expected to discover that a shorter straw will make a higher note. Yet the reasons *why* this might be the case are not explained: unless parents already know this (or can remember it from their own schooling), it is unlikely that they will be able to explain it to their children. Here we have an apparently 'fun' activity which is effectively also a scientific experiment: yet if the scientific principles that the experiment demonstrates are not explained, one might have good reason to doubt its educational value.

In terms of the government's 'social exclusion' agenda, these activities have clearly been designed with some care. While there are some suggestions that parents might purchase books or other commodities, they are urged to buy carefully. In the leaflet on 'Music from around the world', for instance, it is suggested that they might look for 'reasonably priced' tapes or CDs; but they are urged to make sure that they will 'enjoy and make the most of what [they] are buying'. There is much greater emphasis on using public libraries, museums and visitor centres (although, of course, some of these will charge admission); and, as we have seen, most of the domestic activities do not require special equipment. Likewise, while there is reference to the Internet, it is not automatically assumed that families will have access – although of course at present the leaflets are only available via the Internet (unless schools choose to download and distribute them).

On the other hand, as Reay (1998) makes clear, supporting children's learning at home requires resources other than material ones, particularly those of knowledge and time. As we have indicated, the leaflets do not consistently provide parents with the information they might need to 'explain' things to their children. Indeed, in some instances, they make some surprising assumptions about this. The leaflets on the Victorians and the Tudors, for example, clearly presume that parents have studied these periods in history; while those on scientific topics invite questions (for example, about electrical circuits or the spectrum of light) that many parents might find difficult to answer. Meanwhile, elaborate craft skills would clearly be required by parents venturing to make a Roman mosaic, a Tudor maze or a papier-mâché model of a river landscape with their children.

Such activities also make significant demands on parental *time*; and it is here in particular that the booklets' implicit image of family life seems (to say the least) somewhat idealized. Thus, the leaflet on ancient Romans suggests that parents and children might dress up in togas made of old sheets; while the one on Victorians suggests that the family might organize a 'Victorian games day' for their school. Similarly, the leaflet on religious buildings suggests that parents compile an 'I-spy' book in an exercise book for their children to complete; while the one on 'music from around the world' suggests that they assemble their own gamelan orchestra made from everyday objects.

Ultimately, therefore, the materials work to transform the parent into a pedagogue. They effectively provide scripts for parents' interactions with their children, which are expected to permeate their lives outside more specifically 'educational' encounters. Thus, 'good parents' are 'design watchdogs' who discuss the materials and appearance of goods with their children when they are out shopping ('designing and making'). They watch the television news with their children and make lists of the places that are mentioned, and then locate them in an atlas ('settlements'). They go around the house, noting the 'housework actions' associated with each room, and then help their children to choreograph them into a dance sequence ('dance'). They talk about the food they eat, in terms of its appearance, aroma, flavour and texture, and help their children to keep food diaries ('food'). When planning a car journey, they note whether the roads are straight or winding, and whether the town names end with Roman suffixes ('Romans'). And when they are *en route*, they are assiduously looking out for religious symbols, Victorian buildings, street musicians, and evidence of the Tudor period which they can then 'talk about' with their children.

As we will see in more detail in Chapter 10, even the more enthusiastic middle-class parents whom we interviewed were disinclined to identify with this image of family life. They suggested that, while the 'tips' might be helpful for 'other people', they were not necessary for them. Nevertheless, as with other such parental involvement initiatives, there appears to be little evidence that the materials are in fact being used by these 'other' parents. Indeed, this was a possibility that the civil servants responsible for the initiative (whom we interviewed) implicitly accepted. Despite David Blunkett's rhetoric about 'narrowing the gap', they recognized that the initiative might not make much difference to the children who were 'trailing behind', and that it might only be taken up by those 'at the top end [whose] parents are going to buy all this stuff for them anyway'. As one of them pointed out, this was 'not very consistent with the [social] inclusion agenda'; although the fact that some children might do better than they would otherwise have done was still positive in terms of 'the overall standards agenda'.

Of course, much depends upon how these various 'agendas' are defined. 'Social exclusion' is partly a matter of how the materials are made available and their existence is publicized – and in this respect, the fact that the initiative has been advertised in 'down-market' tabloids like the *Sun* and the *News of the World* is to be applauded. At the same time, 'exclusion' is also a matter of the positions that are marked out for parents as potential educators. In many respects, the materials would seem to represent quite an extreme version of the 'curricularizing' of domestic activities, of which critics such as Walkerdine and Lucey (1989) and Brown (1993) complain. They seek not just to transform everyday activities into pedagogy, but to provide parents with what is effectively a set of lesson plans; and in doing so, they construct a position for parents which has to be seen as characteristically 'middle-class'.

Modern times

In some ways, the materials we have been describing here appear to be locked in a kind of time-warp. This is most apparent from the illustrations (http://www.dfes.gov.uk/parents/discover). These are in the form of black-and-white cartoon drawings, which – aside from the occasional non-Caucasian face – would not look out of place in a 1950s children's comic. More significantly, the implicit assumptions about family life that inform the materials also seem to derive from an earlier era. It is as if the writers envisage the child arriving home from school to find mum waiting expectantly to engage them in worthwhile and fun learning activities. The family is constructed here as harmonious and well regulated, an institution in which everyone knows their place. Despite the egalitarian rhetoric about families 'learning together', children are constructed as docile and well disciplined, and parents as caring and diligent agents of the state's education policies. This is a vision of the family that has much in common with that found in other areas of New Labour's social and welfare policy.

However, there is something of a contrast here with some other elements of the Learning Journey initiative, particularly the termly magazine *Parents and Schools*. A glossy, full-colour publication, this is distributed free via supermarkets, and is aimed at parents of children at all stages of education. Like the DfEE's parents' website, the magazine contains advice relating to broadly 'pastoral' aspects of education: for example, there are 'survival guides' on the pressures of returning to school after the summer break, or about problems such as bullying and truancy, as well as information about issues such as special needs, youth training and parent governors. There is less specific advice about home learning of the kind found in the curriculum topic leaflets, although there are features on literacy and maths ('Turn your kid into a smartie pants'), which include suggestions for 'home help', such as number games to play at home or guidance on reading with your child. Such activities are, it would seem, relentless 'fun'. However, the primary emphasis here is on providing information about government campaigns, initiatives and policies. As in the National Curriculum booklets, there is a concerted attempt to make the curriculum – and the process of schooling more broadly – accessible and comprehensible for parents; and the magazine even contains a 'jargon buster' glossary of educational terms and acronyms. While it might be an exaggeration to call this government propaganda, there is certainly no evidence whatsoever that any of these things might be seen as politically controversial. 'Putting the National Curriculum into the hands of parents', as schools minister Jacqui Smith defined it, appears to involve little more than providing them with information about it – and simultaneously proclaiming its virtues.

However, what is most striking about the magazine – particularly in comparison with the topic leaflets – is its 'modern', popular appeal. The busy design resembles that of a mass-market women's magazine, with large, full-colour photographs, short articles, 'tips' and 'hints', graphics and 'sidebars'; and there are competitions, 'give-aways', problem pages, quizzes and readers' letters. Several articles feature 'true life' stories of ordinary parents and children; although media celebrities – including the ubiquitous TV presenter Carol Vorderman – are also strongly featured. In seeking to appeal to a wide readership in this way, the magazine is very clearly attempting to narrow David Blunkett's 'gap'. Yet there is also a strong commercial dimension here. The magazine carries full-page advertisements for products such as mobile phones, cars and financial services, as well as covert advertising in the form of competitions and give-away prizes, and frequent reminders of its commercial sponsors, distributors and partners. In the first issue, for example, books by the information book publisher Dorling Kindersley are offered in three separate 'give-aways', as well as being featured on the front cover; and there is extensive promotion of the government's 'parents online week' – 'in association with BT' – and a positive review of the Sainsbury's Bookstart scheme (Sainsbury's also distribute the magazine, along with a growing range of other high-street outlets featured on the back cover). Likewise, the DfES website contains links to a range of commercial companies, most notably the Disney site.

Of course, education is not the only area in which the boundary between public service and the commercial market is becoming significantly blurred. Yet, as in transport or health or broadcasting, it is vital to consider who benefits from such 'public–private partnerships'. What are the motivations and imperatives of the commercial companies involved, and to what extent do they determine the kinds of services and opportunities that are available? What are the gains and losses for the 'consumer' – not least through being defined as a 'consumer' in the first place? And, in this case, to what extent does the market come to define what *counts* as 'education'? These issues will be addressed in greater detail in the following two chapters, where we look in turn at the production and then the marketing of 'educational' media by commercial companies.

As we have shown in this chapter, the extent to which learning in the home is indeed a means of 'narrowing the gap' between the educational 'haves' and 'have-nots' is certainly debatable. Like many such initiatives, the government's Learning Journey project – and the curriculum materials in particular – would seem to run the risk of preaching to the converted. In doing so, they collude with a more general 'curricularization' of home learning, from which some families stand to gain much more than others. Whether or not the commercial market might provide a more effective way of addressing such educational inequalities – or whether it might widen them yet further – is something that remains to be seen.

CHAPTER 3

PRODUCING LEARNING

The changing face of children's
educational publishing

Debates about the role of the commercial market in education have often been starkly polarized. On one side are those – some of them not far removed from the present British government – who seem to believe that the market will automatically provide solutions for some of the long-standing problems and limitations of state education. On the other are those who implicitly regard commercial corporations as the forces of the devil, who will inevitably undermine public values and public culture in the interests of profit (Buckingham 1997). All too frequently, however, the market is perceived as a singular entity, whose operations are driven by single-minded and straightforward objectives, and whose success in achieving those objectives is largely guaranteed.

In this chapter and the next, we outline a 'political economy' of one aspect of the contemporary education market – namely, the publication of educational resources designed for use in the home. In general, the publishing industry has been relatively neglected by academic research. Literary critics have notoriously failed to address the commercial operations of the book trade, implicitly colluding with the industry's presentation of itself as a kind of charitable service for distressed authors. Yet even in the case of relatively 'sheltered' sectors of the industry, such as children's and educational publishing, economic imperatives are now increasingly in the driving seat. Historically, children's publishing has been a relatively slow-moving area, but it can no longer be seen as an 'old-fashioned gentlemanly profession' (as one of our interviewees described it).

As in many other areas of the media and cultural industries, the overall environment in children's educational publishing has become increasingly competitive and uncertain over the past decade. The deregulation of the retail sector and the rise of new media have both threatened the profits of publishing companies. Many smaller companies have been taken over by larger multinationals with interests in a range of media; while the international market has become increasingly important. In many areas, the key imperative now is to find ways of managing risk. In general, publishers have responded by narrowing their range and focusing on material which they feel confident will sell in large quantities. Series publishing has become the norm (for both books and educational software) and media tie-ins are becoming more important, at least in some areas of non-fiction. New media such as the internet have been seen to offer significant potential in terms of cross-media 'synergy' and in terms of reaching new markets; but there are also considerable risks here, which only the larger publishers are in a position to negotiate.

In this chapter, we begin with a brief description of the different sectors of children's educational publishing with which we are mainly concerned; and we then go on to identify the broader underlying factors in more detail. We consider the increasing concentration of ownership, the changing balance between the retail and publishing sectors, and the impact of globalization and of technological change. We then consider the consequences of these developments in terms of the output of the industry – for example, in the role of cross-media marketing, series publishing and product branding. Finally, we consider the extent to which recent developments in government education policy may or may not be aligned with the commercial imperatives of the industry. Our analysis here and in the following chapter is based on a close reading of the trade press and industry reports, and on a series of more than 25 interviews with key personnel conducted in 2000 and 2001 (interviewees have been anonymized).

Children's educational publishing by sector

The children's educational sector we are concerned with here contains several relatively distinct subsectors. In the case of book publishing, for example, it is important to distinguish between hardback reference books, 'popular' non-fiction books, early learning texts and home study guides. These distinct categories are also, to some extent, replicated in software publishing. While there is obviously some overlap between them, these different types of publications use different formats and styles, and seem to be targeted towards different markets. In particular, they purport to offer different combinations of 'education' and 'entertainment' (or 'learning' and 'fun'). They have also been affected in different ways by the economic and technological changes we will be describing. We will therefore consider each of them briefly in turn.

Reference texts

One of the main staples of the children's non-fiction market is the large format, glossy hardback, such as *The Oxford Illustrated Children's Encyclopedia* or Dorling Kindersley's *Big Book of Knowledge*. These books are highly visual, featuring photographs, artwork and, more recently, computer-generated graphics. They are generally in the higher price range (from about £10 to £25) and sell through traditional bookshops and book clubs. Some of the main UK publishers of hardback non-fiction include Dorling Kindersley, Usborne, Kingfisher, Oxford University Press and Franklin Watts. Reference materials of this kind (particularly encyclopedias) are also published on CD-ROM and the Internet. In recent years, the publisher Parragon has attempted to 'break the mould' in this sector by producing hardback reference books which are much less expensive and which are sold through non-traditional outlets such as supermarkets (see below).

A wide range of subjects is covered in this area of publishing, including history, wildlife, science, space, geography, religion and general reference. Whilst new topics have appeared over the years (for example, computers and technology) there seems to be a strong element of continuity: books on volcanoes and dinosaurs, for example, have appeared on a regular basis over the last 25 years (see Chapter 8). Media tie-ins and licensed characters are a rarity. These books often cover areas of the National Curriculum (like ancient Greece or the Aztecs), but they are not designed specifically for the curriculum of any one country, nor are they marketed as supporting particular aspects of school work. On the contrary, they are designed to appeal to (or to be adapted for) a wide international market.

Unlike some of the more recent genres to emerge in children's non-fiction – like the more 'popular' texts considered below – hardback reference books rarely claim to be entertaining or 'fun'. Instead, they are described as 'fascinating', 'spectacular', 'inspiring' or 'sumptuously illustrated'. 'Edutainment' is not a term which most publishers in this genre would readily apply to their work. As one such publisher told us, their books can be 'visually stunning because the outside world around us is visually stunning – [but] that's not to say it's entertaining exactly'. These books are usually bought by parents and other adults, rather than children themselves.

'Popular' non-fiction

In the last 10–15 years a non-fiction genre has emerged which is the antithesis of the glossy hardback. These books are small-format paperbacks, printed on inexpensive paper, using only black and white cartoon illustrations. They are generally quite cheap (from £1.99 to £3.99) and sell through both traditional bookshops and non-traditional outlets such as supermarkets. Their main market is the UK and they are targeted at children aged between 8 and 12. Their appeal is based on a blend of humour and irreverence towards 'serious' subjects such as history, science and maths. Scholastic's *Horrible Histories* series is effectively the model for this kind of publication. Books from this series appeared regularly in the children's bestseller lists during the 1990s. This phenomenal success prompted Scholastic to produce other series in a similar mould, for example *Horrible Science* and *Murderous Maths*. Inevitably, it also led to 'copycat' publishing by other companies, with the result that there is now a whole range of series which claim to offer 'horrible', 'dreadful' and even 'smelly' accounts of history and other subjects (the highly reputable Oxford University Press, for example, produces a series called *Smelly Old History* which comes complete with 'scratch and sniff' panels).

Unlike the reference texts, these books are primarily marketed to (and bought by) children themselves. While some of these series cover areas of the National Curriculum, they are not marketed as supporting school work. It seems to be assumed that such educational aims are unlikely to persuade children to buy them, and so the books are sold to children primarily as entertainment rather than as education. Although they often take an irreverent approach to their subject matter and to the world of adults (particularly teachers), series such as *Horrible Histories* do not seem to have alienated parents: for the most part, they are willing to buy these books because their children are willing to read them. Our interviews with publishers and with families (see Chapter 10) suggest that parents perceive these books as educational, despite the somewhat unconventional approach. The author/publisher clearly knows where to draw the line between what parents might find acceptable and unacceptable. This appeal to both parents and children is central to the success of these series. As one publisher told us:

> that's the magic of them, that they are worthwhile as well as fun. They are educational as well as fun.

Early learning

The past decade has seen a significant proliferation of books, software and magazines which are targeted at the pre-school/primary school age group and which purport to combine 'learning' and 'fun'. This category is more difficult to define than the previous two because it cuts across different media, retail outlets and price ranges. Nevertheless, these early learning texts share a number of features: they are explicitly marketed as 'fun learning' in a way that the other two categories are not; they are more likely to be based on media tie-ins and licensed characters; they often claim to support the National Curriculum, or the government's literacy or numeracy strategies; there may be some element of assessment and testing; and they are targeted at both parents and children. The marketing rhetoric for many of these products is surprisingly consistent: the words 'fun', 'learning' and (in the case of software) 'interactive' seem to be obligatory. There are quite specific educational goals here: 'learning' is predominantly defined (and indeed assessed) in terms of 'skills' in reading, writing, basic maths and science. These types of publications and software are targeted primarily at children under 8. After this age, any claims to 'make learning fun' tend to disappear.

Within this category, the balance between 'education' and 'entertainment' varies somewhat, particularly since the texts are aimed at both parents and children. One of the main factors which seems to determine this balance is the age group: the younger the child, the more likely there are to be 'fun' elements such as licensed characters. There are also differences between media: for example, software is often more focused on specific objectives (counting, reading, etc.) than some of the pre-school magazines. However, these differences can also be traced to economic aspects of the market. Early learning magazines are sold mainly through supermarkets, are comparatively inexpensive (about £1.50) and are often impulse buys to keep young children quiet during shopping: they therefore have to make a direct appeal to the child. Educational software, on the other hand, is not normally an impulse buy: it is expensive (about £10–£20) and sold in a limited number of specialist outlets. In this case, the parent is seen as the person who instigates the purchase, and therefore educational objectives feature more prominently in the marketing and the content. The product will still have to have some 'fun' elements to make a child want to use it at home, but this will often be a small part of the content. For example, in some software packages the 'fun' seems to come not in the main activities but in the rewards at the end. As one software publisher told us:

> The reward for getting through enough questions is that you get a trailer of – about 30 seconds of a spoof movie, and the guy who wrote it for us . . . he tried it with his tutees and once they realized that there was a little movie at the end of a game, they went through all 26 topics. And wanted to, because they knew there was a reward at the end. And the rewards are the fun.

As we shall see in more detail in Chapters 5 and 7, the learning activities in these materials are often based on 'drill and practice'; and they raise questions as to whether 'fun learning' is anything more than a marketing strategy used to sell products which are in fact more straightforwardly didactic than the packaging suggests.

Study guides

Study guides and revision aids have been on the market for decades, but in the last few years this area of publishing has seen a revival, largely due to changes in educational policy, discussed below (see Sanderson 1999). Traditionally, this type of material was developed for students in the 14–16 age group studying for national examinations, but in recent years a new type of study aid – often referred to as 'home learning' or 'home study' – has emerged which is aimed at a much younger age group. Dorling Kindersley, for example, has designed a range of maths workbooks for pre-school and for Key Stages 1 and 2 (age 5–11). This area of publishing is based on the idea that school work needs to be supplemented in the home: children should be learning before they begin school, in their spare time (including holidays) and even when they are engaged in everyday activities. As in the government materials discussed in the previous chapter, parents are often advised on how to transform everyday activities into 'learning opportunities'.

'Home learning' materials usually cost under £5 and are published as A4-sized paperbacks – and in this respect, they resemble the traditional revision guide. They are stocked in both traditional and non-traditional outlets and, because of their distinctive format, they are usually shelved separately from the other non-fiction materials described above. The layout and content of these publications are quite similar, probably because they are designed to support specific areas of the National Curriculum, usually maths and English. Some look like school textbooks: one of the Dorling Kindersley maths books, for example, is based purely on times tables. Testing and assessment is a standard feature, and certificates or gold star stickers are often provided as a means of motivating users.

Publications aimed at the younger age group adopt some of the rhetoric of the 'fun learning' magazines. However, unlike these magazines, the home learning publications are targeted squarely at the parent: the information on the inside and back covers addresses the parent (offering advice on how to 'help your child'). Guidelines or notes to parents are a standard feature, and in some cases separate titles are produced for parents. The younger the age group, the more extensive these notes are likely to be: for example, six out of the 32 pages in the Letts *Pre-School Skills: Counting* book are parents' notes.

Whilst in the past the sale of home study material was mainly in two periods (back to school and before exams) now there is demand throughout the school year. One publisher – Letts Educational – has even produced series called *Holiday* and *Holiday Extras* which are designed to be used by primary age children over the summer holidays. According to the cover blurb, the *Holiday Extras* series 'bridges the holiday learning gap and ensures school success'. Similarly, the *Holiday* series is described as 'an essential part of your luggage' which will 'reinforce previous learning and will prepare your child – and you – for the approaching school year'. The publishers acknowledge that children may not *want* to 'improve their skills' in reading and maths during their holidays, but parents are encouraged to persevere nonetheless: 'there's no reason why a plan that satisfies both sets of priorities can't be worked out together and enjoyed'.

An uncertain market

While some of the subsectors outlined above have been expanding in recent years, others have stagnated or begun to decline. In the case of books, figures published by Book Marketing Limited suggest that there have been some fluctuations in the children's non-fiction market over the last few years: market value increased from 1997 to 1998 but stayed the same from 1998 to 1999 (see Book Marketing Limited 2000: 8).

According to several publishers whom we interviewed, the market for hardback reference books is now stagnant or even declining. Competition from the Internet, changes in the retail trade, a drop in library funding and an overcrowded market were the main reasons given for this. But while the demand for glossy hardbacks is in decline, other areas of children's publishing are growing, particularly the study guide sector. Publishers attributed this to the culture of assessment and testing in schools, initiatives like the numeracy and literacy strategies, and growing parental concerns about children's education. The demand for 'early learning' magazines and books has also increased, resulting in new titles and series. As one leading publisher told us:

Those early years books got started as a kind of supplementary publishing exercise. We were going to try with one alphabet book. We already had material in-house and we were going to put an alphabet book together as a kind of supplementary book and it really took off. So that we then created a series and went into counting, numbers, shapes, colours and they're going into nurseries and pre-schools. So we started off with just paperbacks, we're now doing big books as well, then we had a spin-off, we did them in board books recently. So there was a market there we didn't expect at the beginning.

The fate of software publishing seems rather less positive, however. The exponential growth of home computing throughout the 1990s, and the insistence of both manufacturers and government that computers were essential for children's learning (see Buckingham *et al.* 2001) led to a rapid expansion in the home market for educational software. Initially, most CD-ROMs were designed for children over the age of 5 – since it was generally believed that younger children would be unable to use them – but by the end of the decade leading companies like The Learning

Company (TLC) and Havas were producing software for children as young as 9 months. However, according to representatives of the main software producers, the market for educational CD-ROMs has started to slow down over the last year, largely due to competition from the Internet (discussed below).

As our brief description of the market implies, there are several inter-locking reasons for this unevenness and uncertainty. To some degree, they can be traced to changes in educational policy and in technology; but they also relate to broader economic and structural changes that are apparent in many other sectors of the cultural industries. It is these changes that we consider in the following sections of this chapter.

Concentration and integration

Many of the main print publishers and software producers in the UK are now part of multinational companies with interests in a range of media. This is most apparent in the case of software. Five companies dominated the UK educational software market by the end of the 1990s: two of these (TLC and Europress) are owned by US toy companies (Mattel and Hasbro, respectively); Havas is owned by the French conglomerate Vivendi; Dorling Kindersley was taken over by Pearson in 2000 and subsequently stopped producing software; and the fifth company is Disney. Prior to its takeover in 1999, Europress had been a family-run business for 30 years; although TLC had already been through several takeovers and mergers. While the book trade is much larger and more diverse, a similar pattern of concen-tration is evident here too. During the past couple of years, several small or medium-sized independents have been taken over by larger compan-ies with interests in other media, notably television; thus, in addition to Pearson's takeover of Dorling Kindersley, Zenith swallowed up Two Can and Granada purchased the long-established revision guide special-ist Letts. With the number of consolidations, buyouts and mergers on the increase, many publishing houses are now a small part of huge international businesses. As the publishing trade paper *The Bookseller* put it:

> As the links in the information ownership chain multiply,
> decisions made in one market can have radical effects on another
> market thousands of miles away. Groups such as Pearson,
> International Thomson and Bertelsmann have global strategies
> in which the UK market sometimes barely registers as a blip.
> (Rickett 2000: 26)

Concentration of ownership and cross-media convergence have been accompanied by vertical integration between producers and distributors. For example, one of the most significant changes in the book trade during 1999 was the acquisition of the publisher Hodder Headline by retailer W.H. Smith, and Hodder's subsequent acquisition of publisher Wayland from Wolters Kluwer. According to reports in the trade press, this acquisition was likely to have a significant effect on the output of Hodder Children's Books: the company plans to develop a range of exclusive titles for W.H. Smith, including both fiction and non-fiction (see Horn 2000).

Meanwhile, publishers and software companies are also finding direct routes to their market. Scholastic, for example, now owns two book clubs, Grolier and Red House. During the 1990s, direct sales by publishers to schools also increased, particularly after the introduction of Local Management of Schools, which allowed schools to buy books from wherever they chose rather than using a local authority service (see Schlesinger 1999). The Booksellers Association's School Suppliers Group has estimated that 50 per cent of educational business now bypasses retailers altogether; and on large orders, publishers often give schools discounts that exceed the basic trade discounts they might offer an independent retailer. This approach also has implications for the home market, as we shall see in the following chapter, where book clubs and schools themselves are increasingly being used as forms of direct marketing that bypass conventional retailers.

The Internet also seems to offer even greater opportunities for large companies to combine production and distribution. Most obviously, it allows companies to sell products directly into the home; but it also permits a profitable 'synergy' between different aspects of publishing and distribution. For example, in 2000 Pearson purchased the US-based Family Education Network. This acquisition was reported to be part of the company's Internet strategy, whereby content from Penguin and Dorling Kindersley would be used in online educational products. As one industry report put it:

> Publisher becomes retailer, bookseller becomes publisher. All this seems to point to a future in which the market will become increasingly fragmented, where the borderlines between the different elements within the industry will become increasingly blurred.
>
> (Schlesinger 1999: 108)

Despite this overall pattern, however, publishing remains relatively less concentrated than other sectors of the cultural industries. This may be a result of the comparatively low costs of entry, for example in comparison with television. Even in the more competitive climate that now prevails, new companies are starting up and surviving. One publisher whom we interviewed compared the book trade to a cottage industry where 'small creative groups' still have an important role. Nevertheless, smaller companies do appear to be much more vulnerable than in the past: the general pattern seems to be that when such companies reach a certain level of success, they are taken over by a larger company, often a multinational.

The role of retail

One additional factor here has been the changing balance of power between publishers and retailers. We will discuss changes in the retail sector in more detail in Chapter 4, but some implications of these for publishers should be identified here. Compared with publishing, the retail sector is more narrowly concentrated; and during the 1990s, the number of takeovers and mergers within the retail sector increased, so that now a small number of companies dominate the market (see Schlesinger 1999). Meanwhile, this decade also saw the demise of the Net Book Agreement, which fixed retail prices for books; and as retailers began to compete on price, they demanded greater discounts from publishers. Getting products into shops has thus become much more expensive, as discounts to retailers now represent a significant proportion of the overall cost of books and software to the consumer.

As a smaller number of companies came to dominate the retail sector, their bargaining power also increased. In 2000 the trade press reported that one leading high-street chain, Waterstone's, was asking independent publishers for a standard discount of 50 per cent (see Kean 2000). This was bad news for publishers, as one informed us:

> The British market at the moment is very, very depressed indeed.
> Partly because of what's going on in Waterstone's . . . the
> managing director of Waterstone's wants British publishers to pay
> an enormous discount to take books into the shops and what it is
> going to mean is that small publishers will go out of business . . .
> W.H. Smith do the same – he's not unusual in that. So life for
> publishers in Britain is hard, very hard.

On the other hand, the retail trade also became more fragmented as non-traditional outlets (such as supermarkets) entered the market. This diversification within retail was a boost for some sections of children's publishing: according to one magazine publisher, the supermarkets' decision to stock pre-school magazines was the most important factor in the growth of this market. Magazine publishers were suddenly able to reach a mass market, and this led to the publication of several new titles. 'Popular' series like *Horrible Histories*, as well as 'fun learning' and study guides, are also sold through some of the supermarkets. On the other hand, supermarkets generally only stock children's books which are priced £5 or under, so this automatically excludes the type of hardback glossy books produced by publishers like Dorling Kindersley and Kingfisher.

However, when Parragon started to produce hardback reference books at a lower price, these were sold through non-traditional outlets, including the supermarkets, Woolworth's and motorway service stations. Their strategy of selling large quantities of books at low prices appears to have worked: according to reports in the trade press, Parragon now dominates the children's non-fiction market (*The Bookseller* 2000a). Not surprisingly, some of the more established publishers are concerned that their market is being undercut by what they regard as cheap imitations, and that this is then forcing them to compromise on quality.

As we shall see in Chapter 4, questions of price and the possibility of finding scarce shelf space in shops have also been a crucial factor in limiting the potential for growth in the software market. The combination of deregulation, concentration of ownership and diversification in the retail sector has therefore had quite different effects on different sectors of children's educational publishing.

Globalization

International markets are increasingly important for some sections of the publishing and software industries. Publishers of glossy hardbacks have come to depend heavily on overseas sales, particularly since their UK market has begun to decline. Books produced by these companies are almost always targeted at an international audience. As one such publisher pointed out:

> we cannot do a book that will only sell in Britain, we have to do books that sell everywhere else as well, because we simply cannot make the margins work unless we sell throughout the world.

The only possible exception to this, according to another publisher, would be if a book was 'absolutely key in the UK and indispensable to the curriculum'.

Books targeted at an international market are usually published as co-editions: a UK publisher will have an overseas partner who publishes the book in that country. Dorling Kindersley, for example, was a co-edition publisher for many years but eventually started to publish on its own. The advantage of co-editions is that production costs can be spread between two or more companies, although of course profits also have to be shared. It is relatively inexpensive for publishers to print foreign-language editions of illustrated books, since only one of the printing plates (with the text) has to be changed; although, of course, the main overseas markets are in English-speaking countries, particularly the USA (which for some publishers is four or five times the size of the UK market).

In this situation, there has been some concern that books are designed with a US audience foremost in the publisher's mind. Several publishers whom we interviewed acknowledged that the books they produce have to be right for the US market; and some suggested that they would be unlikely to publish a book if they felt it would not sell in the USA (for example, one of the proposed titles for a wildlife series was dropped because the animal described is not found in the USA). However, publishers also pointed out that the USA is only one of several markets. The key, they argued, is to produce books which have an *international* appeal.

This has important implications in terms of both subject content and visual imagery. Publishers tend to focus on topics which have a world-wide appeal, and the approach has to be 'non-British' and 'non-Eurocentric'. As one publisher told us:

> We're publishing internationally and that has a huge effect on certain subjects, like history. So, if we're doing a history book, it has to be done from a non-British point of view and non Euro point of view basically. We must not be Eurocentric. We have to take things from an international point of view.

Similarly, images must not be too culturally specific, since they will remain the same even where the text is translated into another language. As we shall see, the quality of the images in reference books is key to their success, and the proportion of image to text has increased steadily over the past 20 years (see Chapter 8). In attempting to appeal to as wide an international audience as possible, the objects featured must be made to appear generic. Anything that is too nationally specific – such as a brand logo on a T-shirt – has to be removed. As one publisher told us:

> We're always very careful with, for example, any pictures we show of homes or costumes or anything like that, that they look generic. So a car, for example, mustn't look like a British car or a German car, it's just got to look like a car, a generic car.

Whilst pictures of objects cannot reflect any one country or culture, pictures of people seem to have to reflect *every* country and race. Children from different ethnic origins are therefore shown; although getting the balance right can be difficult, as some countries have a greater racial mix than others. One way of addressing this issue is to dispense with children altogether and use animals (so that animals are shown, for example, conducting science experiments instead of humans) or close-ups of hands:

> We tend to close up on people's hands, so that you don't always see the child, so that if you're in Scandinavia – Scandinavia, for instance, has a very small black population – it's just unfamiliar . . . We have photographs of different ethnic minorities which appeal to the American market, we have lots of hand shots that appeals to the Scandinavian markets, so it's a kind of a balancing act.

This issue also extends to the *style* of illustrations. For example, photography-based publishers like Dorling Kindersley feel that they have an advantage because photos (in their opinion) tend to travel better than artwork:

> With any kind of artwork style, across fiction or non-fiction, it quite often won't travel – so it's very sensible to use photos if you want, because [when photographed] a tennis ball is a tennis ball is a tennis ball. But a tennis ball drawn by somebody might not appeal.

This issue becomes even more complex with software because there is the added dimension of sound. Clearly both books and CD-ROMs have to be translated into different languages, but software producers also have to address the question of which accent to use. For example, the use of American accents in software marketed in the UK is not very popular amongst parents and teachers; and so producers are now careful to rerecord into a 'non-American' voice.

Another important difference between the book and software market is that the latter usually positions itself as supporting the National Curriculum. Whilst hardback reference books are quite vague about their target readership, the packaging of CD-ROMs is often specific, identifying key stage, school year, age and so on. We found instances of software that had been repackaged for the UK market precisely in order to emphasize its conventional educational value in this way. Furthermore, as we shall see in Chapter 7, software programs use particular pedagogic styles which may be perceived as culturally specific. As one software publisher explained:

> We found a very big issue, for instance, was in the teaching of reading phonics. The American programs we got weren't that concerned about using phonics as a basis for teaching reading – the Scots feel even stronger about it than the English. So we realized if we did reading programmes we had to make them as phonic-based as we could . . . In mathematics, you know, there are not only differences in content but also pedagogical differences.

Establishing an international series brand in educational software can therefore be quite complex, since not all brands will travel. Those which do travel may still have to be modified in some way in order to meet the needs of particular markets. Havas, for example, has a large 'localization centre' for this purpose.

Whilst international markets are very important for hardback reference books and educational software, other areas of non-fiction are more focused on a UK audience. For example the main market for the *Horrible Histories* series is in the UK, though they also sell in Australia and Canada. These types of series are clearly targeted at a UK readership, not only in their content (for example, the focus on British history) but also in the use of slang and references to popular culture, which are an integral part of their appeal (see Chapter 6).

Technological developments

In addition to economic uncertainties, publishers also have to address the consequences of technological change. Competition from digital media is one of the main reasons for the decline in demand for glossy reference books, particularly encyclopedias and atlases. Problems for publishers in this sector started several years ago when CD-ROMs were first developed, and computer companies decided to 'bundle' reference packages (such as *Encarta*) with their computers. Now encyclopedias are available free on the Internet and there are thousands of sites linked to museums, libraries, art galleries and so on which are effectively in direct competition with the reference book market. The Internet also has a number of advantages over print in terms of reference material, for example in providing more powerful search tools and hyperlinks to related sites.

The Internet thus inevitably influences what publishers decide to produce and how they produce it. Some, for example, are reluctant to publish encyclopedias and atlases (since these can be updated on the net) and will avoid subjects like geography where content can be broken down into 'soundbites' suitable for websites. Publishers try not to replicate information which is already on the Internet, or they look for different ways of approaching a subject:

> If you publish non-fiction, at your actual peril you ignore the Internet, I think. I mean, we all have it here and we do research before we do the books and we find out what's on there and what's available easily and we have a jolly good look. The more difficult it is to find one's way around a subject, the more likely it is we'd do a book . . . So things like mind and body, anything like that is a good thing to do a book on. But geography, forget it. I wouldn't go near it.

Despite competition from the Internet, reference publishers are not facing imminent ruin. Books in particular still have many advantages over digital media – they are portable, easily accessible and (according to publishers) have greater authority because they have been through an editorial process. Furthermore, some parents are wary about letting their children use the Internet, or may not have access to the Internet for economic reasons (although, by the same token, these parents may also be unable to afford books). Nevertheless, the advantages of CD-ROMs as compared to the Internet are rather more difficult to identify. The slow-down in sales of educational software in recent years is largely due to competition from the Internet, and this market seems set to decline quite rapidly in the next few years.

The most obvious strategy for publishers and software companies here is to find ways of using the Internet to their own advantage. Some are developing their own sites or becoming content providers for others – effectively using it as another means of distributing content. Others are building connections between books or CD-ROMs and dedicated websites, to which purchasers will have restricted access. Overall, publishers seem to be rethinking their role, and reinventing themselves as information providers across different media. As one well-established traditional publisher told us:

> I think we're in a transition stage at the moment. I think the way we have previously gone about it is no longer viable. I think we're going to have to do things differently . . . the way we'll go about it is by having a much more flexible approach about what we do with information. Not procuring information specifically for a particular book but having a much more flexible approach about how we'd use that material in different media, different formats. Basically, [we will be] acquiring information which is kept up to date and maybe packaging it in books or maybe putting it online or maybe CD-ROMs or licensing it to people in various formats.

Nevertheless, this is a market with relatively high costs of entry, in which established content providers in other media are particularly well favoured. Concerns about quality control on the Internet mean that companies with an established brand in other areas of the media or education (such as the BBC) have a distinct advantage if they develop websites. Multimedia conglomerates like Pearson or Vivendi are also in an ideal position to create educational sites because they already have access to content through their ownership of publishing and software companies. For example, when the educational website education.com was created in 2001, it was able to draw on a number of properties owned by its parent company, Vivendi. According to information on the site, 'education.com offers rich and varied content from major print publishers Chambers-Harrap, Kingfisher, Larousse, Retz; and multimedia publishers Coktel and its famous characters Adi and Adiboo, Knowledge Adventure and its Jump Ahead and Blaster ranges'. Similarly, Pearson is able to use content from its publishing subsidiaries Penguin and Dorling Kindersley in its online education material. In this respect, technological changes reinforce the tendency of changing patterns of ownership to create a more centralized, less diverse industry.

However, e-learning and e-publishing are still in the developmental stage, and one of the main issues facing commercial companies is how to make a return on their investment. Subscription and advertising are two of the leading possibilities, but there are also examples of companies developing sites which effectively have to be used in conjunction with other media, either print or digital. So, for example, Pearson have launched a new study guides package, comprising online testing and resources which can be accessed only by students who have purchased the book. Meanwhile, software producers are developing CD-ROMs which allow users to download additional content from the Internet.

Finally, it is possible that the increasing convergence of media may also have consequences in terms of the visual style of print texts, and the ways in which they structure the reader's access to information. For example, a representative of one of the main reference publishers in the UK told us they were planning to use more computer graphics in their books, because children are so familiar with these types of images. The idea is to make the transition from computer screens to books seem less great:

> We wanted something the kids were going to be instantly familiar with. And we have another series . . . that was all done on screen, or a lot of it was done on screen. To adults it looks inaccessible but you show it to a child and they're totally familiar with it, they get it immediately. Because they're so *au fait* with computer games.

These issues will be addressed further in our discussion of educational software in Chapter 7.

Multimedia synergies

Perhaps the most notable consequence of this multimedia 'synergy', however, is the rise of what has been termed 'multi-media intertextuality' (Kinder 1991). As companies increasingly have interests across a range of media, they are bound to exploit the potential connections between them. In the case of children, this is particularly apparent in the use of licensed characters who can be used across media formats. The advantages of this approach are self-evident: when a character is known from TV, cinema or toys, children often want to buy other products associated with that character. Thus, as we shall see in more detail in Chapter 5, almost all 'educational' pre-school magazines are based on TV programmes. Popular characters like Bob the Builder and the Tweenies are displayed prominently on magazine covers, so that even children who cannot read will want to buy them. As one magazine publisher told us:

> Invariably they are character-driven, that is how we come about making or publishing pre-school magazines. I think we all know young kids are very influenced by TV and so their favourite characters, that is what would encourage them to want to get a

magazine out. A lot of them can't read at that age, so it is purely interest in the character rather than actually having a physical magazine.

The use of licensed characters in educational software has been fairly limited, partly because of the prohibitive cost of licences. However, in the last few years two of the main software producers (TLC and Europress) were taken over by toy companies, giving them access to a whole range of licensed characters. This is particularly advantageous for software companies because the toys indirectly advertise the software, as one publisher pointed out:

> The toy market is much, much bigger than the CD-ROM market. So the toy market will advertise a toy, Action Man toy, or whatever toy. And if there's a CD-ROM to match it, somebody goes round the store, they will be aware of toys and then they'll probably see that and think, 'well, if I can't buy the doll (which is what Action Man is) I might buy the CD-ROMs'. So that's subliminal advertising in a way.

Book publishing is also beginning to be affected by this trend. Licensed characters and media tie-ins are very apparent in 'fun learning' materials and are becoming evident in study guides also. For example, the publisher Two Can broadened its product range to include popular TV brands following its purchase by media group Zenith. Meanwhile, some publishers have enlisted TV and sporting celebrities in order to sell study guides and related products. In 1999 Dorling Kindersley launched its *Maths Made Easy* range of workbooks, endorsed by Carol Vorderman, best known to the public as a presenter on the TV quiz show, *Countdown*. Similarly, two premier league football clubs – Manchester United and Liverpool – are used in the Letts' Key Stage 2 series on maths and English. Photographs of players, fans and stadiums feature throughout these books and most activities are centred around a football theme. So, for example, children have 'pre-match adjectives training' or 'pre-match suffixes training' followed by an exercise in which each question answered correctly earns a goal for Manchester United against a rival team. The authors contrive to bring football into most of the 'training' and exercises: for example, readers are asked to list the names and nationalities of Manchester United players, while pronouns, compound words, collective nouns and antonyms are explained using examples from football (e.g. 'team' is an example of a collective noun).

Despite the commercial possibilities, many publishers and software companies are still reluctant to use licensed characters. There are a number of reasons for this. Licences are expensive, and it is difficult to anticipate what will be popular and how long that popularity will last. Making the wrong choice can have disastrous results. The most spectacular failure in tie-in publishing in recent years was Dorling Kindersley's *Star Wars* venture, which effectively resulted in its demise as an independent company. In 2000 Dorling Kindersley bought the non-fiction rights for *The Phantom Menace* and subsequently published a book on the making of this film. However, the film did not do as well at the box office as had been expected, Dorling Kindersley vastly overestimated the demand for its book and ended up with a rumoured 10 million unsold copies. The company made huge losses on this venture and was eventually taken over by Pearson. Commenting on Dorling Kindersley's predicament, *The Bookseller* (2000b: 28) summed up the problems which publishers can encounter when they venture into the uncertain world of tie-in publishing:

> Some publishers at the more literary end of the market like to think that tie-in publishing is like falling off a log. To be sure, they say, you need to act quickly to grab a commercial opportunity; but, once the deal is done, all you have to do is get the books out and watch the money roll in. But tie-ins are risky properties that require fine commercial skills: a sure instinct for market trends, an enthusiasm for hype combined with an ability to predict whether it is justified, and a gambler's luck.

Apart from the question of how popular a film or character is, publishers and software producers also have to decide which ones are most appropriate for their particular products. One software publisher pointed out that there are some brands which are 'truly inappropriate for educational software'. He went on to say that while his company would use *Sesame Street* characters in their early learning ranges, they would not use Pokémon because the latter was 'more of a fun brand' – even though Pokémon at this time was significantly more popular than *Sesame Street*. This question of 'appropriateness' may relate more to the perceptions of parents rather than children, although it also reflects a concern about achieving the right balance between 'entertainment' and 'education'. Thus, one software publisher claimed that they wanted to use popular characters for learning purposes, but at the same time they did not want to 'spoil' the character from the point of view of their parent company, which owned the rights:

> What we have to be very aware of, and we are, because we've thought about this at some length, is we've not got to spoil the character in the child's mind – so you can't have Action Man being a schoolteacher. If you're going to do education with Action Man it's still got to be an action adventure but with an educational bias. As opposed to doing a 'shoot-em-up' game. It's – when it comes to education you actually don't do a 'shoot-em-up'. It's a game, which still has him as the action hero but with an educational bias to it as opposed to just a more fun bias.

Remaining faithful to a character's TV image is even more important in pre-school magazines, where the purchase is usually instigated by children themselves. So for example magazines featuring Thomas the Tank Engine may have a moral overtone because Thomas is a 'pro-social' character, while a magazine based on less obviously 'worthy' characters may need to adopt a different approach (see Chapter 5).

Series and branding

Character licensing could be seen as one way of attempting to manage risk – which, as we have argued, has become an increasingly important consideration as the market becomes more competitive. Another way for publishers to capitalize on a successful brand is by focusing on series rather than on individual titles.

Over the past decade, series publishing has increasingly become the norm in all areas of non-fiction. An analysis of the book catalogues produced by five of the main UK publishers for 2001 revealed that the large major- ity of new titles were part of series. Similarly, much educational software is produced in ranges, like *Reader Rabbit* (TLC), *Adi* (Knowledge Adventure) and *Learning Ladder* (Dorling Kindersley). Some of the publishers whom we interviewed felt that there was still some scope for one-off titles; although if a one-off title is successful, it will often be turned into a series.

One of the main differences between book series and software ranges is that the latter tend to go across different age groups in a way that books do not. For example, all of the *Horrible Histories* titles are geared towards one age group (8–12) and there is no follow-up series for older children. Software ranges, on the other hand, are based on the idea of progression from one age group to the next, and effectively attempt to build 'brand loyalty' over the longer term. For example, there are eight different titles in the *Adi Maths and English* range, one for each school year between 7 and 15. The only area of book publishing where there is a comparable progression from one clearly defined age group to the next is in the study guides, which are obviously very specific about key stages, school year and age group.

Series publishing is a form of branding which has obvious commercial advantages. Publishers and retailers can promote several titles at once rather than having to start from scratch with each new title. Once a series like Scholastic's *Horrible Histories* or Dorling Kindersley's *Eyewitness Guides* has become established, retailers and customers tend to go on buying new titles on the strength of the series' reputation. (The latter is the most extensive non-fiction series, with over 100 different titles published.) As one retailer told us: 'now we just buy whatever the latest *Horrible History* is . . . regardless of what subject it's on, we buy it. We know it will sell.' Another factor is what this retailer called the 'appeal of critical mass' – in other words, that children like to build up collections of books. Retailers both in the UK and overseas often prefer series as they encourage repeat purchases. In the USA, for example, books are often sold as 'continuity series', whereby customers subscribe in much the same way they would to a magazine or a newspaper. On the production side, there are also a number of advantages to series publishing. Once a formula is in place, new titles can simply be 'churned out', as one publisher put it:

> There are all sorts of economies of scale there, and you've got designers briefed and the design set up. You've got the point of sales set up, you've got the illustrator set up, so you can just churn them out quickly and efficiently and once you're on a roll it does help to sell more of the same. You've got a following.

Popular series like the *Horrible Histories* often have the same author for most or all of their titles. And once a series is successful, the tendency is simply to go on adding new titles: as one publisher pointed out, 'if you've got a good thing, why give it up?'

Although branded series are becoming more important in both fiction and non-fiction, company branding is less evident. At a *Bookseller* conference in 2000, Cassell managing director John Mitchinson bemoaned the scarcity of big brand names in the book trade in comparison with those from other sectors (such as Gap, Guinness and Virgin), arguing that there are only five 'genuine' book trade brands: Dorling Kindersley, Penguin, Amazon.com, Waterstone's and Oxford University Press (*The Bookseller* 2000c: 18). However, several of the publishers and retailers whom we interviewed were critical of strong company branding in the book and software trade. They acknowledged the importance of establishing a reputation, but felt that it was a mistake for publishers to create a company brand by using the same distinctive style across all their material, in the way that Dorling Kindersley had done. Although this strategy can work very successfully for a time, eventually retailers and customers tire of a particular style. One software producer pointed out that companies with a distinctive brand find it hard to go beyond this: effectively they have only one range and one thing to sell, which makes them vulnerable. Indeed, some commentators have argued that this (in combination with the *Star Wars* debacle) was part of the explanation for the demise of Dorling Kindersley. By contrast, creating a range of different branded *series* allows publishers to generate a following, while also permitting a degree of flexibility.

The place of research

In other sectors of the cultural industries, such as television, market research has become increasingly significant as a further means of attempting to manage risk (see Buckingham *et al.* 1999). While there are some indications of this in publishing, market research remains fairly undeveloped, particularly in the children's educational sector. Most publishers seem to rely largely on instinct, experience and their own sales figures, rather than on specific research. Where market research is undertaken, it is often in the form of focus groups. Nevertheless, publishers are generally becoming more cautious about what they will publish, and research forms part of this, as one publisher told us:

> We do quite a lot of research. We always have done research, but we are just more cautious, we turn away things when we are not 100 per cent convinced we are going to sell it . . . We are very much more cautious than we used to be about every single title that we do and we look under stones and we look all around. And who knows what we might have published had the world been more stable? We might have published a few things that deserved to be published.

In general, however, the publishers whom we interviewed claimed that the creative process of publishing did not lend itself to market research; and asking children what they like was not necessarily going to help publishers plan ahead, as fashions change so quickly. Nevertheless, it is easier to predict what will sell in educational publishing than in other areas of children's publishing. As one publisher pointed out:

> The big difference between children's publishing and educational publishing [is that] in educational publishing you know what the changes in the legislation are, you know what the curriculum is going to be, you can tailor your material to it. You know, you've got a fairly long time. In children's publishing – it's about fads. You've just got to have that bone in your body that – that radar that spots the next fad. And no market research in the world will tell you what the next fad is going to be . . . I don't know any children's publisher who really goes in for market research. Except to spot what the opposition is doing and copy it.

Government policy

As this final comment implies, government policy on education does exert a very significant influence on children's educational publishing, even in relation to material that is designed for use in the home. This applies not just to the subject matter of publications, but also to how they define what *counts* as 'educational' in the first place. This is partly an ideological process, in the sense that parents as consumers may be more or less persuaded to fall in line with the government's current educational ethos or priorities. However, it is also an economic process, in that publishers are increasingly confined to publishing material which they believe (or hope) is guaranteed to generate a profit. While there clearly are books and software packages that are exclusively intended for school use, many are aimed at both home and school markets. Since the school market is more predictable, and since publishers are increasingly 'playing safe', it is likely that these two markets will be ever more closely aligned.

The book trade received a boost in the late 1990s when – after many years of underfunding of school libraries – the government provided grants for books to support the introduction of the National Literacy Strategy. Although publishers benefited from this additional funding, it was not the huge windfall which some had expected, leading to speculation that not all of the money earmarked for this purpose was actually spent on books. At present, there are concerns that now that schools have stocked up on books, government funding will drop.

However, direct funding for books and libraries is only one of the ways in which government policy affects the book trade. The educational initiatives of the past decade have meant that publishers (not just those in the schools market) have had to respond to ever-changing circumstances. The National Curriculum, introduced in 1990, laid down very specific requirements on subject content, narrowing the range of books being produced and in turn making the market more competitive. Publishers now have to work hard to distinguish their products from those of their competitors, whereas in the past they had a much freer rein over content. As one told us:

> Well, the National Curriculum is much more specific – if you look at an area like history, it is very much more specific. Before you used to be able to publish books about all sorts of different periods of history and sell them all equally. And personally I have a real grudge against the National Curriculum for History Key Stage II, because I think it is missing opportunities of exciting children in history because it doesn't look at the history that is all around them. We can't sell books about the Middle Ages, about knights and castles, because it is not taught at Key Stage II, so nobody will buy the books at the 8–11 age range.

The emphasis which successive governments have placed on assessment has also fuelled the demand for curriculum-related books. The introduction of Standard Assessment Tests (SATs) and other regular testing in schools, as well as initiatives like the National Numeracy and Literacy strategies, has been particularly significant in this respect (*Back to School Bookseller* 2000). This has been particularly evident in the massive expansion of the study guides market, as one leading publisher (quoted in Sanderson 1999: 14) explained: 'Study guides are riding the crest of a wave. The British government's emphasis on standards means that at the moment, the market is growing to such an extent that there's room for everyone.'

As we indicated in Chapter 2, parents are being placed under increasing pressure to support what children are doing in school, and this fact has not been lost on commercial publishers. This in turn has reinforced the competitive, assessment-driven aspects of the government's strategy. According to one major publisher:

> Parents began to supplement areas of the curriculum they felt were being neglected. They looked for workbooks on tables and spelling, phonics and handwriting, and this accelerated into the whole 'back to basics' movement. Publishers and book sellers were not slow to pursue the opportunity here: we all produced home learning workbooks, with straightforward text and no-nonsense design, to reinforce traditional values.
>
> (*Back to School Bookseller* 2000: 20)

Not surprisingly then, books, magazines and software in the 'fun learning' and study aid categories almost always claim to support the National Curriculum or the Numeracy and Literacy Strategies. Linking content to school work (however tenuously) has become an important marketing strategy for materials designed for use in the home – although, as we have noted, this is less apparent in the case of reference books, which are in any case designed for an international market.

Nevertheless, there are inevitable tensions here, which the rhetoric of 'fun learning' only partly resolves. For example, focus group research undertaken by Ladybird before the launch of their *Success at School* series in 2000 found that parents were 'feeling pressured with the demands of homework'. However, it was also noted that 'they want learning at home to be fun and don't want their children to be presented with more school-like work' (*The Bookseller* 2000d: 4). Likewise, the *Janet and John* series revived by the Star Kids imprint (also in 2000) represented another attempt to square the circle, not least by combining an assumed parental nostalgia for the 1960s originals with the use of the Internet. According to the publisher, 'the books are simple and free from ideology and jargon, and with a direct appeal to children's own experiences' (www.janetandjohn.com). And yet, it seemed, parents had to be reassured that their children would actually *want* to use the workbooks: 'Janet and John activity books make learning at home a fun experience . . . These are books your child will want to have at home.'

Conclusion

Contemporary developments in educational publishing could be seen to reflect broader changes in the relationship between the public and the private spheres. Of course, this market exists primarily in order to generate commercial profit for shareholders; but it seeks to do so by attempting to meet parents' and children's expectations and aspirations regarding education – in other words, by providing a form of 'public good'. In this sense, it is not dissimilar to the institution of public service broadcasting. And yet, as is the case in broadcasting, both the nature of commercial imperatives and the dominant definition of the 'public good' – and the relationship between them – are currently subject to significant change (cf. Buckingham *et al.* 1999).

To some degree, these forces appear to be working in concert. As we have shown, the competitive pressures of the marketplace are increasingly resulting in a reduction of the range and variety of material available; and in general, this can only be reinforced by the narrowing emphases of current educational policy. On the other hand, new tensions may be arising here, not so much in the range of material as in its character – and not least in the awkward relationship between 'education' and 'entertainment'. This issue is one that will be taken up in our analyses of specific texts in Part Two. Before doing so, however, we need to consider the other side of the industry, that of retailing and distribution.

CHAPTER 4

SELLING LEARNING
Developments in the retail trade

The means by which books, magazines and software are marketed significantly determine the kinds of consumers that can be reached, and hence the potential for commercial profit by publishers. Of course, consumers are more likely to purchase material that is made widely available – and in this way, retailing can be seen to play a significant part in determining what gets produced in the first place.

In this chapter, we outline some broad changes in the retailing of children's educational texts, focusing primarily on books and software. The first part of the chapter looks at three broad tendencies within this sector, which to some extent parallel those described in the previous chapter: the concentration of ownership; the diversification of retail outlets; and the changing nature of the shopping experience. In the second part of the chapter, we provide four brief case studies of different approaches to book and software retailing, focusing both on the commercial strategies adopted in different sectors of the business, and on the marketing rhetoric that characterizes them. We begin, however, with some brief general observations on the changing nature of the retailing sector.

An awkward market

Selling educational books and software into the home market represents something of a challenge for retailers. Compared with alternative products, the potential for profit is limited, and so there may be little incentive to carry a wide-ranging stock of titles. This is particularly the case in relation to educational software, but it also applies to books. Within the book trade, children's books generally come a distant second to the adult market. Books bought for children tend to be cheaper than those purchased for adults: the average prices paid in 1999 were £3.55 and £6.95 respectively, while books costing £10 or more accounted for 44 per cent of the value of books bought for adults, compared to 17 per cent of those bought for children (Book Marketing Limited 2000). As with adults, the leading genre bought for children is fiction. However, the ultimate consumer of a children's book is not generally the person who pays for it, so the question of how retailers appeal to the consumer is a complex one. According to research carried out by Book Marketing Limited (2000), only 8 per cent of books bought for children are bought by children themselves. The retailer therefore needs to appeal to a dual audience.

As we described in Chapter 3, some sections of the children's non-fiction market are stagnant at the moment, while others appear to be booming. Although sales of encyclopaedias and general reference books are in decline, the growing pressures of national testing are fuelling the market for revision aids and study guides: one independent retailer whom we interviewed claimed that she could fill her shop with these kinds of publications, such was the demand. According to one high-street chain, teachers are now far more likely to recommend study guides than they were in the past, and parents appear to be more susceptible to these recommendations:

> We get an awful lot of parents who come in clutching the back
> of an envelope with something they've scribbled down at Parents'
> Evening and they don't want anything else, because they only
> want the particular product recommended by the teacher. And
> that has become increasingly important.

In this context, the incentive to offer a broader range of non-fiction stock is bound to be limited, particularly for non-specialist outlets.

Meanwhile, as we have noted, the industry is beginning to see a significant slow-down in sales of educational CD-ROM packages. While this is largely due to competition from the Internet, it is also a result of long-standing difficulties in terms of retailing. This is partly a matter of the limited number of retail outlets through which software is sold. Whereas there are many specialist bookshop chains in the UK, there is only one specialist software retail chain – Electronics Boutique – whose main business is obviously in games. CD-ROMs are sold mainly through computer hardware shops (such as PC World), general electrical retailers (such as Currys) and mixed retailers (such as W.H. Smith and Woolworth's). There is no more than a handful of independent software retailers, excluding specialist games shops. In addition, several of these outlets are not very well suited to some sections of the target audience, particularly mothers with young children. As one software publisher pointed out:

I think a lot of women will find PC World offputting – they're not a female environment. They're a male, boy one. You get to the door and you're greeted by a young lad who says 'do you know what you want?' basically. They're big cavernous places and there's lots of noise because you've got demos of games and things, so people are not going to rush to those . . . We do a lot of business through them [PC World] – but I think there are lots of other avenues to the market, because the market has not grown to the size that one would have expected three or four years ago.

Traditional bookshops have generally been reluctant to stock educational CD-ROMs, although elsewhere in Europe this is quite common. As one software publisher told us:

Bookshops tinkered with it five years ago, they used to put it in corners, they didn't really know what to do with it, and then it didn't sell, and therefore they didn't want to have it.

With the downturn in the market for educational software, it now seems even less likely that shops will expand into this area.

Supermarkets or general chains like W.H. Smith are seen as a more desirable outlet by software producers because they have the potential to reach a wider market. However, the range of software which such retailers can stock is also limited by the amount of shelf space which CD-ROM boxes require: the packaging is much bigger than the product. However, packaging, cover blurb and pictures are very important for selling software because customers are not able to try the software before they buy it. As one retailer explained:

The argument could be that you get one chance – you see the front of the box, you make a strike in front of the box, and the front of the box is important. They will pick it up, you turn it round and you have the back of the box to sell what is the equivalent of several books usually and it's very difficult. You've got to get it across on the back of the box. A few pictures, some text, and bullet points – why that product is the one you should have.

The final constraint here is that of price: software packages are often very expensive and are therefore unlikely to attract 'impulse' purchases. This in turn makes it less likely for them to be stocked by supermarkets or other general-purpose outlets, which can gain a quicker return by using their shelf space in other ways.

Concentration of ownership

To an even greater extent than publishing, the retail sector has seen a significant concentration of ownership over the past decade. During the late 1990s there was a series of high-profile mergers and acquisitions (Schlesinger 1999). In 1998 alone, W.H. Smith bought John Menzies and the Internet Bookshop, Dillons merged with Waterstone's and they were jointly acquired by the HMV Media Group, Hammicks was bought by the Millennium Entertainment Group Africa (MEGA), and Bookpages was bought by Amazon.com. The following year Bertrams merged with Cypher and Heffers was sold to Blackwells. The 1990s also saw significant foreign investment in UK bookselling, including the sale of Books Etc. to the US company Borders in 1997. As well as these big takeovers, smaller companies like Austicks and Thornes were being absorbed into expanding chains. Most of the mergers and takeovers of the 1990s were followed by the opening of new and bigger stores. In the process, the book trade has become polarised between small to medium-sized retailers on the one hand, and very big groups on the other. There is, for example, a huge gap between the two main booksellers – Waterstone's and W.H. Smith – and the next band of companies (Schlesinger 1999). It appears to be the medium-sized chains that have reduced most in recent years, either because they have been taken over or because they have expanded and so moved up into the next grouping. Nevertheless, some new chains have appeared or are expanding.

In this rapidly changing environment, independent booksellers seem to be particularly vulnerable. In the late 1990s, there were indicators that the overall size of the independent sector had not altered significantly (Schlesinger 1999). However, more recent reports suggest that independent booksellers fared badly during 2000, with sales slipping by almost 10 per cent (Bookseller Publications 2001). The independents still have some advantages over the chains, and tend to emphasize local knowledge and personal service. Whilst the larger retailers tend to order stock centrally, independents (and some medium-sized book chains like Ottakar's) have a localized system of stock buying, which enables them to take into account local considerations. Nevertheless, as the retail market becomes more competitive, the independents seem to be facing an uncertain future.

Many publishers initially welcomed the changes taking place in the retail sector, particularly the opening of superstores and the prospect of more retail space being devoted to books. However, there has also been a down-side for publishers. As we noted in Chapter 3, the balance of power in the trade has steadily shifted from publishers to retailers, and this has been accentuated by the concentration of ownership in the retail sector and the demise of the Net Book Agreement (NBA). The major retail chains now have such enormous purchasing power that they can demand better terms from publishers: in the process, these companies can make greater cost savings and so become even more profitable. In effect, publishers are being forced to buy shelf space in order to get their goods to potential customers. In the process, the formerly good relationship between retailers and publishers has started to deteriorate. As one publisher put it:

> There used to be almost a partnership between the bookseller and publisher and now I think that partnership has gone and it is dog eat dog. There is a lot of concern, worry, and embattled feelings on both sides. It used to be a gentler industry. I think a lot of industries are probably going through a similar kind of thing. Anything to do with retail is really difficult at the moment.

Diversification of outlets

Although the retail sector polarized during the 1990s, it also became more fragmented as non-traditional outlets entered the market. Books are now increasingly sold in a whole range of shops, including department stores, health food shops, garden centres, DIY shops, and so on. Research carried out by KPMG found that although 25 retailers accounted for 70 per cent of UK sales, the remaining 30 per cent was generated by about 3285 different outlets (Schlesinger 1999). For some of these outlets, books still form a minor proportion of business and the threat to the specialist sector is probably minimal. However, the decision by supermarkets to increase their book range is a cause of concern for mixed retailers like W.H. Smith, which cater for a similar market.

This diversification was undoubtedly encouraged by the collapse of the NBA. Under the terms of the NBA, supermarkets had not been able to discount books in the way that they would other products, and therefore tended to stock a very limited range, mainly of 'bargain' books. Once the NBA collapsed, supermarkets such as Asda and Tesco began to devote more space to books. However, this interest in books is also part of a wider strategy. According to one supermarket book buyer whom we interviewed, the food market is saturated and there is no longer room for any real growth in this area. In order to survive and expand, supermarkets are now looking for new markets in non-food products, including books, videos and software. Supermarkets are in a strong position to move into these areas because they already have millions of customers every day. Yet although some supermarkets are planning to devote more space to books, they cannot (and do not currently intend to) compete with the specialists in terms of range. For the reasons identified earlier, software forms a small part of the supermarkets' non-food range; however, according to one buyer whom we interviewed, this is a growing area.

Meanwhile, the last decade has also seen the advent of online shopping; and bookselling is considered to be one of the success stories of Internet retail, even though online companies have been slow to generate profit. Increased book sales have been attributed to the convenience of online shopping, the offer of discounts and the huge choice of titles available. In addition to books, some retailers offer a range of other media (including videos, CD-ROMs and DVDs), although the sale of software through the Internet is reported to be far behind that of books. Book clubs – having experienced growth in the 1990s – are particularly vulnerable in the face of competition from the Internet, as a recent industry report suggested:

> The demise of the NBA and that new champion of the armchair shopper, the Internet, have effectively robbed the book clubs of their discounting monopoly and, at the same time, left some of them with apparent disadvantage of a membership requirement to buy a certain number of titles each year . . . The clubs face a new challenge: their marketing bywords of convenience and choice have been well and truly appropriated by the Internet bookseller; book clubs cannot compete with the range of titles offered by the likes of Amazon.com.
>
> (Schlesinger 1999: 96–8)

However, there are a number of factors which still limit the level of online shopping: not everyone has access to the Internet, there are concerns about security, and some people simply prefer to shop in high-street outlets where they can look at a book or CD-ROM before they buy it. Bricks-and-mortar shops have responded to competition from online-only retailers by setting up their own Internet sites and, as we shall see below, by attempting to change the character of the 'shopping experience'.

As the chain booksellers expand and more non-traditional outlets diversify into bookselling, some commentators have predicted that supply will soon outstrip demand and this will eventually lead to widespread closures. According to Martin Grindley, president of the Booksellers' Association, there is now 'too much floor space chasing too few customers' (Clee 2000: 32). On the other hand, it could be argued that non-traditional outlets are helping to expand the market for books (or at least particular kinds of books) rather than simply diverting sales away from other outlets. For example, book purchases in supermarkets are often impulse buys by people who would not normally go to traditional bookshops. Similarly, the Internet offers access to books which might otherwise be hard to find in local shops (e.g. specialist titles, out-of-print books) and it is therefore possible that additional sales are being made. There is also some evidence to suggest that, because it is so easy to buy on the Internet, people are buying more books than they might otherwise have done in bricks-and-mortar shops (Schlesinger 1999). Nevertheless, the long-term impact of this kind of retail diversification on the book trade is difficult to assess at this stage, partly because it is a relatively recent phenomenon and also because the future commitment of such non-traditional outlets to selling books is not certain.

The impact on the children's educational market

These changes in the overall book market have had particular implications for children's retail. The entry of non-traditional outlets means that children's books are now sold in a wide range of locations, including supermarkets, toy shops and department stores. The 1999 *Books and the Consumer* survey, for example, found that the distribution of the children's market is more diverse than for adults, with bookshops, book/ stationery stores and book clubs accounting for just over half of books bought for children, compared to nearly three-quarters of purchases for adults (Book Marketing Limited 2000). In the case of supermarkets, children's books are now one of the main genres stocked, along with best-selling adult fiction and cookery. The supermarkets tend not to compete with the specialist sector in terms of range or subject expertise, preferring to target customers who do not go to bookshops or who purchase on impulse, as one supermarket buyer told us:

> Where we can offer something over and above a traditional
> bookshop is that – again, our research shows us that there are
> a very high proportion of people who don't go into traditional
> bookshops because they feel intimidated by the atmosphere. It's
> partly to do with the amount of range that's there, they think,
> 'how can I find the one book that I want when there are thousands
> here?', and often they're quite dark, and they're quiet, and they can
> be quite overwhelming if it's not something that you've grown up
> with. And the great thing about a supermarket is that people are
> incredibly familiar with it . . . And they don't have to select from a
> huge range. I mean, we have preselected and what they do, they trust
> us to have selected the best on the market, so we don't offer choice.

On one level, then, it could be argued that diversification has made children's books accessible to a much wider market; although the range and type of material that is being offered are quite restricted. However, the supermarkets' entry into the market may have helped to create a demand for certain types of publications that did not exist before, as in the case of educational magazines aimed at younger children (see Chapter 3). According to one publisher, the supermarkets' decision to stock pre-school magazines was *the* most important factor in the growth in sales, and this in turn led to the publication of new titles. In many ways, supermarkets are an ideal outlet for magazines or books which combine education and entertainment. Many parents shop with their children, and so supermarkets tend to stock titles which will have an immediate appeal to the child and which will be seen by parents as better than sweets and cheaper than toys. Book and magazine sales through these outlets tend to be 'impulse' buys rather than planned purchases, and they are generally seen as something to keep children quiet during shopping.

This impulse aspect in part dictates the kind of books which the supermarkets will sell. For example, price is important, and most children's books stocked in supermarkets are under £5. Magazines or books will have to be 'fun' to appeal to the child but maybe also have an educational element to please the parent. Titles like Scholastic's *Horrible Histories* are ideally suited to supermarket retail because they are inexpensive, part of an immediately recognizable series, and combine education and entertainment. As one supermarket buyer told us:

> What Scholastic have done is to do what we're trying to do with education, which is to create the sort of 'fun to learn' idea. So to be able to sell products which are appealing to children – they don't seem dry, but parents perceive the educational benefit – and so they kind of deliver two things. They deliver fun for the child and they deliver the educational benefit, and parents feel good about buying books for their children . . . It's better than buying them comics, or sweets or lots of other things.

Some commentators have suggested that because supermarkets and other mixed retailers focus on inexpensive paperbacks, best-sellers and series they may have a stifling effect on publishing, resulting in 'fiction by the yard' (see Horn 1997a; 1998a). There have also been concerns that the non-traditional outlets would add to an already competitive retail sector. Yet despite the perceived threat, research carried out by Book Marketing Limited, (2000) suggests that there was little change in the supermarkets' volume share of the book market from 1997 to 1999. The supermarkets are more likely to represent a threat to other mixed retailers rather than specialist bookshops, because they are targeting a similar clientele; and this became particularly apparent when the supermarkets moved into the 'early learning' market. While the range of books available in supermarkets is very limited, they clearly are having a significant impact on trade in certain key areas.

As we have noted, the impact of concentration in the retail sector has led to concern about the fate of independent booksellers. Nevertheless, the two specialist children's bookshop managers whom we interviewed reported that their sales had remained constant or even increased over the last few years. They felt that this was partly due to their location (in affluent areas of London) and a middle-class clientele who were interested in books. Neither of these shops tried to compete with the chains on discounts: because of their size, they are not in a position to negotiate better terms from publishers, as Waterstone's has attempted to do. They try to differentiate themselves from the chains by focusing on personal service, subject knowledge and book range. Customer loyalty and building up a profile within the community were also important. Both shops had close links to the local schools, tailoring their stock to meet their needs as well as organizing events like author visits to schools.

The retail experience

As the retail trade becomes more competitive and fragmented, booksellers have looked for new ways in which to attract customers. In addition to discounting, retailers have also focused on improving the shop environment and services in order to make shopping a more enjoyable experience, for example by providing coffee/soda bars, seating areas and computer terminals. Booksellers have paid increasing attention to the ways in which items are displayed, and introduced different products alongside books. This new approach to retail has been influenced by the American model where the huge bookstores such as Borders and Barnes and Noble have 'virtually become community centres', offering a range of services and entertainment options (Schlesinger 1999: 26).

This new emphasis has led to various initiatives specifically designed to appeal to the children's market. Traditionally, the big chains have dealt with children's books in much the same way as they dealt with every other kind of book. However, children are now increasingly being targeted as a niche market, and a new rhetoric is emerging about the importance of 'respecting their needs'. According to Carol Gill the merchandising manager of W.H. Smith (quoted in *The Children's Bookseller*, 1999: 18):

> The critical challenge facing booksellers, publishers and authors
> alike is, therefore, to understand the importance of children as a
> consumer group in their own right and to ensure that children,
> of their own volition, choose to read books in the future. Above
> all else, children demand respect. To succeed in the next
> millennium, we must first respect children as an important
> consumer group in their own right, by understanding and
> embracing their needs.

Providing a multi-product environment is one strategy used to target children and their parents. In the last few years children's retailers (in common with retailers more generally) have begun to talk about providing 'solutions' rather than just products: 'We are looking more and more at cross-merchandising because customers are not looking for a speculative book, they are looking for a solution for, say, the concept of geography for their son' (Clea Ewing, quoted in McCabe 1997: 14). It was also felt that books could do well in a multi-product environment because toys and videos would attract children to the books area. Some retailers have started to provide in-store entertainment (like storytelling), juice bars and seating areas in an effort to turn shopping into a 'leisure experience'. Daisy and Tom, the up-market department store for children set up by Tim Waterstone, and now owned by the HMV Media Group, encapsulates this new approach to children's retailing, as we shall describe below.

Specialist booksellers have also re-examined the way in which they target the child market, though some are more committed to this idea than others. There is very little difference between the way in which adult and children's books are sold in Waterstone's, for example. Indeed, when Waterstone's and Dillons merged there were concerns that children's bookselling would suffer from the rebranding of Dillons stores as Waterstone's, since Dillons had been perceived as the stronger of the two chains in children's retail (see Horn 1998b). Waterstone's have countered criticisms of their policy by pointing out that children's departments should not be treated as 'a kind of remedial section': 'We have the philosophy that it is the books themselves that are interesting, so we don't want lots of gimmicks in the children's section. We have the confidence that the books will sell themselves' (Martin Lee, quoted in Horn 1998b: 23).

Nevertheless, other retailers have experimented with changes to store layout, displays and product range in order to target children and parents more directly. In 1997, W.H. Smith introduced a multi-product children's area, 'Discovery', in 13 of its shops. The strategy here was to shift the emphasis from the product to the subject matter: instead of displaying books with books, software with software, and so on, different products were displayed together around a particular theme, for example science. However, the project soon ran into problems, partly because customers were not used to shopping in this way, and found it difficult to find what they wanted. This problem was accentuated by the fact that the Discovery area was usually located at the back of the store. Furthermore, older children did not like the idea of being in a separate area to adults, while some parents started to use it as a sort of crèche where they could leave their children while they went shopping, raising concerns about safety. Nevertheless, the failure of 'Discovery' has not discouraged others: as we shall see below, Ottakar's went on to trial a similar initiative in five of its stores.

Meanwhile, the idea of selling different products together as a pack became more popular a few years ago. For example, Playmobil produced a book-plus-toy range (see *The Children's Bookseller* 1998). However, this concept seems to have had fairly limited success. The software company Europress, for example, had hoped to combine educational CD-ROMs and books, but found that the retail sector was not very interested in this kind of product. There were practical problems such as how to shelve non-standard-shaped items, and some shops (particularly the small independents) did not have the space to expand their product range. Combining products also raises the price threshold, so the supermarkets and general retailers are less likely to stock them; and some traditional outlets seem to object to book-plus-product ranges because they are not seen as 'appropriate'. This reluctance on the part of traditional booksellers may be because they regard the multi-product approach as a form of 'dumbing down', particularly if it involves toys and novelty items. Not surprisingly, the shops which are most likely to stock multi-product ranges are the shops which already have a multi-product environment, like Daisy and Tom.

Retailing: four case studies

Having outlined the broader tendencies within the retail sector, we now move on to describe a series of case studies of different types of retailers. Our focus here is twofold: we look both at the commercial strategy of these companies and at their marketing discourse – and in particular, at the way they attempt to appeal to parents' educational aspirations for their children.

Daisy and Tom

Daisy and Tom is a kind of children's department store, which provides a range of products (e.g. toys, books and clothes), services (such as a children's hairdresser) and in-store entertainment all under one roof. The shop aims to provide 'a one-stop shopping experience' which is convenient and enjoyable for both parents and children (see Horn 1997b). The first Daisy and Tom store was opened in London in 1997 by Tim Waterstone, controversial managing director of the Waterstone's book-shop chain; and it became part of the HMV Media Group in 1998. Despite early predictions that Daisy and Tom would expand in the UK and Europe, only two stores have so far opened in the UK.

In her book on the toy industry, Ellen Seiter (1993) distinguishes be-tween retailers which sell mass-market promotional toys (like Toys R Us) and smaller up-market toy stores which focus on 'educational' or 'classic' toys targeted at the well-educated middle-class parent. In terms of prod-uct mix, Daisy and Tom seems to be a compromise between these two types of retailer. A large proportion of the toys are of the mass-market variety: for example, they are based on licensed characters, including the long-running Barbie and Action-Man ranges, as well as more recent crazes like Bob the Builder, the Tweenies and Pikachu. However, Daisy and Tom also stocks a range of 'classic' toys which include mahogany rock-ing horses (£2400), European dolls and teddies (priced from £65 to £250 and displayed in a locked cabinet), hobby horses and other wooden toys, and soft toys based on classic fiction, such as Paddington Bear. This diversity is also reflected in the book section, which ranges from classic children's fiction to books based on popular licensed characters (such as Pokémon) – although, interestingly, the latter are displayed on a shelf specifically labelled 'media tie-ins'. The price range goes from paperbacks for 99p to glossy hardbacks for over £25. However, at the time of our first visit, classic fiction (for example, *The Chronicles of Narnia*) and picture books seemed to be more prominently displayed than in other bookshops; and while many other bookstores were in the grip of 'Pottermania', the promotion of the fourth Harry Potter book was more subdued here than it was elsewhere. A number of books designed for the under-five age group are sold in conjunction with other products, mainly toys or cups. There is also a range of study guides and revision aids, though these are at the back of the store. Clearly, some of the more expensive or 'classic' items in the store would be selected by the parent, rather than the child. For example, the shop sells navy blue *Mary Poppins*-style prams, rather than buggies or push-chairs; and some of the children's clothes are from Baby Dior and French Connection.

Although the children's product range at Daisy and Tom is fairly diverse, the shop environment is quite different from that of the major book and toy chains. There is none of the brashness of Toys R Us, for example: instead, we have mellow music, subtle lighting, light-coloured wooden floors and shelves, and spacious aisles. While bookshops like Ottakar's claim to provide 'exciting in-store interactive stations' (see below), Daisy and Tom seems to have taken its inspiration from an old-fashioned fairground and a rather nostalgic view of childhood. There is a small carousel consisting of wooden horses and roosters, each of which has its own name. This is located in a circular room, the ceiling of which is shaped like a circus tent with blue and white stripes going up to the centre. A countryside scene is painted across the wall, showing two smiling children being carried up into the air by their kite. Below them there are rolling green hills and little houses, whilst above there is a perfect blue sky and a smiling yellow sun (the same image is shown on the shop's carrier bags). Two giant-sized bears dressed in military uniform stand on either side of the exit from this room: one is a guardsman bear and the other a household cavalry bear. Elsewhere in the shop there is a puppet show, and in the centre of the book room there is a display based on a European-style clock tower, with two figures in traditional dress. Although many of the products reflect the latest fashion, the overall shop environment seems to hark back to some idealized bygone age.

While Daisy and Tom is not exclusive (you can buy a plastic sword for under £3), it certainly is not a mass-market store. However, this is reflected more in its location (on London's King's Road) and the shop environment than in its product mix. Although the clientele is likely to be middle- or upper middle-class, the shop cannot afford to confine itself to parental tastes. With the rise of the child as 'sovereign consumer' (Buckingham, 2000b), it may be difficult for any shops (even those in the most up-market areas) to ignore mass-market phenomena like Bob the Builder or Pokémon.

Ottakar's

Ottakar's was set up in 1987 and expanded rapidly to become one of the main bookselling chains in the UK. The majority of branches are located in towns, small cities and city suburbs. According to their children's books manager, Ottakar's has positioned itself between W.H. Smith (the leading books-and-stationery retailer) and Waterstone's (the leading bookshop chain) and is particularly committed to the children's book market. In general, there is no central buying apart from opening and promotions stock. Ottakar's stock CD-ROMs, although they do not see this as a growing area because of competition from the Internet.

At the time of our research, Ottakar's was trialling a project called 'Launch Pad', which brought together a range of books and educational toys with a product mix of about 60:40 in favour of books. Launch Pad replaced children's departments in five stores, while the specialist children's store in Sheffield was based entirely on the Launch Pad concept. By broadening its product base to include toys, the chain hoped to attract new customers, including children who do not necessarily like books. According to the children's books manager, the project was designed to provide 'a complete education offering' based on the idea that 'children learn best when they are having fun'.

The Sheffield branch (which is called Launch Pad rather than Ottakar's) exemplifies this 'fun' approach to education and shopping. According to their website (www.ottakers.co.uk/Internet/shopfinder/shopdetails.jsp?shop10=OTT096), the shop provides 'an amazing range of children's books and educational toys, from Roald Dahl to rockets' as well as 'exciting in-store interactive stations', making Launch Pad 'the place to be!'. Events in the store include not only the usual book-based events (such as story-telling and author signings) but also a variety of activities including an Easter egg hunt, making Easter cards, and visits from Peter Rabbit, Spot the Dog, Maisy Mouse and various other characters. The language in which these events are promoted (e.g. 'join the fun and mayhem') seems designed to dispel the idea that bookshops are boring. The 'fun' principle is supposed to be part of children's departments in all Ottakar's stores, not just those involved in Launch Pad, as their children's books manager told us:

> First of all, we make the children's department as fun and as exciting as we can. Lots of events to introduce people to the culture of a bookshop, dispel any myths about it being stuffy or libraryish. They are entertainment zones as well as an opportunity to sell books . . . The look and the design of the children's department is bright and inviting so children feel very at home. In all stores there are various degrees of interactivity from a car to a truck to a rocking horse to big interactives that we have got together with the Science Museum to produce, so it is very much entertainment value . . . that entices people into our stores.

Another way in which Ottakar's targets the parent and child market is through its collaboration with schools. Various events are organized with local schools, including competitions, author visits, storytelling and book reviews. In a more direct form of marketing they will 'pursue teachers for reading lists for the courses and persuade the teachers to recommend Ottakar's to their students'. The local branch will then stock as many books as possible from this list. As we have noted, this ability to respond to local circumstances is one of the advantages of decentralized book buying: neither W.H. Smith, the supermarkets nor some of the other chains would have this level of flexibility. Ottakar's also sells into the schools market, arranging evenings when teachers can browse through the books and meet publishers' representatives and authors: they are given a 10 per cent discount not only on books purchased for the school but also on any books which they buy for themselves. These events are usually held after the store has closed, and refreshments (wine and cheese) are provided.

Albeit in a very different way from Daisy and Tom, there is a key emphasis here on the 'shopping experience', which is reflected in the atmosphere of the store and its attempt to offer opportunities for consumer participation and identification. As with many of the publishers, the inseparability of 'fun' and 'learning' is seen to provide a crucial means of addressing children and parents simultaneously.

Tesco

Tesco is the largest food retailer in the UK and also has branches in Europe and Asia. Like many other large corporations, it is keen to present itself as a company with a social conscience. It has a broad-ranging 'Corporate Social Responsibility' programme which covers education, local communities, the environment and farming. Education appears to be a particularly popular 'cause' amongst supermarkets in general. For example, Sainsbury's (one of Tesco's main rivals) sponsored Bookstart, a scheme which provides free books for babies; while Tesco has been particularly successful in branding itself as 'the education supermarket'. Perhaps the most widely known initiative here is its 'Computers for Schools' scheme (whereby Tesco issues shoppers with vouchers that can contribute to the purchase of computers for local schools); but it has supported a number of other educational projects, including the 'Learning Zone' at the Millennium Dome, the 'Green Code' programme, and 'Our School Awards'. Tesco also offers advice to parents on child development, health and education via its extensive website (www.tesco.com/youandyourchild). The site features 'survival tips for first time dads', a 'what mums say' panel, the 'Tesco Toddlers Club', links to a chat room, and offers of a free magazine 'packed with advice from experts'. Interspersed with the advice pages are the inevitable sales pitches ('Now your little treasure is an active toddler, it's a relief to know that Tesco can meet all your shopping needs in one place.').

Of course, this interest in education is not wholly altruistic. Unlike some other charitable causes, education carries a fairly unambiguous 'feel-good factor'; and families with children are an important sector of the food retail market. According to a Tesco representative whom we interviewed, the company derives 'a soft benefit rather than a direct one' from supporting these educational initiatives: they help to establish the company's profile in the community and build up customer loyalty. Obviously, such initiatives can generate valuable publicity: for example, the Tesco website contains a feature on how Prime Minister Tony Blair launched the tenth year of the Computers in Schools scheme in Sedgefield 'by cutting a special 10th birthday cake with local school children'.

Until the 1990s, Tesco, like other supermarkets, focused almost exclusively on the food market. With the collapse of the Net Book Agreement and the saturation of the food market, the company started to diversify into non-food products including books and software, and now stocks a range of educational books, toys and CD-ROMs. In the last five years it has expanded the number and range of such items, although it does not see itself as being in competition with the specialist sector: as their representative put it, the aim is to become a small version of W.H. Smith rather than a branch of Waterstone's. Here again, the company is particularly interested in the 'fun to learn' concept, and stocks a range of magazines and early learning materials for the pre-school market.

Tesco's approach to bookselling seems to reflect its overall approach to retail: books are just one of the many products on sale and tend to be marketed in much the same way. Competitive pricing is one of the main features of supermarket retail and so the majority of children's books are at the lower end of the price range. As with other products, Tesco has developed its 'own brand' books (primarily in the 'early learning' area), and there is a centralized system of book buying so that stock tends to be the same regardless of shop location (though shop size may limit the range). Although Tesco has increased its range in this sector over the last five years, there are difficulties in expanding further. The company fears that – despite its strongly 'responsible' branding – some parents are not inclined to trust a food retailer when it comes to education and books in general. Tesco therefore faces a dilemma: it has to increase its range in order to be taken seriously as a bookseller, but it does not want to expand too much as it may lose the advantage of being more accessible than specialist shops. Securing an appropriate and commercially viable market position in this sector is therefore a difficult balancing act.

Brainworks

Our final case study looks at one attempt to solve the difficult problem of retailing educational software. Brainworks is a software distribution company that operates in much the same way as a book club. Its catalogue (the one we refer to here is dated spring 2000) is primarily distributed via broadsheet newspapers. Brainworks markets heavily discounted CD-ROMs produced by a range of software publishers, and offers a 'Home Learning Plan' which entitles subscribers to further discounts. The catalogue features illustrated descriptions of the software packages, complete with endorsements from parents, teachers and 'experts'.

The cover of the catalogue features a child dressed as an archetypal 'swot', complete with large spectacles, slicked-down preppy hairstyle, formal shirt and bow tie. It purports to contain no fewer than '287 ways to boost your child's schoolwork'. Two representative quotations can also be found on the front cover:

> 'I used to think homework was boring – but with my new maths CD-ROM, it's much more interesting and fun!' David Oliver, Aged 8

> 'My children have really leapt ahead with their classwork since we joined Brainworks. They are excited by learning because its [*sic*] fun.' James Derwent, Parent

These quotations signal two key themes that recur throughout the catalogue: the notion of gaining competitive advantage for your children, and the relationship between learning and 'fun'.

The claim that using such software will give your child a 'head start' in the educational race is quite unashamed. A message from Anne Civardi, editorial director, emphasizes that the primary aim of Brainworks is to 'help your children do better at school and in their exams'. Thus, among the software included in the catalogue, *Jump Ahead Year 1* offers your child '18 ways to get ahead in school', while *Maths Blaster* will 'start your child's journey to becoming a maths genius'. While some of the software is designed explicitly to assist children in preparing for tests, even apparently entertainment-based productions are defined in these terms: *Fireman Sam* will 'really help build on classwork in Key Stage 1', while *Noddy* contains 'new assessment technology' that will 'show your children's progress'. In thus capitalizing on parental anxieties about testing, the catalogue clearly positions its ideal reader as a 'concerned parent'. The good parent will be the one who completes the application form for the Home Learning Plan:

> Yes, I am interested in giving my child a better education. Please enrol me in the Brainworks Home Learning Plan.

The relationship between 'learning' and 'fun' is the other major theme in the catalogue as a whole. These terms almost invariably occur together. Thus, *Talking Tables* is a 'fun learning program that takes away some of the drudgery of learning those dreaded tables'; *Freddi Fish* will 'keep your children immersed in learning fun'; while *Carmen Sandiego* 'really does teach world history the fun way'. Yet despite the persistent coupling of these terms, different values are associated with each. Thus, *learning* is a matter of acquiring 'essential skills', 'mastering games based on reading fundamentals' and 'following respected teaching methods'. The software is 'terrific for reinforcing language and phonic activities', 'a fantastic way to introduce the vital building blocks of reading skills' or a way of gaining practice in 'solving intriguing maths assignments'. Through its use of these terms, the catalogue represents education as a highly instructional process, a matter of acquiring and practising disembodied 'skills', albeit in a palatable and entertaining manner. Meanwhile, *fun* is associated with quite different terms: it is about 'excitement', 'adventure', 'magic' and 'enchantment'. Thus, *Star Wars Yoda's Challenge* invites you to 'explore a galaxy of fun and learning'; while *Jump Ahead* will 'make learning to read a great adventure' and offer 'fundamental maths – made fun'.

As this implies, there is in fact a fundamental opposition here between *work* and *play*. Learning is work; while play is something parents might (perhaps reluctantly) allow their children to do when their work is done. Learning is what responsible parents want to encourage; but in order to do so, they have to present it in the context of pleasure and play. They have to add some sugar to the pill. Despite the rhetoric of 'fun learning' and 'learning fun', this approach thus effectively reinscribes oppositions between education and entertainment – and indeed, sustains a hierarchy in which educational 'work' is seen as the only truly worthwhile pursuit for children.

Our research on the market in educational software suggests that the titles which sell most effectively are those which make the strongest educational claims, particularly if they relate to testing and other government policies such as the National Literacy Strategy. Titles which make more 'progressive' claims – which represent learning as a matter of open-ended 'discovery' – are less likely to succeed. In some instances, changing the packaging in order to emphasize such traditionally educational claims – 'covers the whole Key Stage 1 Maths curriculum' – has resulted in significant increases in sales. Here again, there is an interesting coincidence between market strategies and educational policies, which contrives to sustain a highly reductive conception of what counts as 'education'.

Interestingly, some companies such as Granada are now offering special deals to schools and colleges to promote their educational CD-ROMs to parents. In a digital version of the Tupperware party, institutions 'keen to encourage the use of quality software in the home' are offered a 'Home Version Sales Kit' and free software vouchers as an incentive for multiple sales. In this approach, teachers are not merely a market: they have, in effect, become marketers themselves.

Conclusion

Over the past decade, technological and economic changes have fundamentally transformed the structure of the media and cultural industries. Despite retaining vestiges of a genteel public image, publishing has been no exception to this. The developments we have described in this and the previous chapter suggest that the market in children's educational materials is now increasingly governed by commercial imperatives. In the attempt to cope with growing competition and reducing profit margins, the scope for innovation and risk-taking among publishers has been significantly reduced. In this uncertain world, the logical response is to play safe, and to rely on tried and tested formulae; and, where relevant, to allow the dictates of government policy to provide a degree of predictability and security. While the diversification of retail outlets has enabled publishers to reach new markets, the growing degree of concentration within retailing is bound to result in a narrowing in the range of products available to the consumer. In all these respects, the market would seem to exercise a constraining, conservative influence on the provision of educational goods and services.

Nevertheless, the commercial marketplace can also be seen as an arena in which popular wants and needs are expressed. This is a market in which children's sovereignty is increasingly being acknowledged – and, in some quarters, positively celebrated. In this context, parental (and indeed governmental) notions of what counts as learning cannot reign unchallenged. In attempting to engage with the changing enthusiasms of children, educational publishers have been obliged to rethink their approach; and while some of these changes have undoubtedly been superficial, others may have been rather more profound. As such, the growing significance of commercial appeals is bound to have implications in terms of the pedagogic strategies these books, magazines and software are likely to adopt – and particularly in terms of the relationships between 'education' and 'entertainment'. How these relationships are configured and defined at the level of specific texts is the focus of the four chapters that follow.

PART TWO

CHAPTER 5

PARENTAL PEDAGOGIES
Edutainment and early learning

This chapter is the first of four case studies looking at the ways in which learning is constructed, packaged and sold to parents and children. The chapters that make up this part of the book cover a range of media, including magazines, books and educational software. Cutting across the specific instances we discuss is a series of overarching concerns. How do these texts define 'education' and 'entertainment', and seek to combine them? How do they set out to teach, and what kinds of learning do they promote? How do they position the user in relation to knowledge and information? What roles or identities do they mark out for children and parents?

In this chapter, we focus specifically on 'edutainment' magazines aimed at pre-school children. While educational magazines of this kind have existed for some time, the pre-school market has expanded at a remarkable rate over the past five years. As we have implied, this expansion is partly a response to changes in government policy on education; but it is also a consequence of economic changes in publishing and retailing. These magazines are thus a paradoxical development. On the one hand, they represent the growing 'curricularization' of learning in the home; and yet they also reflect the growth of commercial influences on the lives of very young children. They address parents as pedagogues, who should be responsible for ensuring that their children acquire the 'skills' they will need for educational success; and yet they also address parents and children as consumers, and indeed as active participants in a global multimedia market.

Most of the titles in this field are based on children's television programmes and characters. We therefore begin by describing the expansion of this market in the context of the broader commercialization of children's media culture and the growth in cross-media merchandising. We then provide an analysis of the educational rhetoric of the magazines, as embodied in their sales pitches and pedagogic advice to parents. Finally, the pedagogic strategies of the magazines are analysed, through an account of their mode of address and their positioning of the child reader. On the one hand, we suggest, many of these magazines are informed by a reductive and disciplinary conception of learning – not least in their appeals to parents; yet on the other, there is an apparently contradictory emphasis on entertainment and 'fun'. As we have implied, this combination may be symptomatic of broader changes in the forms and sites of learning in contemporary society.

An outline of the magazines

Educational magazines for young children have existed for decades, although the range of titles available has expanded significantly in recent years. Of the 19 different titles we were able to obtain from a range of high-street newsagents in early 2000, only two (the BBC's *Playdays* and *Toybox*) date back to the early 1990s. The others are all much more recent in origin, although several of them recycle old material, in some cases from as far back as the 1980s. (For a list of titles analysed, see Table 1.)

Such magazines can be purchased on subscription or in local newsagents, but they are also increasingly appearing in less traditional outlets such as supermarkets. They generally cost between £1 and £1.30 each, although a couple of titles (both produced by smaller independent publishers) are more expensive: *3Rs Budgie* is £1.90, while *Learning Land* (which incorporates a CD-ROM) is £3.99. The magazines are generally

Table 1   List of titles analysed, with publishers

Sesame Street (Panini UK Ltd)	*Play and Learn: Thomas and Friends*
Learning Land (De Agostini UK Ltd)	(Egmont Fleetway)
Noddy (BBC)	*CiTV Telly Tots* (Egmont Fleetway)
Spot (BBC)	*3Rs Budgie* (Practical Publications Ltd)
Playdays (BBC)	*Tots TV* (Redan)
Teletubbies (BBC)	*Friends* (Redan)
Toybox (BBC)	*Bananas in Pyjamas* (Redan)
Tweenies (BBC)	*Barney* (Redan)
Bob the Builder (BBC)	*Fireman Sam* (Redan)
Tell Me Why (BBC)	*Jellikins* (Burghley Publishing)

Note: Some of the magazines are undated, but all were purchased in early to mid-2000. Comics or other magazines that did not make explicit 'educational' claims were excluded from the analysis.

published monthly or every two or three weeks. They often incorporate 'free gifts', such as sets of crayons, fridge magnets, badges or stickers.

As is apparent from Table 1, the market is dominated by the BBC, who at the time of writing (mid-2000) publish eight separate titles. According to the BBC's Annual Report, their annual turnover in this area is approximately £12 million. Their major rival is Redan, whose *Fun To Learn* series relates to independent (commercial) television programmes. Other publishers include Egmont Fleetway, a major international publisher specializing in comics and teen magazines; Panini, who are major players in the lucrative sticker albums market; and a few smaller independent publishers. With the exception of *Learning Land* and the BBC's *Tell Me Why*, all the titles are related to children's television programmes and characters, or (in a couple of instances) to popular book series.

While there are obviously some differences in the content and format of these magazines, similar activities and features occur throughout. These include: illustrated stories; rhymes and songs; colouring-in and join-the-dots pictures; mazes; counting activities; sorting and matching exercises; 'make-and-do' assignments; exercises involving finding or identifying objects; information-giving features; board games; writing activities; cut-out-and-collect pictures or posters; activities based on the alphabet and letter recognition; competitions; drawings sent in by readers; and, of course, advertisements. Several of the Redan *Fun To Learn* titles include pull-out 'workbooks'. In addition, most of the magazines provide guidance for parents, in the form of messages on each page and/or separate pages aimed specifically at parents. Most of the magazines are either 24 or 32 pages in length, of which an average of two or three pages are taken by advertising.

The learning business

On one level, these magazines are symptomatic of what the US critic Marsha Kinder (1991) has called 'trans-media intertextuality'. In recent decades, media aimed at children have increasingly been characterized by integrated marketing. Television programmes are no longer just television programmes: they are also films, records, books, comics and magazines, computer games and toys – not to mention T-shirts, posters, lunchboxes, drinks, sticker albums, food, and a myriad of other products. The key children's media successes of the 1980s and 1990s – *Teenage Mutant Ninja Turtles*, *Super Mario Brothers*, *Mighty Morphin' Power Rangers* and now *Pokémon* – have all been packaged and marketed as multimedia phenomena in this way.

Among younger children, this market is largely driven by licensed characters: Barney, Postman Pat, Fireman Sam, Noddy, Budgie the Little Helicopter, Thomas the Tank Engine, Bob the Builder, Spot and friends are recognized by children around the world, and are used to brand a whole range of products. This is, without doubt, an increasingly lucrative business. In the USA alone, children under 12 are estimated to spend $11 billion each year, and to influence the purchase of more than $160 billion in family goods and services. The market is estimated to be growing at around 2 per cent per year (Del Vecchio 1997: 20). Nearly all the most popular toys are TV-related, as are many of the most popular books bought for this age group (Kline 1993; Seiter 1993; Hilton 1996).

However, this development is not confined to the work of exclusively 'commercial' corporations, or indeed to children's 'entertainment'. In the USA, Public Broadcasting Service (PBS) productions such as *Sesame Street* (produced by the not-for-profit organization Children's Television Workshop, and screened on PBS channels) have always depended on ancillary merchandise and 'spin-offs' in other media. The same is true of *Barney*, also screened on PBS. Both programmes have associated 'educational' magazines published in the UK by Redan, as well as generating a range of books and 'educational' toys.

In recent years, this integrated marketing approach has also been increasingly adopted by the BBC. BBC executives continue to assert that commercial activities take second place to editorial (and, in this case, educational) concerns; yet the involvement of the BBC's commercial subsidiary, BBC Worldwide (which publishes the magazines considered here), is increasingly seen as a prerequisite, particularly for major new investments in programming (Home 1995). The success of the BBC's latest pre-school series, *Teletubbies*, is a revealing case in point (see Buckingham 2002b). *Teletubbies* would not have existed without the possibility of overseas sales (it is currently sold in more than 60 countries); and a major merchandising operation was planned by BBC Worldwide from the very beginning. The list of *Teletubbies* products either licensed by the BBC or marketed directly is ever-growing: it includes a magazine, books, audio- and videotapes, computer games, posters, toys, clothing, watches, food and confectionery, mugs and crockery, stationery and games – as well as more unexpected artefacts such as computer mouse mats. According to the BBC's Annual Report, £330 million was generated overall during the programme's first two years, with £23 million going directly to the BBC in 1998 (43 per cent of which came from sales of videotapes, a market dominated by products aimed at pre-schoolers).

As this implies, very young children are a key market here; and broadly 'educational' magazines are a significant part of this. Such magazines capitalize on children's enthusiasm for the characters and programmes, while simultaneously addressing parental anxieties about education. In the case of the BBC, the magazines are intended to be complementary to the programmes, particularly in the sense that they add an 'educational' dimension to programmes that might otherwise be perceived as merely 'entertaining' (and hence be open to criticism from some parents).

According to one executive whom we interviewed, they 'use the pro-gramme and the characters to introduce children into a learning state of mind'. For the BBC, currently struggling to retain its audience share (and hence the legitimacy of the licence fee through which it is funded), 'education' is a central aspect of its brand identity in an increasingly competitive international market. Attempting to capitalize on its reputation for education and 'quality', while simultaneously avoiding the charge that it is merely 'exploiting' children, inevitably creates significant tensions – as the continuing controversy surrounding the educational merits (or lack of them) of *Teletubbies* clearly demonstrates.

These magazines are therefore part of an overall integrated marketing enterprise. Some of the merchandise is licensed by the BBC and/or the copyright holders to commercial companies. In the BBC's *Noddy* maga-zine, for example, there is a full-page advertisement on the back cover for Noddy merchandise sold through the mail order and online com-pany Character Warehouse: this includes Noddy dolls and soft toys, a train set, a toy mobile video phone, a cassette recorder and a scooter. In other instances, the merchandise is sold directly by the production companies themselves. Redan's *Tots TV*, for example, features a full-page advertisement for merchandise based on *Tots TV*, *Rosie and Jim* and *Teletubbies* sold directly by Ragdoll, the production company. Some of these items cost as much as £50 each.

Another, less direct form of merchandising is by means of competi-tions. Thus, Egmont Fleetway's *Play and Learn: Thomas and Friends* uses a competition to publicize Thomas the Tank Engine toys: 'Alexander wins one of these splendid engines from Heart Character Toys. Heart Char-acter Toys stock over 250 Thomas products in their mail order catalogue [pictured]. For your free copy, call . . .'. In other instances, it seems that companies are 'generously donating' products in order to generate some cheap advertising: *CiTV Telly Tots*, for example, announces that 'Thanks to the kind folk at Dorling Kindersley, Telly Tots have 40 fantastic *Mopatop's Shop* book sets to win!' (*Mopatop's Shop* being a programme currently broadcast on Children's ITV).

While there is some 'external' advertising here (e.g. for sweets or foodstuffs), most of it takes the form of cross-promotion. In a sense, any magazine based on a television programme is by its very nature an advertisement for that programme – just as the programme is effectively an advertisement for the magazine. However, in the BBC's case, the magazines include several advertisements for other BBC magazines or videotapes, sold via BBC Worldwide and available from the BBC's online shop. *CiTV Telly Tots* – probably the least overtly didactic of these maga-zines (see below) – is effectively a pre-schoolers' TV listings magazine: in addition to showing the channel and time of the programmes relating to each item in the magazine, it directs readers to its website, and offers a 'CiTV Favourites' video as a competition prize. In this TV-centric world, children are 'telly tots' and their parents are 'grown-up telly tots'; while competition winners are pictured with speech bubbles identifying their favourite Children's ITV programmes.

In some respects, these phenomena are merely symptomatic of the increasingly competitive, commercial nature of children's media culture (see Buckingham 2000b). Children and their parents – who are, after all, the most likely purchasers of these magazines – are clearly positioned here as *consumers*. The magazines are commodities themselves; and they both mediate and promise access to other commodities. In this self-promotional world, every text effectively becomes an advertisement for every other text. Nevertheless, this is not to say that readers are, in any simple sense, 'passive' consumers. Beyond the advertising itself, the magazines offer children the pleasure of recognizing familiar characters and comprehensible narratives; but they also provide the more active engagement of solving puzzles and playing games related to the programmes. They extend the world of television into the realm of everyday life, allowing children to relive the pleasures and to engage with the characters in potentially different circumstances. This is not yet *inter*active; but it is more than simply a matter of imprinting fixed meanings onto inert minds.

At the same time, however, these magazines are making explicit *educational* claims. They purport to encourage or bring about learning that will be of benefit to the child. These are claims which, for more traditional critics, are essentially incompatible with the imperatives of consumer culture. According to authors such as Stephen Kline (1993), for example, 'consumerism' and the maximization of profit are necessarily at odds with positive educational and cultural objectives. From this perspective, 'education' and 'entertainment' are often seen to be fundamentally incompatible: using the devices of entertainment media for educational ends – or even to put children in 'a learning state of mind' – inevitably represents a form of 'dumbing down'. In our view, however, the relationships between 'education' and 'entertainment' are both more complex and more paradoxical than this argument would suggest. 'Education' in any form is inevitably 'entertaining', in the sense that it has to engage and interest us; just as 'entertainment' is bound to be 'educational', in the sense that we cannot help but learn from it. Children are not merely 'passive consumers' of media entertainment – or indeed of education. Yet, as we shall indicate, the magazines effectively sell education *to parents* as a kind of commodity – and in doing so, they reflect the wider commodification of learning which is characteristic of current trends in educational policy.

Selling education

In recent years, the education and care of very young children has gradually been drawn into the government's broader educational regime. As

Anning (1998) observes, pre-school provision in the UK has increasingly moved towards a subject-based curriculum. Formal schooling now effectively begins at the age of 4 (two years earlier than in most other industrialized countries); and the early years curriculum is now dominated by the need to prepare children for government-dictated 'strategies' on literacy and numeracy that occupy much of the classroom time in primary schools. Testing also now begins at the point of entry into school, resulting in additional pressure on teachers to 'cover' a tightly prescribed curriculum. Despite research evidence pointing to the value of practical, experiential learning for children of this age (see Anning 1998), the government emphasizes 'expository', whole-class teaching and the need for drilling children in disembodied 'skills'.

The government's recently published guidance for what is now known as the 'Foundation Stage' (Qualifications and Curriculum Authority 2000) explicitly sets out to raise 'standards of learning and teaching' in this field. It describes a highly regulated world of 'well-planned, purposeful activity', in which 'a carefully structured curriculum' leads inevitably to 'effective learning and development'. 'Practitioners' are seen to be 'implementing curriculum requirements' and 'using assessment to evaluate the quality of provision'. The document's goals for early learning are somewhat cutely described as 'stepping stones', but they are effectively the same kind of prescriptive 'attainment targets' (or behavioural objectives) as found in the National Curriculum documents for older children. Despite the assertion that these are not age-related, it is these targets that will be applied in the 'baseline' tests on which children are now assessed on entry to school at age 4.

Needless to say, perhaps, there is no recognition whatsoever in this document of the fact that young children already live in a commercially based media culture. Information and communication technologies (ICTs) are effectively equated with computers, which are seen as an unproblematic benefit to learning; while television and video are mentioned only briefly, and in the context of children 'finding things out'. Learning is a form of 'work' that seems to proceed in ignorance of much of young children's everyday lives and cultural experiences.

As we have indicated, children's participation in consumer culture is centrally recognized in the magazines; but (perhaps paradoxically) so are the kinds of educational claims represented in government documents. The titles of the magazines themselves, or the series titles, frequently indicate as much: *Fun to Learn*, *Play and Learn*, *Learning Land*. *3Rs Budgie*, the most overtly didactic of these titles, leaves little room for doubt with its heading above the main title: 'READING, WRITING & ARITHMETIC'. Many of the magazines also signal their educational intent via slogans on the front cover: 'BBC Children's Magazines . . . make learning fun!' (*Spot* and others); 'Educational support for the early years' (*Tell Me Why*); 'Giving our children a head start in life' (*3Rs Budgie*). Finally, many of the titles use the logo and slogan for the National Year of Reading or the National Reading Campaign; while the Redan titles proclaim that they are 'Compatible with the National Curriculum'.

Much of the content of the magazines themselves is obviously 'educational', yet this has to be explicitly asserted through messages addressed to parents. According to BBC Worldwide executives, these instructions are included in order to ensure that parents obtain the maximum 'educational value' from the magazines, rather than their children simply 'doing what is said'. Thus, most of the magazines have messages to parents on the inside front cover or on page 3, which point out their educational benefits. These are often defined in terms of 'developing skills', and in some cases are directly linked with particular school subjects or key stages of the National Curriculum. Thus, for example:

> Play and Learn Thomas and Friends magazine is full of activities and stories involving children's favourite Thomas characters. It is a valuable companion to Key Stage 1 programmes of study and will introduce children to the skills required in English, Mathematics and Art in an entertaining and fun way.

Less frequently, there are claims about the magazines' role in encouraging 'creativity' and personal, social and (in one case) moral development – although, symptomatically, these too are often defined in terms of 'skills'. Thus, in *Play and Learn*,

> 'the simple activities and stories are also designed to teach children basic moral and social skills and are all based on the findings of academic research.'

As if this reassurance were not sufficient in itself, nearly all the magazines provide more detailed information for parents about each activity or section. In the case of the BBC's *Tell Me Why*, this information occupies most of the inside front cover. Like its sister publication *Learning is Fun* (aimed at children aged 5–7), this magazine claims that it 'covers the curriculum' for children at the appropriate stage. Its 'Notes for Parents' are in six sections, corresponding to the six areas identified in the government's curriculum guidance (Qualifications and Curriculum Authority 2000); and in each case, the parent reader is directed to the relevant activities in the magazine itself. Meanwhile, the magazine also includes a separate advice page, full of information about 'early learning goals', authored by Education Editor Ann Smith, whose credentials as a former headteacher and Ofsted inspector are identified. In most other cases, however, these messages to parents are given in small print at the bottom of the relevant page.

This information serves two main purposes: firstly, to define the educational aims or rationale for the materials; and secondly, to give suggestions about how they should be used. In providing an educational rationale, these messages use a quasi-scientific pedagogic discourse, with its own specialized vocabulary. Children 'extend activities', 'develop understanding', 'grasp concepts', 'compare and contrast', undertake experiments and 'creative activities' and practise 'skills'. Familiar everyday activities, described in the directions to the children as 'colouring in', 'drawing' or 'playing', are recontextualized in this discourse as a matter of 'developing skills' in problem-solving, observation, manipulation and so on. Thus, parents are informed that 'colouring in helps children to develop colour and design skills and to practise pencil control'; while drawing a picture of a pet 'will help develop observational and imaginative skills' (*Fun to Learn: Friends*). Even apparently 'fun' activities will develop skills that can be used in more obviously educational activities at a later stage. Thus, in finding their way through a maze in *Playdays*, 'young children have a chance to practice manipulative control for developing their handwriting'; and in playing hide-and-seek in *Tell Me Why* children are developing 'awareness of space' in line with the government's recommendations on 'physical development'.

In the case of the BBC magazines and *Learning Land*, these notes extend to providing suggestions to parents about ways of helping their children with the activity, or continuing to practice the same 'skills' at other times. Thus, in *Playdays* parents are urged to 'encourage [children] to be inquisitive, noticing things and asking questions'; and to use 'mathematical vocabulary' in 'everyday situations' in order that children can hear and understand it. Children are to be urged to spot and identify insects in the garden or park, and make a book with pictures of insects, giving details of where and when they were found. In the case of *Learning Land*, these suggestions are particularly extensive, occupying a separate panel headed 'Dear Parent' at the side of each page. They are typically written in imperative mode:

> Dear Parent, This activity encourages your child to think about how plants grow and to explain a simple life-cycle. Share a practical activity with your child. Sprinkle some cress seeds on damp cotton wool. Talk about what happens each day as tiny sprouts, and then green leaves appear. Explain that plants need different things in order to grow, similar to human beings. Most plants need soil, sunlight and water. Talk to your child about how useful plants are . . .

These instructions effectively provide parents with a lesson plan, and a script for interacting with their child, which will explain the fundamental principles of plant biology.

Like a great deal of parenting advice, instructions of this kind seem almost designed to induce feelings of inadequacy and guilt (cf. Urwin 1985). The adoption of a potentially intimidating specialist vocabulary, combined with suggestions that require significant additional investments of time and resources, may lead many parents to feel that they are simply 'failed teachers'. As in some current initiatives in relation to 'family literacy', there is a sense in which parents are implicitly defined as deficient in pedagogic skills.

In one or two instances, potential anxieties that parents might feel about the inadequacies of their own knowledge are forestalled:

> The scientific reasons why this ('FREE') magnifying glass makes things look bigger are probably quite difficult to explain to young children. However, at this stage it is enough that they use it, appreciate that it does change the size of things and are interested enough to ask why.

Ultimately, however, it is not enough for parents simply to allow their children to make their own way through the magazine. Parents must be on hand to help, answer questions, correct mistakes, explain and reinforce the major learning points – and in the case of the more elaborate 'make and do' activities, to actually perform the tasks themselves while their children look on. One of the words most frequently used to describe parental activity (particularly in the BBC magazines) is 'encourage': thus, for example, parents are frequently told to 'encourage' children to 'practise their maths skills' (*Noddy*) or to 'develop their speaking skills and increase their vocabulary' (*Toybox*). Quite how parents might deal with children who do not respond appropriately to such 'encouragement' is not addressed.

The magazines thus clearly position the parent as a pedagogue or teacher – albeit one of a relatively traditional kind. This is nowhere more explicit than in *Tell Me Why*, which comes complete with a ('FREE') set of reward stickers:

> If you buy *BBC Tell Me Why* magazine for a year it will help your child work their way through the early learning goals for the nursery and reception curriculum. Reward your child with a smiley face sticker when they finish each activity.

In other instances, such as the National Curriculum compatible 'workbooks' accompanying the Redan *Fun to Learn* titles, children are invited to become self-regulating learners, ticking the activities they have completed on a checklist and cutting out their own 'certificate of fun' (and then collecting the set). In some instances, parents or children are enabled to mark the work using the answers provided. Despite the fun and the smiley faces, learning is clearly defined here as a matter of *work* – indeed, of children 'working their way through the early learning goals for the curriculum'.

As Walkerdine and Lucey (1989) argue, such an approach serves to regulate the activities, not just of children but also of parents. 'Good' parents are those who use everyday activities – playing in the park, cooking or shopping – as opportunities for pedagogy. The 'skills' (such as those of numeracy or literacy) that are entailed in such activities are no longer incidental, but instead become the main focus and rationale of the task. In the process, everyday activities are 'curricularized': that is, they are recontextualized in terms of pedagogic discourse (cf. Bernstein 1996), and broken down into component 'skills' that can be identified and assessed (whether formally or informally). In Walkerdine and Lucey's study, this pedagogic mode was particularly characteristic of middle-class mothers, who are more likely to be constructed by researchers and educational professionals as 'sensitive' parents, while working-class mothers, more preoccupied with the demands of work, are judged to be wanting. In this way, they argue, mothers are made to bear the entire responsibility for their children's later educational success: the regulation of children thus becomes simultaneously the regulation of mothers.

Popular pedagogies

If these magazines are effectively selling a particular version of 'education' to parents – who are, in effect, their primary target market – what do they offer to children themselves? In fact, there is some diversity in the pedagogic strategies adopted by the titles we have surveyed.

At one end of the scale is *3Rs Budgie*, which (as its title suggests) adopts a no-nonsense approach to teaching what it calls 'the basics of education'. The magazine is aimed at 'Key Stage 1: 3–7 Years' (although in fact that key stage is 5–7); and according to the slogan on the front cover, it is about 'Giving our children a head start in life'. Unlike many of the BBC and Redan magazines, however, *3Rs Budgie* contains virtually no guidance for parents. In a sense, its educational 'pitch' is obvious. The magazine is organized in three sections, labelled 'Reading', 'wRiting' and 'aRithmetic'. Each section is clearly separated on the contents page; the bottom of each page has a colour-coded strip with the relevant 'R'; and each section also has a distinctive background colour and design (letters on an orange background for reading, numbers on a blue background for arithmetic). Each of the three Rs is thus clearly defined as a discrete 'skill' or curriculum area; and it seems to be vital for children to be reminded which of them they are practising in any given activity.

The reading section contains four stories. The most substantial of these features the character of Budgie the Little Helicopter (from the books written by Sarah Ferguson, Duchess of York, and now the hero of a children's television series). In 'Budgie and the Big Wheel', Budgie and his aeroplane friends Pippa and Chuck ('the big American Helicopter') are assigned by Lionel ('the Aircraft in Charge') to help at the national glider championships at Barnsdale Airfield. Once their work is complete, they decide to fly over to look at the funfair, going against Lionel's instructions. There, they discover that the big wheel is stuck and people are trapped. They radio Lionel, who arranges for the fire engines to come, and the people are rescued. On their return to the airfield, Lionel tells them off for going against his instructions; but he is also pleased that they have made it possible for the people to be rescued.

The structure of this story is repeated in two of the other stories in this section: 'The Magician's Apprentice' and 'Ostrich Learns a Lesson' (which is a version of the fable of the hare and the tortoise). In all three cases, children (or surrogate children) are shown to be in the wrong: like Budgie, they fail to follow adults' instructions, or they think they are more capable than they are, and so discover the error of their ways. The world of Budgie, like that of Thomas the Tank Engine, Noddy and others, has an almost feudal hierarchy, as perhaps befits their exclusively rural settings. Lionel (the equivalent of Thomas's Fat Controller) enjoys unquestioned authority, and sports a handlebar moustache to prove it; while Pippa (like the female train carriages in *Thomas*) simpers uncertainly, with her blonde hair tied in a pink polka-dot bow. Significantly, the Budgie story is followed by a series of nine comprehension questions, set by Lionel: 'Lionel is the Aircraft in Charge at Harefield Airfield. He likes everything to be well understood. See if you understood the story by answering his questions.'

This highly didactic approach is reflected throughout the magazine. Narratives and images are used as a pretext for practising decontextualized language and arithmetical skills. In the writing section, for example, readers are invited to 'take a coloured pencil and underline all the words in the story beginning with T or t'; while another story is used as the basis for a cloze exercise. There is also a considerable amount of copying of single words: 'Read the words and find them in the picture. Now copy the words onto the dotted lines.' 'Drilling and skilling' of this kind is even more apparent in the arithmetic section. While there is some minimal attempt to put the activities into an 'everyday' setting – 'Patsy has 22 coloured pencils. If she gives half of them to her sister, how many will each of the girls have?' – many of the questions are simply in the form of abstract sums – '£1.30 + 52p = . . .'. This section concludes with two pages of multiplication tables and an answer page. A couple of invitations to draw pictures, and a 'pinboard' of readers' efforts, are included as little more than an afterthought.

At the other end of the pedagogic scale is *CiTV Telly Tots*. While this magazine (like *3Rs Budgie*) bears the logo of the National Reading Campaign, its educational intentions are much less overt. There are no references to National Curriculum key stages, or to specific areas of the curriculum; nor is there any reference to 'learning' or helping your child 'get ahead'. The contents are identified by title, and there are no sections for different 'skills'. On the inside front cover is 'a note to Grown-up Telly Tots':

We hope that you find plenty in CiTV Telly Tots Magazine to entertain and stimulate young minds. Your help and involvement makes all the difference to encourage confidence and an inquisitive nature. At first your child may just enjoy looking at the pictures and talking about them, However, here are a few suggestions to get the most from these pages . . .

- Go at your child's own pace.
- Offer lots of praise.
- Point to the page numbers and say them out loud.
- Point to the objects in the pictures, this helps to develop observational skills.

As this implies, the pedagogy here is much less didactic. It is primarily concerned with building young children's confidence and self-esteem. 'Skills' of observation or number recognition are of secondary import-ance. In fact, the activities in the magazine are similar to those in many of the others: there are stories with comprehension (or 'what can you remember?') questions; pictures with things to point out and name; and matching and colouring-in activities. On the other hand, there are none of the workbook-type activities of *3Rs Budgie*, such as pages of sums or lists of words to copy. While the 'note' above clearly implies a pedagogic role for parents, there are many fewer pedagogic instructions addressed directly to children, of the kind that appear in many of the other magazines.

Significantly, the magazine also has a much more personal address. On the inside front cover, four children's TV presenters introduce them-selves and welcome the reader to the magazine; and they recur on sev-eral other pages. (Only two magazines in our sample feature pictures of their editors, the BBC's *Toybox* and *Tell Me Why*; and in both these cases, their address is more directed towards parents.) This is also one of the very few magazines in our sample to feature photographs of its child readers, on a 'Tots Topics' write-in page; and here again, children are invited to write to two of the presenters, rather than to a faceless editor.

This informality also extends to the visual design. The layout of the cover and the first inside pages of *CiTV Telly Tots* is much less segmented and orderly than most of the other magazines. Images of the characters break out of their frames, and there is heavy use of circles and ovals rather than squares and rectangles. Throughout the magazine, coloured balls and stars float across the page, and much of the text is set on wavy lines rather than straight horizontals. The uneven 'bubble-writing' typeface used for the magazine title and for many of the stories is also less formal than those used in many of the other magazines.

Finally, the stories themselves avoid the moralizing tone identified in *3Rs Budgie*. Indeed, few of the stories feature adult figures at all; and where they do appear, their authority is frequently undermined. Thus, in 'Dog and Duck', a group of toys come to life and play games when their owners' backs are turned; and in 'Sooty Heights', the puppets get up to their familiar anarchic tricks at the expense both of the hotel's owners and of Albert Bottomley, the pompous hotel critic from the local newspaper.

In all these respects, therefore, the approach of *CiTV Telly Tots* is much less formal and didactic than that of *3Rs Budgie*. The learner constructed by this magazine is more autonomously 'active' than the passive recipient of the *3Rs* tests. Yet the irony, of course, is that this apparent pedagogic progressivism arises in the context of a much more overtly commercial product. As noted above, *CiTV Telly Tots* is effectively a collection of trailers for ITV children's programmes. The world that is referenced here is not, by and large, the real world of children's lives, or even the notional reality of school textbooks (Patsy and her 22 coloured pencils). On the contrary, it is the imaginary world of Sooty Heights and Mopatop's Shop. *CiTV Telly Tots* positions the children and parents who read it not primarily as students and teachers, but as fellow consumers of media culture. There is a form of 'active learning' here, but it is one which is carried out almost wholly within the fictional universe of the television characters.

The BBC's magazines could be situated around the middle of a continuum between these two approaches. In comparison with *3Rs Budgie*, the style of illustration is more contemporary (and more studiously multicultural) and the stories are less moralistic. These magazines generally take a broader view of the pre-school curriculum, and the rhetoric of the advice to parents (like that of *CiTV Telly Tots*) is relatively liberal. The emphasis here is very much on proceeding at the 'child's own pace', and on 'fun' as well as 'developing skills'. Nevertheless, parents are clearly intended (as it says in *Bob the Builder* magazine) to 'work through' the magazine with their children in order to capitalize on the 'good educational opportunities' it provides. Thus, standard primary school classroom activities such as comprehension, sequencing, counting and handwriting exercises are regular features. Similarly, the magazines present information in a declarative way that is characteristic of school textbooks: they use short, active sentences in the present tense in order to establish the unambiguously factual nature of what they describe (cf. MacLure and Elliott 1992). This factuality is supported by high-quality colour photographs, which serve as incontestable evidence of 'the world around'. Questions to the reader are mostly on the level of information retrieval ('can you spot the stick insect in this picture?'): there are few open invitations to speculate here, and no sense in which knowledge might be seen as controversial or open to debate.

On the face of it, however, the learner constructed by these magazines is distinctly 'active'. While character-based magazines like *Noddy* and *Spot* tend to carry more stories, most of the BBC magazines contain several time-consuming 'make-and-do' activities, many of which would require extensive parental involvement. Thus, in addition to colouring-in, matching and writing activities, for example, our edition of *Tweenies* encourages children to make a family tree with photographs, and to cut out and stick in a series of pictures of 'modern inventions' in the playroom. As befits its theme, *Bob the Builder* contains even more elaborate activities, although parents are advised to warn their children about the dangers of playing near building sites or copying 'anything that they read about'. In some cases, these activities receive curriculum justification: thus, according to the BBC's *Toybox*, making Christmas cards 'involves DESIGN and TECHNOLOGY' [*sic*] – although, as they admit, 'younger children will need some help to make the card'. It is in these activities in particular, perhaps, that the domestic regulation of children's learning is simultaneously the regulation of parenting (cf. Walkerdine and Lucey 1989).

Of course, some of these differences between these magazines might be explained in terms of the target age group. While *3Rs Budgie* claims to be directed at children aged 3–7, it is perhaps implicitly targeting the older end of this age group. *CiTV Telly Tots* makes fewer assumptions, for example, about its readers' ability to read or write (let alone subtract or multiply). In general, the magazines in our sample aimed at younger children tend to be less overtly didactic. The BBC's *Teletubbies* magazine, for example, is clearly aimed at younger children: according to its advice for parents, its emphasis is on play, imagination and creativity, providing a 'foundation for future learning' rather than explicitly teaching curriculum-related skills. By contrast, its *Bob the Builder* magazine is explicitly directed towards developing skills in literacy and numeracy, in addition to touching on curriculum areas such as science and history. Nevertheless, there seems to be considerable latitude in terms of how the publishers define their target audience – not least for economic reasons. Young children are, by definition, a small market; and the more publishers seek to cater for distinctions *within* that market, the smaller it becomes. To acknowledge the considerable differences between two-year-olds and five-year-olds would, in these terms, be a very costly move. Judging by the readers' letters pages, all these magazines seem to be read by (or at least purchased for) a broad age range between 3 and 7.

Questions about how these magazines might be used and interpreted are ultimately beyond the scope of this chapter. To be sure, such texts could be seen as powerful sources of identity formation: they effectively 'position' parents and children as subjects of a particular form of educational discourse. By exploiting anxieties (among parents) and capitalizing on the pleasures of popular television (for children), they offer a potent combination of 'education' and 'entertainment' that helps to reinforce particular definitions of what counts as legitimate knowledge. The pedagogies they embody can thus be described as forms of 'regulation' – both for parents and for children (cf. Walkerdine and Lucey 1989).

However, this is not to say that they are necessarily effective in what they set out to achieve. Parents' and children's readings of this kind of material are likely to be diverse; and they will not necessarily correspond to the intentions of their producers. Parents may buy the magazines out of a sense of educational responsibility, or simply of guilt – or just to keep their children quiet as they wheel them around the supermarket. Parents and children may 'work through' them studiously from cover to cover – or they may just glance at them in an odd moment, pausing only to look at the pictures. The 'educational' elements may be a convenient alibi for parents, who need to be reassured that they are adequately performing their role; while for children, the 'entertainment' aspects may provide the necessary sugar for the pill of learning. Children (and indeed parents) may actively resist the pedagogic positions they are encouraged to occupy: they may read 'critically', against the grain of the magazines' educational intentions, or merely with a degree of casual indifference. In the end, how 'education' and 'entertainment' are defined will depend, not just on the texts themselves, but on the everyday negotiations of family life and on the everyday practices of readers.

Conclusion

So how do we understand this recent proliferation of 'edutainment' magazines aimed at pre-school children? On the one hand, we can see it as a consequence of the increasing commercialization of children's media culture, and the need to exploit successful copyrights across a range of media. On the other, we can also see it as a consequence of the growing competitiveness generated by government policy on education, and the increasing levels of anxiety and guilt this produces among parents. The point here is that – far from being opposed – these two aspects of the phenomenon are intimately related. Both are a matter of *selling* – selling entertainment to children, and selling education to parents. Far from entailing a form of passive consumption, both also involve a form of *activity* – activity that is simultaneously 'educational' and 'entertaining'.

CHAPTER 6

POPULAR HISTORIES

Education and entertainment in
information books

In this chapter, we move on to consider educational materials aimed at an older age group, and in a different medium. Our focus is on popular information books about history intended for use in the home. Specifically, we look at four contrasting books about the ancient Romans, a well-established primary school 'topic' now formally enshrined in the National Curriculum. As in the previous chapter, our primary emphasis is not so much on the *content* of these books as on their *pedagogy*: we are more interested in *how* these texts are teaching than in *what* they are teaching. Our analysis focuses on three interrelated aspects of these pedagogic strategies. We are concerned, first, with the ways in which these texts 'position' their readers in relation to sources of knowledge – in effect, with their epistemology or historiography. Second, we consider how the texts address their readers, for example through the use of narrative or expository language. Finally, we look at how they establish the relationship between 'education' and 'entertainment', and the implications this might have for different readers.

Making histories

Over the past thirty years, there have been significant changes in the academic study of history, in terms of its content, methodology and philosophical foundations. During the 1970s and 1980s there was a widespread reaction against the traditional paradigm which saw history as essentially concerned with politics, wars and the 'great deeds of great men' (Burke 1991a). By contrast, 'new' history encompasses a much wider range of subjects including, for example, the history of the family, of culture and beliefs, and of groups previously hidden from history such as women, children and the poor. Whereas traditional history focused on the 'view from above', a growing number of historians have become interested in 'history from below' (Sharp 1991). This broadening of the subject content has also resulted in the use of a wider variety of sources of evidence, including oral and visual sources.

Another important difference between proponents of traditional and new history is in their understanding of the nature of historical knowledge. Broadly speaking, the traditional paradigm sees history as objective: the historian's task is simply to present readers with the facts. By contrast, new history is based on the idea that reality is socially or culturally constructed: it is not something which the historian simply uncovers. As Burke (1991a) has suggested, there is now a greater acceptance that historians do not reproduce 'what actually happened' so much as represent it from a particular point of view.

There has also been a parallel debate about the nature and content of history teaching in schools. For much of the twentieth century, school history was based on what David Sylvester (1994: 9) has called the 'great tradition', in which the role of the teacher was to 'give pupils the facts of historical knowledge' – a body of knowledge that in practice consisted mainly of British political history. Over the past thirty years, there has been a gradual move away from this 'great tradition' towards a more interpretative, source-based approach to school history. The subject content has also been broadened to include social, economic and (to a lesser extent) cultural history. Nevertheless, the transition from 'old' to 'new' history was not an easy one, and the debate over the history curriculum became increasingly politicized during the 1980s and early 1990s (see Crawford 1995; Foster 1998). The National Curriculum and its subsequent revisions have been widely seen as a compromise, combining the emphasis on skills such as source analysis with a more traditional focus on the acquisition of factual knowledge (Huggins 1996; McAleavy 1998).

Research carried out during the 1980s suggested that school textbooks were not yet reflecting the 'new' approach to history. These books did not, for example, mention historical sources; or if they did, they failed to acknowledge their problematic nature. According to Cairns and Inglis (1989), such books generally construct history as a given body of knowledge. However, a couple of years later, Maw (1991) found that some textbook writers and publishers were beginning to respond to changes in the history curriculum by including more source materials, and encouraging a more questioning approach.

As we shall indicate, these epistemological or historiographical issues may be explicitly raised in texts themselves; yet they are also more implicitly reflected in the ways in which material is presented (both verbally and visually) and in the ways in which the reader is addressed or 'positioned' by the text (cf. Ellsworth 1997). To what extent, for example, is the reader positioned as merely a witness or observer of life in earlier times? Is the reader invited to question particular interpretations of history, or to consider how and why they have been produced? How does the author attempt to 'draw in' the reader, or assume the reader's point of view? To what extent, and in what ways, are readers invited to draw on their own experience? In what ways does the text seek to 'entertain' (literally, to engage or 'hold') the reader, for example by making use of fictional or popular genres? These are the kinds of pedagogic questions we address in our analysis below.

History as 'edutainment': four case studies

Academic debates about the nature of history and changes in educational policy are not the only developments which influence the production of history books, however. As we have indicated in Chapters 3 and 4, the commercial imperatives of publishing and retailing have diverse implications in terms of the form and presentation of educational texts. The four titles we have selected for analysis illustrate some of the contrasting strategies publishers have adopted here.

At one end of the scale is *Ancient Rome* by Simon James, published by Dorling Kindersley (1990). This is a glossy, large-format hardback book of 64 pages, published in association with the British Museum. It costs £9.99, and is in Dorling Kindersley's extensive *Eyewitness Guides* series. According to the publisher, this series is suitable for anyone from 'eight to eighty', though in practice they are marketed as children's reference books and retailers shelve them with books aimed at the 9–12 age group. *Ancient Rome*'s back cover blurb describes it as 'a spectacular and informative guide to the fascinating story of ancient Rome. Superb colour photographs of Roman armour, tools, jewellery, and more, give the reader a unique "eyewitness" insight into the history of the Roman Empire'.

At the other end of the scale is John Farman's *Romans* (1998), published in Macmillan's *History in a Hurry* series and targeted at children aged 7 and over. This is a small, 64-page paperback, printed on inexpensive paper, costing £1.99. Its only illustrations are black-and-white cartoons. Its back cover describes it as 'very good, very short (and very cheap)': '*History in a Hurry* is so short that there just isn't room for any boring bits! All you need to know (and a little bit less) about the Romans. (Quite a lot less, actually. Ed.).'

Terry Deary's *Horrible Histories* series, published by Scholastic, is effectively the model for this kind of publication (see Chapter 3). The series is targeted mainly at the 8–12 age group. In our analysis here, we have included Deary's *The Rotten Romans* (1994). At £3.50, it contains 128 pages, again with only black-and-white cartoon illustrations and on inexpensive paper. Its cover blurb claims to offer 'history with the nasty bits left in': 'The Rotten Romans follows life for folk in Roman Britain from Nasty Nero and other awful emperors, to Brave Boudicca and the poor old peasants, who tried to send the Romans right back where they came from . . .'.

Finally, we also consider *The Roman Empire* by Nigel Kelly, Rosemary Rees and Jane Shuter, published in Heinemann's *Living through History* series (1997), designed for the 11–12 age group. Published in hardback and paperback, it contains 64 pages with colour drawings, maps and photographs, although the production values and paper quality are not as high as Dorling Kindersley's *Ancient Rome*. Our paperback copy cost £6.99. Unlike the three books described above, *Living through History* is marketed primarily to schools, though it is also available in some high-street shops. We included *Living through History* in our analysis partly because it attempts to incorporate some of the features of 'edutainment' texts, for example cartoon characters and humour. Its cover blurb claims that '*Living through History* is a history series with a difference': 'As well as giving you the historical narrative alongside source materials, it brings history to life by telling you many of the weird, wonderful and some-times gory stories behind people and events.' Furthermore, we were in-terested to see how a book produced primarily for the school market would compare with those produced for the home market. (In order to distinguish between books with similar titles, we will refer to *The Roman Empire*, *Ancient Rome* and *Romans* by their series titles, i.e. *Living through History*, *Eyewitness* and *History in a Hurry*.)

As this brief description implies, there are significant differences be-tween these books in terms of the appeals they are making to readers. However, there are many overlaps in terms of content. *The Rotten Romans* focuses more on what it calls 'gory' stories, while *Eyewitness* is based primarily on glossy photographs of artefacts and buildings. However, all four books outline the political and military history of Rome, covering the rise and fall of the empire, the organization of the Roman army and the form of government. All four also place a central emphasis on social history, for example covering topics such as education, religion, enter-tainment, food, sanitation and living conditions. Although the books describe 'the great deeds of great men', they are also concerned with groups which would traditionally have been marginalized, including women, children, slaves and 'ordinary' people. All the books (particu-larly *History in a Hurry* and *The Rotten Romans*) appear preoccupied with the minutiae of everyday life: for example, all four mention the fascinat-ing fact that the Romans used sponges instead of toilet paper.

Of course, there are also differences in content. Economic history is largely overlooked by *The Rotten Romans* and *Living through History*, whereas *Eyewitness* includes sections on 'transport, travel and trade' and 'life in the countryside'. By comparison with the others, *Eyewitness* and *History in a Hurry* focus more on social and cultural aspects: only eight out of the 28 sections in *Eyewitness* and three of the 11 chapters in *History in a Hurry* are concerned with political and military matters. Unlike these books, *The Rotten Romans* and *Living through History* give quite detailed accounts of the Roman invasion of Britain; although the absence of such material in the Dorling Kindersley book probably reflects the fact that it is aimed at an international readership (see Chapter 3).

To a large extent, however, all these books reflect the changing balance of content in history teaching. As Cairns and Inglis (1989) suggest, the emphasis in contemporary history teaching is on building connections with children's own experience by focusing more on the everyday lives of people in the past. To a greater or lesser extent, this is something all these books achieve. However, the *ways* in which it is achieved are crucial: it is certainly possible to change the content – for example, to include the perspectives and experiences of hitherto excluded groups – without necessarily changing the ways in which students (or, in this case, readers) are given access to that content, or positioned in relation to it.

In this respect, the most significant differences between these books are to do with their *pedagogy* rather than their *content*. Of course, these differences are partly a reflection of the fact that they are designed to appeal to different markets – as their cover prices would suggest. As one of the publishers at Dorling Kindersley told us, their books are normally purchased by parents and therefore need to appear 'authoritative'. By contrast, *Horrible Histories* are clearly intended to be purchased directly by children, and indeed collected along with popular fictional book series such as *Point Horror* and *Goosebumps*, also published by Scholastic. Thus, whilst the cartoon illustrations of *History in a Hurry* and *The Rotten Romans* are similar to those in children's comics, the glossy photographs of *Eyewitness* are reminiscent of adults' coffee-table books and magazines. The irreverent approach to historical knowledge in *History in a Hurry* and *The Rotten Romans* is completely at odds with the respectful tone of *Eyewitness*. Meanwhile, as its cover blurb suggests, *Living through History* attempts to appeal to both markets, containing cartoon stories of the life of Caesar alongside maps of the growth of the empire and colour photographs of Roman artefacts.

Sources of knowledge

Yet if these differences are partly a matter of marketing, they also raise much broader questions about epistemology and pedagogy – questions that are inevitably at stake in the attempt to popularize learning. In her analysis of school history textbooks, Janet Maw (1991) develops a typology involving two related axes. First, she distinguishes between source-based texts and texts which make little or no explicit use of source materials. As an advocate of 'new' history, Maw emphasizes the use of a range of source materials as a means of encouraging a more questioning approach. Second, she distinguishes between didactic texts (in which the interpretation is closed) and exploratory texts (in which the interpretation is open). A textbook which is didactic *and* makes little use of source materials is described in the following terms:

> The language can be emotive and is often judgemental, the interpretation authoritative in that judgement is given, not justified. Questions are normally set to test comprehension. The question sections sometimes include very brief quotations from sources, but these invariably support the narrative . . . Often vividly written and attractively presented, it does very little indeed to encourage the reader to reflect upon the interpretation set out.
>
> (Maw 1991: 165)

Maw argues that the inclusion of source material creates the *potential* for a more exploratory approach, and hence the opportunity for pupils to question their own and the writer's assumptions. However, the use of source materials does not guarantee such an approach, as the evidence itself 'may be biased or idiosyncratic in ways that are not made clear to the reader' or the evidence may simply reinforce the interpretation of the main text (Maw 1991: 164).

Applying Maw's typology to our titles, both *The Rotten Romans* and *Living through History* have some of the features of an exploratory text. Both books begin with a discussion about the nature of history and historical sources. In the case of *Living through History*, this takes up the entire first chapter (eight pages), and covers the following themes:

- How do we find out about history?
- What can archaeology tell us?
- Can you always trust historical sources?
- What will the future make of us?

In the section on 'How do we find out about history?' the authors describe how the skeleton of a prehistoric man was found, the various tests which were carried out to establish the date and cause of death, and what this discovery tells us about prehistoric life. History is shown as a process in which archaeologists, scientists and historians try to construct meaning from objects. As the authors points out, 'it is not just a matter of digging things up and writing down what you see' (p. 6). The text illustrates some of the challenges which historians face in interpreting source materials and invites readers to think about what future generations might make of objects from the 1990s. However, these issues are not linked to sources used later in the text. The result is that although readers are made aware of the problematic nature of source material *in general*, they are given little indication of how this applies to a study of Roman history specifically.

The opening discussion of the nature of history in *The Rotten Romans* is much shorter than that in *Living through History*, but it also questions the idea that history is about uncovering 'facts'. The author points out that:

> In maths, two and two is usually four – and in science water is always made up of hydrogen and oxygen. But in history things aren't that simple. In history a 'fact' is sometimes not a fact at all. Really it's just someone's 'opinion'. And opinions can be different for different people.

(p. 5)

The Rotten Romans illustrates the importance of taking into consideration the context in which source materials were produced. Documents may, for example, have been written for political reasons: the author suggests that the historian Tacitus exaggerated the scale of Boudicca's defeat in order to glorify the Roman army. Readers are warned: 'Don't believe everything you read in your history books. If the Brits had been able to write then, they would have given a very different account of the battle' (p. 45). The idea that there are different interpretations of events is further illustrated by a cartoon argument between a Roman and a Briton over who was to blame for the conflict between Rome and Boudicca. However, the book fails to consider how historians treat these (apparently) conflicting sources of evidence, and as a result some readers may be confused as to how historians reach *any* conclusions about the past.

Overall, *The Rotten Romans* makes little use of source materials, and these usually consist of short quotations. Nevertheless, the questioning of sources in *The Rotten Romans* is presented as a form of defiance against teachers and the hegemony of history textbooks. The author implies that teachers censor information and fail to acknowledge that history is based on opinions rather than facts: 'teachers', it asserts, 'will try to tell you there are "right" and "wrong" answers even if there aren't' (p. 5). There is thus an implicit conflict established between the author's approach to history and (what he defines as) the position taken by schools. As we shall see below, this apparently 'subversive' stance is a key aspect of the book's address to its readers.

Certain linguistic features of the text also serve to encourage this more sceptical stance towards information. The use of modal verbs ('may', 'might') and other hedges (like 'perhaps', 'to some degree') indicate a degree of uncertainty, encouraging readers to regard the text more as an interpretation than a factual account. These characteristics are particularly apparent in the language of *Living through History*. By comparison, Dorling Kindersley's *Eyewitness* is characterized by low modality (that is, less uncertainty) and fewer linguistic hedges.

Eyewitness is in some respects 'source-based', although its source materials are in the form of photographs of artefacts and buildings, and there are no extracts from written sources. The book is divided into double-page spreads with, on average, two-thirds of the spread taken up by pictures and captions, and the remainder by the main written text. Each picture and caption forms its own unit of information, so that it is not necessary to read the main text in order to make sense of the illustrations. As Meek (1996: 41) has pointed out, the written text in these kinds of illustrated topic books is 'a kind of adjunct' to the pictures. The fact that photographs and captions form their own self-contained units makes the book ideal for browsing through, a feature it shares both with teenage magazines and adult coffee-table books.

The dominance of illustrations in this and other Dorling Kindersley books may reflect a wider trend whereby visual communication is becoming more important in school textbooks, newspapers and other print media (Kress and van Leeuwen, 1996). In the case of history textbooks, there certainly appears to be an increased emphasis on the use of visual materials as sources of historical evidence (Osler 1994). However, there is a danger that, whilst written sources are subject to investigation and critique, visual materials are often presented as unchallenged evidence (David 2000). In the case of *Eyewitness*, there is little sense in which the reader is invited to question the meaning and the reliability of source materials. The captions which accompany the photographs seem to imply that there can be only one possible meaning. For example, the images of Roman life given in mosaics, statues, carvings and other works of art are described but not questioned in terms of their reliability. Clearly, images provide a particular representation of the past; and it is vital for historians to 'consider the circumstances in which the picture was created, the cultural conventions that dictated the format of the finished product, the creator's purpose in creating the picture, [and] the audience for which it was created' (David 2000: 235). Only on a couple of occasions, however, does the author of *Eyewitness* suggest that what is shown in pictures and artefacts may not be a reliable representation of life in Rome; and even here, the reader is not told how or why this might be so. For example:

> This wild entanglement of limbs, horses and armour is a relief
> from a stone coffin showing Roman cavalry in combat with
> Northern barbarians. Although the artist did not depict the
> soldiers very accurately, he gives a fine impression of the bloody
> chaos of war.
>
> (p. 13)

In contrast to *Living Through History*, *Eyewitness* does not describe how historic objects are found or analysed. In effect, *Eyewitness* is a museum display recreated in a book: it presents history as a matter of studying objects whose origins and provenance are not revealed. This sense of objectivity is emphasized by the use of high-quality colour photography. As Kress and van Leeuwen (1996) observe, colour photography is traditionally seen as capable of 'capturing' reality. By contrast, sketched illustrations of the kind found in *Horrible Histories* and *History in a Hurry* have a higher modality than photographs. As Smith (1995) points out, the status of drawn illustrations 'is that of a "version" rather than a reality'. Thus, in *Eyewitness*, the dominance of photographs seems to increase the sense of the factuality of history: statements about the past appear to be backed up by hard evidence. The lavish, full-colour photographs have an almost sensory appeal, and are reminiscent of the type of photography used in glossy magazines. According to Kress and van Leeuwen (1996), these types of 'hyper-real' photographs appeal to the senses and create an illusion of touch, colour and feel. By contrast, all of the images in *The Rotten Romans* and *History in a Hurry* are sketches, which tend to be comic rather than realistic. Their purpose does not seem to be to accurately recreate history, but to encourage a somewhat irreverent approach to the subject.

Positioning the author and reader

One of the means by which information can be made to appear factual is by creating a distance between the author and the reader. Olson (1980: 192) suggests that school textbooks 'separate speech from speaker, and that separation in itself may make the words impersonal, objective, and above criticism'. Similarly, Nichols (1981) has described the use of voice-over in traditional documentaries as 'the voice of God': like the impersonal voice of the textbook, it represents a claim to authority and neutrality. By contrast, the use of the personal voice in texts may make information appear more subjective and increase the solidarity between readers and writers (van de Kopple and Crismore 1990). Academic historians have also argued in favour of a more direct, personal address in order to remind readers that what they are reading is a particular point of view (Burke 1991b).

The personal voice ('I') is not used in *Living through History* or *Eyewitness*. Readers are addressed directly, either as 'you' or as 'we', but only on a few occasions. When the audience is addressed directly in *Living through History* it is usually for pedagogic reasons, for example to summarize at the end of a chapter or remind readers of what they have just learned: 'The first eight pages in this book have helped you understand some of the problems historians face' (p. 11). On the few occasions on which readers are addressed in *Eyewitness*, it is usually to invite them to compare some aspect of the ancient world with modern society.

By contrast, the personal voice is used more frequently in *The Rotten Romans*, and particularly in *History in a Hurry*. Both books attempt to construct a persona for the author: the authors are given their own characters, opinions and, in the case of *History in a Hurry*, a personal life (he refers to his editor, his daughter and his parents). Both texts also address readers directly as 'you', or occasionally as 'we'; and *The Rotten Romans* creates what Kress and van Leeuwen (1996) have described as a 'visual you', whereby a sketched character appears to be addressing the reader directly. However, both these texts go beyond simply acknowledging the presence of a writer and a reader: they also seem to want to *identify* with their readers, to build up a rapport or solidarity with them. In a sense, they are seeking to bridge the inevitable gap that exists between the adult writer and the child reader – a gap that is characteristic of children's literature and media more broadly (Rose 1984; Buckingham 1995).

Thus, one significant characteristic which both narrators share is their opposition to authority figures. In the case of *The Rotten Romans*, authority is represented by teachers (as noted above), while in *History in a Hurry* it is the author's 'fussy editor'. (Indeed, as in the cover blurb quoted above, the editor occasionally 'intervenes' in the text to set the author straight.) The narrators distance themselves from such authority figures, possibly on the assumption that (as children) their readers will be able to relate to this. Thus, the author of *The Rotten Romans* adopts a conspiratorial tone, promising to tell readers all the interesting – 'horrible' and 'gory' – parts of history which boring teachers leave out; while the author of *History in a Hurry* also wants to tell us 'more dreadful things', although his editor won't let him. *The Rotten Romans* even encourages readers to test their teachers on the 'gory' parts of Roman history – on the assumption that they will not know the answer. Challenging the authority of teachers in this way may help to establish a degree of solidarity between author and reader, but it also serves as a useful means of reassuring the reader about the author's lack of ('boring') educational intentions: at least *he* is not trying to teach you something!

This impression of solidarity is also fostered by the use of informal language. *The Rotten Romans* and *History in a Hurry* both use casual, colloquial language, with a good deal of slang. As in many advertisements, 'chummy' language is used to address us as friends or intimates (even though we are not) and to undermine any impression of authoritarianism. Humour (or the semblance of humour) abounds. Thus, for example, in *History in a Hurry*, we are told that:

> Mark Anthony, Augustus' partner in world domination (they soon got rid of old Lapidus), was a bit of a lad by all accounts, and he fell hook, line and sinker for a flash babe called Cleopatra (queen of Egypt).
>
> (p. 47)

A similarly irreverent, 'laddish' tone is evident in the description of the prizes given to gladiators:

The standing-up chaps would then saunter cockily over to the
royal box for a few kind words, a bag of gold and some poxy old
laurel reef (is that right? Ed.) from the boss.

(p. 31)

As we shall see below, this sense of solidarity is also reinforced by the use
of references to football, pop music, television, films and other aspects of
popular culture which readers are expected to be familiar with.

Finally, it is worth noting that this impression of formality or informality is also manifested in the visual design of the texts. In general, the
design of *Living through History* and *Eyewitness* is more schematic and
regimented. The former, in particular, uses rectangular blocks of text and
colour-coding in a manner that is characteristic of school textbooks. Key
terms are highlighted in bold type, and the sources in each section are
identified by letters. On the other hand, it also contains a couple of
more informally designed sections (notably a cartoon of the life of Julius
Caesar) that seem to have strayed in from a different type of text. As we
have noted, the layout of *Eyewitness* subordinates written text to images,
and avoids substantial blocks of text. As such, it tends to invite a more
casual engagement, although (when seen in the context of Dorling
Kindersley productions *en masse*), it is highly formulaic. Each theme is
presented in the form of one or two double-page spreads. A few paragraphs of text (mainly on the left-hand page) introduce the theme; while
photographs and illustrations are located at the bottom and to the side
of this page and on the right-hand page.

Of course, *The Rotten Romans* and *History in a Hurry* are no less formulaic, although the visual style is certainly more informal. *The Rotten
Romans*, for example, contains cartoons, hand-drawn maps and recipes, a
fake newspaper article and an extensive handwritten diary by the British
leader Caractacus. Information is presented in speech bubbles, and the
text is interspersed at irregular intervals by cartoons with handwritten
captions. Even on pages where there are no illustrations, the text is
broken down into bullet points or numbered lists, and there are several
quizzes. The text of *History in a Hurry* is also interspersed with short
sections labelled (for example) 'Useless Fact No. 439'. As with *Eyewitness*
– albeit in a very different way – the underlying assumption is that
information needs to be broken down into smaller units for readers, and
that they need variation to keep their attention. Indeed, as we have seen,
History in a Hurry sells itself on being 'so short that there just isn't room
for any boring bits'.

In refusing the formal and authoritative mode of address that is apparent in *Living through History* and *Eyewitness*, and in seeking to break
down the distance between the reader and the (fictitious) author, these
texts are clearly seeking to promote a less reverential approach to history. Of course, this studied informality is highly contrived; yet it could

be argued that books like *The Rotten Romans* are at least 'upfront' and explicit about what they believe their readers' intentions to be, and how they intend to address them.

Narrative, exposition and learning

A further key distinction that recurs in analyses of information texts is that between narrative and exposition. According to McPartland (1998: 343):

> In narrative, the person involved in recounting the narrative
> to the reader or listener is either the central participant in the
> discourse or recounts the events of the narrative from the
> perspective of an observer (first or third person); the statements are
> explicitly oriented to the actors in the narrative (agent oriented),
> rather than, for example, the subject matter of the discourse; the
> statements relate to the past (accomplished time) and they are
> linked chronologically.

By contrast, expository text is

> expressed in impersonal terms, is oriented towards its subject
> matter, its facts, concepts or principles; the temporal dimension is
> centrally important to this mode of discourse and it adopts logical
> rather than chronological linkages in its sequence of statements.

Recent debates have focused on the relative educational merits of these two contrasting forms, both in textbooks and in classroom discourse. On the one hand, some writers have argued that children find expository texts difficult and that narrative is the most appropriate genre, particularly in early schooling when children are learning to read (Meek 1996). By contrast, other researchers suggest that even the youngest school children are capable of understanding expository forms, and that some may even prefer these to narrative (Duke and Kays 1998). According to this view, children will have difficulty in transferring from narrative to expository texts in later stages of schooling if they have had very little experience of these kinds of texts early on.

Another issue addressed in the literature concerns the use of narrative in helping students to gain a better understanding of their subject. McPartland (1998: 341), for example, argues that the purpose of using narrative in teaching geography is 'to stimulate the geographical imagination, to act as a vehicle for the transmission of geographical values and to promote geographical knowledge and understanding'. Meek (1996) also suggests that narrative gives history greater cohesion and is preferable to presenting unconnected 'bits of information'. On the other hand, Wignell (1994) is critical of what he sees as the dominance of narrative or action-based forms in classroom teaching because when it comes to testing, students are expected to produce texts which are more abstract and 'interpretative'.

Among the texts under consideration here, *History in a Hurry* and *The Rotten Romans* combine expository and narrative forms, though the latter tend to dominate. *The Rotten Romans*, for example, is divided into different sections (the Roman army, the Celts, etc.) most of which include a general introduction to the theme followed by descriptions of specific events and individuals. The events described are usually battles, whilst the individuals tend to be military or political leaders. The section on 'Battling Britons', for example, includes detailed accounts of Boudicca's and Caractacus's campaigns against the Romans. In addition to anecdotes about historical figures, there are numerous legends about giants and gods, one of which even starts with the phrase 'once upon a long time ago'. Nevertheless, the stories in *The Rotten Romans* take different forms, including imaginary diaries, newspaper articles and comic strips.

Living through History also combines expository and narrative text, though the two are more equally balanced than in *The Rotten Romans*. Here again, each chapter provides a broad outline of a particular theme (for example, 'Rome's Rise to Power') and follows this with descriptions of specific events and individuals who are seen as central to this theme. In some cases, these are contained in separate colour-coded boxes. Again, the individuals described are almost always military or political leaders, with particularly detailed accounts of Hannibal, Boudicca and Julius Caesar.

By contrast, *Eyewitness* contains almost no narrative text. This may be partly due to the fact that its emphasis is more on social history, which does not lend itself so easily to a narrative format: even *Living through History* and *The Rotten Romans* tend to use more expository forms when describing issues such as childhood, education and the lives of women. However, even those chapters of *Eyewitness* which are dedicated to political and military history rarely mention historical figures (the exceptions being Hannibal and Julius Caesar) and there are no chronological accounts of lives or military campaigns such as those found in the other books. *Eyewitness* offers a general outline of each theme, but instead of following this with accounts of specific individuals and events, it uses photographs and descriptions of objects from that period. While each of these books moves from the general to the specific, therefore, they do so in quite different ways.

Although *Eyewitness* has little in common with the action-based or narrative forms identified by Wignell (1994), this does not necessarily make the text interpretative or explanatory. In fact, the text in this book tends to describe rather than explain; and if an explanation is given, it is implicit rather than explicit. For example:

One of Diocletian's successors, Constantine, believed that he came to power with the help of the Christian god, and by his death in A.D. 337 Christianity had not only emerged from the shadows but had become the state religion.

(p. 62)

The connection between the emperor Constantine's beliefs and the subsequent spread of Christianity is not made clear here. This lack of interpretative text and a reliance on visual images may make it difficult for readers to form any coherent understanding of the past. Margaret Meek (1996) has criticized some of these picture-based topic books on these grounds, arguing that they present disconnected 'bits of information' rather than fully developed explanations:

New printing techniques produce illustrations of such high quality that original documents, photographs of contemporary artefacts, and pictures of famous men and women seem to make the-past-in-the-present more immediate. But the result may be a shortening of interpretative text that would fit the bits of information together, and so make possible more coherent understandings in the readers.

(Meek 1996: 61)

However, this apparent avoidance of explanation may reflect a broader difficulty in the teaching of history: research carried out by Lee *et al.* (1996), for example, indicated that some primary school children do not distinguish between statements of fact and explanations.

Education and entertainment

As we have noted, the more 'child-oriented' mode of address of *The Rotten Romans* and *History in a Hurry* is also reflected in their use of references to popular culture. For example, in *The Rotten Romans* there are references to sport ('off-side', 'Rome 1 Carthage 0'); television (a *This is Your Life* feature on Boudicca); and popular books and films (*The Eagle has Landed*). Unlike these more generic references, many of those in *History in a Hurry* are clearly from the 1990s, such as the Spice Girls, Oasis and Riverdance.

The entertainment element of these texts is most strongly manifested in their blend of humour and horror. In this respect, these series pick up on the broader popularity of horror with the target age group, reflected in book (and television) series such as *Goosebumps*. While the focus here is obviously not on the supernatural, the elements of physical disgust and spectacular violence are equally strong – albeit diluted by humour. Thus, one of the explicit assumptions which informs both series (particularly *Horrible Histories*) is that children like to read 'gory' details about the past. As a result, they contain numerous descriptions of battles, human sacrifices, gladiators, crucifixions, the ill-treatment of slaves, the cruelty of the emperors, and so on. *Living through History* and *Eyewitness* also mention some of these subjects, but the descriptions are not as graphic. Whilst *Eyewitness* describes gladiator fights with disapproval, *The Rotten Romans* and *History in a Hurry* do so with relish. Apart from blood and guts, the latter series also focus on what contemporary readers would regard as unusual eating habits and sanitation.

The 'horror' in *The Rotten Romans* and *History in a Hurry* is to some extent mitigated by the use of humour and cartoon-style illustrations. For example, an account of a slave uprising which resulted in hundreds of crucifixions is accompanied by a cartoon character saying 'you just can't get the staff these days'. Another comic feature of *The Rotten Romans* is the way in which animated Roman characters are made to speak like people in modern Britain, using contemporary slang. It is possible that this humorous style may be confusing for some young readers, however. For example, one illustration in *The Rotten Romans* seems to imply that the Eiffel Tower existed in Roman times; while another shows a daily newspaper from ancient Britain. The strong reliance on narrative here may also create some uncertainty about whether the text is fact or fiction.

Although the *Horrible Histories* pride themselves on their shock value, there are certain boundaries they are not willing to cross. For example, there are no references to anything sexual in *The Rotten Romans*; and the closest it comes to 'bad' language is some innocuous name-calling, like 'smelly-knickers' or 'gorilla-features'. By contrast, *History in a Hurry* includes stories about the Romans' sex lives and there is also a certain amount of sexual innuendo. A good example of how the two series differ is in their descriptions of the lives of the emperors. Whilst *The Rotten Romans* focuses on the emperors' cruelty, *History in a Hurry* also looks at their sex lives – including incest, adultery, orgies, prostitution and bisexuality, all of which are described in the same irreverent, humorous tone as the rest of the book.

By contrast, *Eyewitness* is resolutely serious. It seeks to appeal to the child's sense of wonder rather than their sense of humour or their fascination with violence. As we have noted, the cover blurb claims that the book will be a 'spectacular and informative guide', offering a 'unique eyewitness insight'. Here, and implicitly in the lavish style of the illustrations, it creates an image of the child as inquisitive and eager to learn. The Roman empire itself is described with reverence and awe:

> The colosseum in Rome is the greatest of the many amphitheatres
> of the Empire, and a marvel of Roman engineering. Opened by the
> emperor Titus in A.D. 80, it held about 50,000 people and was

designed so well that everyone could have got out of the building in a few minutes.

(p. 28)

Living through History attempts a compromise between these two styles, resulting in a certain awkwardness at times. As we have indicated, its humorous cartoons – a life of Caesar, for example, or images of Romulus and Remus – seem out of character with the formal textbook style of the rest of the book. Significantly, its cover blurb claims that 'it brings history to life by telling you many of the weird, wonderful and sometimes gory stories behind people and events'. The publishers implicitly recognize that, in attempting to appeal to children, 'gore' and humour sell books – as the long-running and much-imitated success of *Horrible Histories* clearly demonstrates.

Here again, therefore, these books appear to construct a very different image of their 'implied reader'. *The Rotten Romans* and *History in a Hurry* define the child as anarchic and subversive of authority; while *Eyewitness* defines the child as innocent and full of wonder. While the former seems to encourage the active agency of the child reader, the latter positions the child as a docile recipient of revealed truth.

However, the implied reader of texts like *The Rotten Romans* and *History in a Hurry* also appears to be implicitly male. Osler (1994) has criticized a similar text for adopting 'a style reminiscent of traditional boys' comics, with cartoons and jokes presented from a male perspective, largely featuring male characters'. The targeting of a male readership is particularly evident in *History in a Hurry*. The book is narrated from a stereotypical male heterosexual perspective. Women are referred to as 'babes', and a 'slave-babe' is shown standing naked in front of a group of men. The author even makes clear his own preferences:

Men's clothes were always white (sometimes with the odd coloured band) and they wore them short, but women (who could wear tasteful colours) had to wear them to their feet, which I think is the wrong way round.

(p. 17)

Occasionally the address is specifically to a male audience, for example:

Girls in ancient Rome were regarded as rather a burden (no comment, eh lads?) . . .

(p. 35)

The author does address the female audience at one point, but not in the conspiratorial, laddish way that he addresses the 'lads'. Before describing the position of women in Roman society he warns: 'If there are any staunch feminists out there, take a deep breath' (p. 28). In common with the majority of textbooks, all these books implicitly prioritize the world of men: apart from a separate section describing the lives of women in ancient Rome, most of the illustrations and text relate to men (cf. Cairns and Inglis 1989).

To some degree, this address to boys may be symptomatic of broader assumptions about gender and reading. Conventional wisdom among teachers – and a good deal of research – suggests that boys are less interested in reading than girls, and are more likely to express a preference for non-fiction (Millard 1997). In seeking to reach out to the boys' market, publishers are bound to take this into account: as in the case of children's television (Seiter 1993), girls may well be more likely to read material aimed at boys, while the reverse is less likely to be the case. In this respect, the marginalization of females in the text and the implicit address to male readers could itself be seen as a response to market forces.

Conclusion

The books we have analysed in this chapter were chosen as case studies designed to illustrate broader tendencies, not just in the production of books about history but also in children's information books in general. Like the majority of contemporary information books, the titles we have considered all attempt to combine elements of 'education' and 'entertainment'. While this is most obvious in the case of books aimed directly at children (such as *The Rotten Romans* and *History in a Hurry*), it also applies to the other texts we have considered. Some school textbooks, like *Living through History*, have tried to incorporate elements of edutainment in the form of cartoon characters and humour; while reference texts such as Dorling Kindersley's *Eyewitness* seek popular appeal on the basis of their glossy photographs rather than of making history 'fun'. Some critics would argue that, in their different ways, both approaches represent a form of 'dumbing down', in which serious subjects are trivialized or rendered merely 'spectacular'. Publishers and retailers, on the other hand, would defend them on the grounds that they make history more entertaining and therefore more accessible to children who might otherwise have little interest in the subject.

To a greater or lesser extent, all four books reflect the changing balance of content in contemporary history teaching. They all contain an emphasis on social history of the kind that is characteristic of 'new' history. However, the ways in which they present this material, and how they position the reader in relation to it, are quite different. The distinction between the informal, irreverent approach of *The Rotten Romans* and the more authoritative (and indeed authoritarian) approach of Dorling Kindersley's *Eyewitness* is particularly striking here. The latter is a highly didactic text, in which history is presented as a series of objective facts, not as something which is open to different interpretations. Yet while the author of *The Rotten Romans* makes some attempt to alert readers to the problematic nature of historical sources, there are considerable limitations to the way in which this is done – not least because readers are given few opportunities to interrogate such sources themselves.

Indeed, when compared with a modern school textbook (in this case *Living through History*) it becomes apparent that 'popular' history books like *The Rotten Romans*, *History in a Hurry* and *Eyewitness* have little interest in questioning the nature of history as a discipline or form of knowledge. It might be argued that these issues are too complex to address in books which are designed for leisure reading – although, as we shall indicate in Chapter 8, popular books about *natural* history often include detailed descriptions of the methodology of disciplines such as palaeontology. Ultimately, the 'child-oriented' approach of popular series, like the Horrible Histories could be described as a form of rhetorical populism: its primary function is to draw the child reader into a kind of anti-authoritarian complicity with the author, rather than promoting more general critique. While school history and school textbooks may have changed their focus over the last few decades, this has only been superficially reflected in history books designed for use in the home.

CHAPTER 7

GOING INTERACTIVE
The pedagogy of edutainment software

The exponential growth of home computing is inextricably entwined with many of the broader developments we are addressing in this book. While some have argued that the market is now approaching saturation, the proportion of households with computers continues to rise. Of course, there are many reasons for this. As the equipment has fallen in price and become more 'user-friendly', the Internet in particular is increasingly being utilized as a medium for entertainment – for leisure interests, home shopping and personal communication. Yet the potential role of home computers in children's education is undoubtedly a key explanation for their rapid dissemination.

Of course, children are a primary market for computer-based entertainment, which is largely delivered through dedicated games consoles. But when it comes to the PC, it is the *educational* potential of computing that is most strongly emphasized in the advertising and in public debate. Indeed, the home computer could be seen as one of the indispensable 'symbolic goods' of contemporary parenting (Cawson *et al.* 1995). Investing in computers is, so parents are told, a way of investing in your children's future. Computers give children access to worlds of knowledge that would otherwise be denied to them; and, so it is argued, they give children control of their own learning. Education and parenting *without* technology thereby come to be seen as at least conservative, if not downright reactionary. It is the fundamental responsibility of good parents and teachers to 'catch up' with the children who are in their charge (Buckingham 2000b).

In her research on the marketing of computer hardware and software in Australia in the mid-1990s, Helen Nixon (1998) points to the emergence of a new range of specialist magazines aimed specifically at the family market, with titles like *Computer Living, Family PC* and *Parents and Computers*. As Nixon shows, these magazines and the advertising they carried featured prominent images of 'happy techno-families'; and they played particularly on parents' anxieties about their children's education. Computers were represented as a key tool in the drive for educational success: they would give children an 'educational edge' on the competition and help them 'move to the front of the class'.

As we indicated in Chapter 4, these discourses are still apparent in a good deal of marketing and consumer advice material aimed at parents. Parents must be persuaded of the unique educational benefits of home computing, and simultaneously reassured about the fact that their children can be protected from harm (Buckingham *et al.* 2001). Nevertheless, in third-millennium Britain, there are signs that the promotional era is already over. There no longer seems to be any need to persuade parents of the educational value of home computers *per se*. The challenge now is to get them to invest in the software.

And yet – as we have seen in Chapters 3 and 4 – the domestic market for educational software now seems to be faltering. This is partly a result of competition from the Internet, but it also reflects some endemic problems in the promotion, distribution and retailing of educational packages. As we will see in Chapter 10, parents do not necessarily know about the software that is available, or where to obtain it; and the fact that it cannot generally be previewed prior to purchase is a significant disincentive, as compared with books. Several of the parents and children whom we interviewed had invested in software that turned out to be of poor quality, or did not live up to the promises of its packaging. Most had bought little beyond the packages that came 'bundled' with the computer itself.

These findings echo those of previous research. In an early study, conducted well before the popularization of the Internet, Giacquinta *et al.* (1993) found that uses of educational software in the home were extremely limited, even in families with relatively high levels of enthusiasm and technical knowledge. All the research would suggest that children's use of computers in the home is massively dominated by playing games; and that the use of specifically educational software remains relatively limited (Harris 1999; Livingstone and Bovill 1999; National Center for Education Statistics 2000; Papadakis 2001).

These questions about the uses of software will be taken up in more detail in Part Three of this book. In this chapter, we would like to identify and discuss some of the characteristics of educational CD-ROM 'texts' themselves. Rather than focusing in detail on specific case studies, we will look briefly at several titles aimed at children between 5 and 12 years of age, ranging from 'drill-and-practice' packages to more game-like products. As in previous chapters, we will focus specifically on the *pedagogy* of this material – that is, the relationships between 'teachers' and 'learners' that it attempts to establish. Our key concern here will be the notion of 'interactivity' – a quality which is often trumpeted as one of the unique benefits of educational software, yet in our view is rarely well defined.

The decline and fall of interactivity?

Advocates of digital technology in education are often dismissive of the majority of commercially produced CD-ROMs, and of the 'marketing hype' that surrounds them. Aldrich *et al.* (1998: 321), for example, claim that such packages are 'poorly constructed, consisting simply of a mishmash of images, sounds and video that offer little more than light entertainment'. Lydia Plowman (1996a: 263) argues that educational packages are often no more than 'electronic books . . . betraying the material's origin in a different format and failing to maximise the potential of a new medium'. Seymour Papert (1996) likewise condemns the more popular 'instructional', back-to-basics software packages, particularly those which attempt to 'deceive' children into believing that they are simply playing a game.

The consensus here seems to be that (with some rare exceptions) the software that now dominates the market represents a kind of betrayal of the educational promise of computers. In some cases, there is a kind of nostalgia for a past 'golden age' of educational software. Thus, John Robertson (1998) offers a representative personal account of what he calls the 'paradise lost' of educational computing. He argues that in the early days of information technology in schools (in the 1980s), the software in use was 'highly interactive and pupil-empowering'. In more recent years, largely as a result of commercial pressures and changing government policies, the software has become much less adventurous. Robertson argues that the multimedia encyclopaedias and reference books that now dominate computer use in schools have a degree of superficial sophistication, but are much less 'interactive' and 'empowering'. These packages contain much more information, but they typically allow the learner very little control over the nature of the learning situation or the purpose of the interaction.

While there is a considerable amount of truth in this view, there are also some problems with it. As the quotations above would suggest, the argument seems to reflect a suspicion of 'entertainment' *per se*, on the grounds that it necessarily represents a form of 'dumbing down'; and it is clearly informed by a particular 'constructivist' ideology that some at least would find questionable. Perhaps more significantly, Robertson and others are not comparing like with like. The early software packages they favour (such as databases, word-processors, spreadsheets and LOGO) could be broadly defined as *tools*: they are packages that enable the user to achieve other things, such as solve problems, create multimedia texts, or handle data. The more recent packages are different in kind: they are essentially *media* – that is, means of 'delivering' or providing access to information that is contained in the package itself. Of course, the 'tool' programs are still being used in schools and homes; and some at least do seem to offer new creative possibilities, for example in terms of image manipulation and animation (Sefton-Green and Parker 1999). Nevertheless, it is important to make distinctions between the different types of educational software available, and the different functions they seek to perform.

From this perspective, the place of the domestic market is rather paradoxical. On the one hand, it could be argued that parents are likely to be more vulnerable than teachers to the inflated claims of marketeers – not least because they have fewer sources of independent advice. Yet, on the other hand, it may be that they are in a better position to exploit the more 'empowering' possibilities of computers. Many critics have argued that the institutional constraints of schooling make it fundamentally incapable of exploiting the potential of new media technology (Cuban 1986); and for some, the home represents a more promising site for development. Jerry Wellington (2001), for example, believes that the technology inherently fosters a more flexible, open-ended, student-led style of learning; and he suggests that this 'marvellous platform for learning' is more attuned to the 'informal' learning style of the home than that of the school, which he characterizes as rigid and conformist. Indeed, he suggests that it may be for this reason that computers are now being taken up much more rapidly in homes than in schools.

However, this view seems somewhat essentialist in its depiction of these different learning styles: the notion that learning with information and communication technology is *inherently* any more 'open-ended' or 'free-ranging' than learning in school (as the author alleges) can quickly be dispelled by a brief glance at the software packages on sale in any high-street store. Indeed, as in the other areas we have been discussing, there is a growing pressure to align the learning style of the home more closely with the learning style of the school – and this realignment is bound to be reflected in the kinds of software available on the market.

Gaming and learning

A key aspect of the domestic context – and one which educationists frequently neglect – is the fact that most children's primary experience of home computing is that of playing games. Most children come to educational software with a wealth of experience of 'entertainment' software. The study of computer games is still relatively underdeveloped (see

Buckingham 2002a, for a review); but the key characteristics of successful computer games are fairly self-evident. Many games are extremely complex, 'multimodal' environments, which use sophisticated three-dimensional visual imagery. They offer many choices and routes for exploration; they contain complex and negotiable systems of rules to be mastered; and they generally involve a challenging goal or task, which requires long-term engagement to achieve. Many game genres require a whole range of cognitive activities: gathering and applying new information, memory, problem-solving, using tools, strategic planning and hypothesis testing. Furthermore, games are a key dimension of many children's peer-group culture: they are part of collaborative play or social activities, and they are integrated within a broader, intertextual multimedia environment. For all these reasons, games are self-evidently compelling and motivating, not just intellectually, but also emotionally and physiologically. By contrast, most so-called educational software possesses *none* of these characteristics.

Of course, the reasons for this are partly economic. Computer games are a major global industry, whose profits have recently begun to outstrip those of Hollywood. It would clearly be impossible for educational software designers to avoid using some of the tropes and devices of computer games – even if some would see this as a concession to 'entertainment'. Nevertheless, the budgets available to them are likely to be minuscule in comparison with those of even the more modest computer games. The gap between the two will be glaringly apparent to most children, however much their parents may encourage them to play educational games on the computer. To move from *Tomb Raider* to *Become a World Explorer* (Dorling Kindersley (DK)), or from *The Adventures of Zelda* to *Adi's Attic* (Knowledge Adventure) is to move from a world that is challenging and compulsive to one that must quickly seem impoverished and constraining.

On the other hand, whatever expertise they may develop through their experience of games, it is not necessarily true that children are automatically skilful users of educational CD-ROMs. As Plowman and her colleagues have discovered through observation in schools, many children struggle to retrieve information from CD-ROMs, because they may not be familiar with the conventions of interface design: much of their discussion focuses not on the content, but on the mechanical operation (Plowman 1996a; Laurillard *et al.* 2000). Perhaps because they do not have large production budgets, educational CD-ROMs themselves are frequently lacking in this respect. In using these packages, we ourselves encountered problems that will be familiar to many users, and which were echoed by some of the parents whom we asked to evaluate them: programs would refuse to install (or uninstall); they would shut down unexpectedly because an error of type 67 occurred; or they would plague the user with seemingly arbitrary menus or instructions. In several instances, so-called 'intuitive' interfaces appeared to leave too much to the imagination: we were occasionally left facing a frozen screen, not knowing where to click in order to proceed; or alternatively were carried along on a particular sequence, not knowing how to escape from it. Even when one has mastered the interface, there is a sense in which much of the content of a CD-ROM is discovered quite accidentally: there are often 'secrets' in multimedia whose existence may not be known, and which may therefore be impossible to discover (Plowman 1996b). This combination of poor interface design and user inexperience tends to result in a disorienting and fragmented experience that is far from being a 'marvellous platform for learning'.

Educational multimedia genres

As we have noted, it is important to make some fundamental distinctions here, at least in terms of the different genres of educational software. It is possible to identify some broad categories, as follows:

- drill-and-practice (including revision aids), e.g. *Test for Success, Times Key Stage 2 Science, Mega Maths Blaster*;
- fun learning (compilations, including games, quizzes and puzzles, aimed at teaching early maths or reading), e.g. *The Jolly Postman, Bananas in Pyjamas, Play with the Teletubbies*;
- living books (fictional stories featuring animation), e.g. *Arthur's Teacher Trouble, Amanda Stories*;
- reference works (encyclopaedias, dictionaries, atlases), e.g. *DK Children's Encyclopaedia, My First Incredible Amazing Dictionary, Eyewitness History of the World*;
- exploration (involving the exploration of a location or space), e.g. *World Explorer, Castle Explorer, The Ultimate Human Body*;
- educational games (mystery, puzzle or simulation games), e.g. *The Logical Journey of the Zoombinis, Sim Town, The Great Treasure Hunt, featuring Skipper and Skeeto*;
- tools (word-processors, databases, design/drawing, animation), e.g. *Kidpix Studio, Disney Complete Animator, Art Attack*.

Of course, many CD-ROMs are packages containing several different types of software; and there are many packages that could be seen as generic 'hybrids'. Dorling Kindersley's *World Explorer*, for example, contains the following: a 'globetrotting' journey, in which users can freely explore an animated world map, collecting 'stickers' as they go; a game, in which the user is sent on a mission to follow a particularly elusive 'friend' through several locations (in the manner of *Where in the World is Carmen Sandiego?*); a collection of multiple-choice quizzes about countries, flags and so on; and a searchable reference text, complete with video extracts and hyperlinks. Likewise, GSP's *The Great Treasure Hunt* is primarily a mystery game, in which the user has to discover hidden treasure using a range of enigmatic clues; although along the way, it includes puzzles, quizzes and lessons about the solar system. Even drill-and-practice packages like *Adi's English and Maths Year 6* (Knowledge Adventure) contain games, small-scale simulations, design tools, and reference resources. All three packages also feature links to selected Internet sites.

Fairly self-evidently, the majority of these genres are derived or adapted from genres in other media: drill-and-practice books, 'fun learning' magazines, reference books, TV programmes, children's story books, and so on. The fundamental difference – at least outwardly – is that these packages purport to be 'interactive'. Indeed, it is this interactivity that is frequently seen as the guarantee of 'fun' and of children's motivation to learn. Dorling Kindersley's publicity trailers, for example, repeatedly claim that its packages offer 'a truly interactive learning experience'; and it is this that apparently enables 'fun and education [to] come together effortlessly'. Precisely what forms this interactivity takes, and its implications for learning, are the focus of the remainder of this chapter.

Dimensions of interactivity

Several authors have attempted to develop taxonomies of interactivity in relation to educational media. Laurillard (1987) and Bartolome (1992) distinguish different 'levels' of interactivity in terms of the degree of control or autonomy they offer the learner. Thus, at the lowest level are media that are more didactic or 'instructional', and offer relatively little control (as in a TV broadcast); while at the highest level are relatively unstructured or open-ended media that enable learners to find their own way through different sources of information at their own pace (as with the World Wide Web). Between these two are media such as programmed learning texts, which offer the learner a more limited range of choices within a predetermined framework, and may allow more or less control over the sequence of activities or the kind of response. (These three levels of interactivity are sometimes termed 'reactive', 'proactive' and 'coactive', respectively.) While these authors acknowledge that different degrees of interactivity may be appropriate for different educational aims, they nevertheless clearly favour a maximizing of interactivity, representing it (in Laurillard's terms) as a form of 'emancipation'.

However, Aldrich *et al.* (1998) argue that much of the interactivity on offer in commercial CD-ROMs is relatively superficial. It is a matter of 'physical activities at the interface': the user 'acts' (for example, by clicking a button) and the computer responds. They refer to this as 'reactive interactivity', and argue that in some instances it can be quite gratuitous: the user clicks aimlessly, more or less at random, and is rewarded with 'humorous' noises and pieces of animation. This is certainly a fair description of the level of interactivity in many so-called 'living books'. Here, each screen (or page) contains a wealth of animated objects that can be activated by the user – although at the expense of becoming distracted from the ongoing narrative.

Rod Sims (1997) offers a more elaborate taxonomy of interactivity, again focusing primarily on the degree of learner control. This ranges from *object* interactivity, of the kind just described, through *linear* and *hierarchical* interactivity (where the user follows a predetermined sequence, or selects from a predefined menu) to more open-ended forms of interactivity, which give the learner much more choice and control. The latter include *construct* interactivity, in which the learner is required to manipulate objects to achieve a particular goal; *simulation* interactivity, in which learners assume the role of 'controller' of a particular operation; *hyperlinked* interactivity, where the learner can navigate at will through a body of information; and *immersive* interactivity, in which the learner is 'projected into a complete computer-generated world which responds to individual movement and actions' (Sims 1997: 168).

As Sims indicates, these different types of interactivity entail different modes of engagement on the part of learners in different types of tasks: learners may be seeking answers to specific questions, or merely 'browsing'; they may be following a navigational path laid out by the system or program, or alternatively defining their own; and there may be one or many solutions to the problems they are presented with. Furthermore, the software itself may offer different types and levels of feedback, ranging from simple help messages (*support* interactivity) to more detailed feedback on performance (*update* interactivity) or more extended opportunities for users to compare their responses with those of 'experts', and to reflect upon them (*reflective* interactivity).

Drilling and skilling

The nature of these distinctions can be illustrated by considering some of the different software 'genres' identified above in a little more detail. At the 'reactive' end of the continuum are the 'drill-and-practice' packages, which are often explicitly intended as a form of revision aid or remedial support. Some of these packages focus on 'skills' – mainly in literacy and numeracy – while others are more concerned with subject content – for example in science or history. Nevertheless, they all entail a form of quiz or test; and in some instances, they contain a 'tracking' facility for the users (or their parents) to assess progress.

In several instances, the 'fun learning' ethos is to the fore. Dorling Kindersley's *Test for Success* series, for example, features 'Seymour Skinless', the animated skeleton from another DK title, *The Amazing Human*

Body. According to the publicity blurb, Seymour is 'the guy who puts the "cool" in school'; and users are expected to be motivated by his 'enthusiasm' and 'schoolboyish sense of humour' – which in practice appears to consist largely of weak puns. This use of tropes and genres from entertainment is clearly intended to offset any suspicion that the content is too closely related to school work. Dorling Kindersley's *I Love Spelling*, for example, is essentially a series of spelling tests in the form of a science-fiction-style game show. Its publicity trailer promises 'endless fun' and 'incredible addictive fun'. Perhaps the most overtly game-like approach is adopted by Knowledge Adventure's *Mega Maths Blaster*, which packages mental arithmetic tasks in the form of a series of science-fiction-themed computer games (simple platform and *Space Invaders*-style games). Speed is of the essence here, as the focus shifts rapidly between multiple-choice tests and games with little or no mathematical content, clearly included as a form of 'reward'.

Dorling Kindersley's *Learning Ladder*, 'a complete learning system for your child', is somewhat more complex in that it aims to *teach* as well as *test*. In the case of the Maths and English sections, the user is first presented with a 'one-to-one lesson' – effectively, a paragraph of text read by an animated child character. This is followed by a practice exercise, and then by a set of five (purportedly 'interactive') graded exercises. The user is also able to request brief back-up explanations. As the tests are completed, the user earns points which accumulate towards the reward of a picture that can be printed out; while it is also possible for the parent to track progress via a series of gauges. The user is led through the package by 'Woody', an animated pencil, who is relentlessly cheery and patronizing. Selecting a particular option (colons and semi-colons, brackets and dashes) results in an excited exclamation from Woody: 'My favourite!', 'Nice choice!' or 'Let's go, champ!' Success is rewarded with encouragement – 'Good work, kiddo!', 'Hey, you know your stuff! Whoo-hoo!' – while failure meets only with a hint of disappointment – 'Let's come back to that later'. The activities also contain an extensive library of 'bells and whistles' (not to mention drumrolls, buzzers, scratches and other sound effects).

Of course, packages of this kind might be condemned for teaching disembodied 'skills', and for doing so in a highly mechanical way. The user is trained to follow the rules, and the rules are taken to be objective and indisputable. Techniques such as punctuation or calculating fractions are entirely removed from any context or real purpose for which they might be used. In these respects, *Learning Ladder* may not be so very different from what now passes for literacy and numeracy in the wake of government-directed 'strategies'. Yet the extent to which a testing package of this kind can be described (as it is in DK's publicity trailer) as 'an unrivalled interactive learning experience' is perhaps more open to debate.

A slightly different approach to 'interactivity' is offered by the Science section of this package, which derives more from the 'exploration' genre identified above. Here, the user explores a three-dimensional 'world' called Science City. Clicking on objects leads you to illustrated information pages; and there are also multiple-choice quizzes. This approach is also followed by *The Times* newspaper's *Key Stage 2 Science* package. Here, the user is invited (by the inevitable animated rodent) to explore 'Domeworld – a land of scientific discovery'. In each of the eight themed domes (for example, woodland, plant world, the body), the user is given a series of quizzes, puzzles and activities. Here again, success enables the user to gather points towards a larger reward – in this case, a 'spectacular' flight to the moon. Each of the tasks is brief, and it is possible to move quite quickly from naming teeth to assembling electrical circuits and spotting camouflaged spaceships. In this package, there appears to be no guidance provided when the user fails to answer correctly.

In terms of the taxonomies introduced above, the 'interactivity' provided by this sort of package is obviously very limited. The 'exploration' structure of the Science packages allows the learner slightly more control over the sequence and selection of the activities; but in general, the approach is clearly linear and hierarchical. While there is some support interactivity (in the form of help messages), update interactivity is limited to checking test scores, and there is no opportunity to reflect or compare one's responses with those of 'experts'. The use of rewards as a form of operant conditioning, the limited nature of the feedback, and the fragmented, atomized nature of the content all imply a narrowly behaviourist conception of learning. While the packages may or may not be 'fun', terms like 'interactive' and 'discovery' seem only marginally appropriate.

Finding out

Somewhere in the middle of this continuum, there is a range of packages that are fundamentally to do with *information retrieval*. These packages include reference works such as dictionaries and encyclopaedias, as well as some we have termed 'exploration' packages. These packages are less overtly 'curriculum-based' (as DK put it); and in the publicity material, the emphasis is more on affective or motivational benefits than on the mastery of skills. Dorling Kindersley's trailer for its *Children's Encyclopaedia*, for example, claims that 'Knowledge is power, and this encyclopaedia is your child's gateway to a world of knowledge and a lifelong passion for learning'. Much is made here of the sheer *quantity* of the information available; of the use of multiple media (including video); and, of course, of 'interactivity'.

In the case of multimedia reference works, the content is frequently drawn directly from books. At its worst, this results in what some in the industry call 'shovelware', implying that content has simply been shov-elled from one medium to the other. In the case of CD-ROMs aimed at children, however, there is generally a more concerted attempt to provide a degree of interactivity. Dorling Kindersley's *History of the World*, for example, contains a range of activities such as quizzes and games that encourage the user to locate information. The package offers a variety of ways of searching, for example by region, time period or theme; and it also contains a more conventional alphabetic index of names and key themes. There are also hypertext links between the various contents, as well as links to external websites. Like a conventional encyclopaedia, much of the information is in the form of relatively decontextualized 'facts'; but there are many more ways of accessing that information than would be possible with a book.

Practice in information retrieval is a key theme in the geographical and historical 'exploration' packages. To some extent, the paradigm for these packages is Broderbund's extremely successful *Where in the World is Carmen Sandiego?* (now marketed by The Learning Company). Here, the user is an employee of a detective agency, and is given the assignment of locating the master criminal Carmen Sandiego. The user follows Carmen through a series of international locations, gathering clues from witnesses and compiling them in an electronic notebook. More recent versions include an 'explore mode' that contains brief fact files on each location. The interactivity of *Carmen Sandiego* is essentially linear: while the user can choose to go to any of the locations listed, the witnesses will only respond if the correct location is chosen.

Dorling Kindersley's *World Explorer* exemplifies the more 'educational' exploration packages. While it contains a simplified Carmen Sandiego-style game, it also functions as a geographical encyclopaedia with a searchable index. Additional elements here include multiple-choice quizzes and games; 'stickers' and 'postcards' to collect; a selection of geographical 'movies'; as well as matching and perspective games. As with some of DK's multimedia encyclopaedias, it is also possible to 'personalize' the package by inserting a name and a photograph of yourself so that you can be 'snapped' in different locations. In addition to following these more structured activities, it is also possible to wander through various locations on a (very simplified) world map. Clicking on images will generate short animations or 'bells and whistles' in the style of a 'talking book' (object interactivity); but it can also lead to information pages with explanatory text and further hyperlinks. This basic formula is also employed in relation to other subject areas in Dorling Kindersley's *History* and *Science Explorer* packages; and, in a somewhat more in-depth way, in its *Castle Explorer*.

Like the multimedia reference works described above, these 'explorer' packages work hard to animate and motivate the process of information retrieval – or to make it 'fun'. As such, they contain a range of different forms of interactivity. While there are elements of linear, hierarchical and object interactivity, there are also limited forms of hyperlinked interactivity – although these are obviously much more constrained than those on the World Wide Web. In some of the more advanced packages (such as *Castle Explorer* and the three-dimensional *Ultimate Human Body*), there is a degree of immersive interactivity, in that the user is able to navigate in a virtual world, crossing space and time (although this is not a genuinely responsive world). Feedback is relatively limited, and is primarily confined to support, with limited updates (for example, in the form of stickers collected).

However, the sheer range of activities available in these packages, combined with the emphasis on more open-ended navigation, contributes to a sense in which the key activity here is that of *browsing* rather than purposeful information retrieval. By contrast, the *Carmen Sandiego* packages establish a much more clearly defined *goal* for the user – and in this sense, they seem closer to a game than an 'educational' package. Nevertheless, all these types of package raise questions about how such information is to be understood and used – in other words, about how *information* might be transformed into *knowledge*. We will return to this issue below.

Game play

Towards the 'proactive' end of our continuum are packages that much more obviously resemble games, and might well be described as such by their users. Of course, as we have indicated, packages like *Mega Maths Blaster* use game formats – even if they are significantly simpler and less compelling than the average PlayStation game. The 'explorer' packages and some of the encyclopaedias also include (extremely simple) games, although these often seem to be included as 'fun' extras or rewards, rather than as key elements. (This is also true of some of the drill-and-practice packages.)

There are several packages that might be categorized as 'educational games' (although, as we shall indicate below, this categorization itself is fairly problematic). Three examples will have to suffice here. GSP's *The Great Treasure Hunt, featuring Skipper and Skeeto*, places the user in a haunted castle, where the object is to hunt for hidden treasure. The user enters different rooms, and is presented with puzzles and riddles to solve, as well as simpler fairground-type games. These have to be completed successfully if the user is to progress to the next clue. Perhaps the best analogy for this package is the adult game *Myst*, in that the user has to piece together the solution from a range of sources, using a variety of different types of evidence. While not as atmospheric and elliptical as *Myst*, *The Great Treasure Hunt* is comparatively challenging for its target age group (6–14).

In *The Logical Journey of the Zoombinis* (Broderbund/The Learning Company), the user attempts to ensure the survival of a group of little creatures as they work their way through a series of tests and obstacles. The user selects the creatures at the start of the game by permuting from among a series of defining characteristics (different hats, noses, etc.); and it is these characteristics (or combinations of them) that subsequently become the basis for the creatures being eliminated from the game. The key to success is to discover the hidden 'rules' of each obstacle or test, through repeatedly and systematically varying the characteristics. As the title suggests, this is essentially an exercise in logic; and it requires considerable skills in terms of memory, hypothesis testing and prediction.

Sim Town (Maxis) is a junior version of the well-known simulation package *Sim City*. Here, the user is required to develop a town using a 'tool box' consisting of roads, buildings, houses, utilities, and so on. People then appear to occupy the town, multiplying seemingly uncontrollably. In effect, the user makes a series of 'town planning' decisions, whose consequences are then revealed – for example in the form of overcrowding, pollution, floods or fires. However, the connections between the user's decisions and their consequences are not made explicit: here too, there are underlying 'rules' or principles that must be identified if the player is to succeed.

In terms of our earlier taxonomy, these packages all appear to offer a considerable amount of choice and control to the user. *Sim Town* is clearly an example of simulation interactivity, which to some degree mimics a real-life situation; while the others might be described as to some extent immersive. Perhaps the most interesting differences here are in terms of the nature of the feedback. Unlike *Sim Town*, the first two packages both impose a specific goal which has to be met; and in the case of *The Great Treasure Hunt*, there is also a time constraint (of one hour). Nevertheless, both effectively rely on a form of trial and error; and in both cases, there is a (potentially frustrating) absence of support interactivity (for example, in the form of help messages). By contrast, while *Sim Town* also lacks support interactivity, it does provide a form of update interactivity (via newspaper headlines) – even if the form of the updates is not explicitly tied to the actions of the user.

To what extent can one describe these packages as *educational* games? As we have implied, *Sim Town* could be seen as an elementary town planning simulation; while *The Zoombinis* is essentially to do with logical thinking. Such a claim is a little more difficult to make in the case of *The Great Treasure Hunt*, although it could certainly be regarded as an exercise in 'visual and creative thinking skills' (as its packaging claims). Interestingly, several of these more game-like programs seem to have been repackaged in recent years in order to emphasize these kinds of 'educational' claims. As we noted in Chapter 4, this seems to be increasingly important in the UK retail market, both for books and software, largely as a result of the growing significance of national testing. Thus, the title of *The Great Treasure Hunt* is now dwarfed by the words 'Play and Learn' on the cover; while *The Logical Journey of the Zoombinis* is marketed in the UK as *Zoombinis Maths Journey*, complete with a 'Supports UK National Curriculum' logo. Likewise, the covers of more recent versions of *Where in the World is Carmen Sandiego?* (and its spin-offs) incorporate a list of the 'skills' the user will 'master' (reading, deductive reasoning, logic, combining information, etc.), along with the invitation to 'Study 50 countries and cultures'. Here too, the buyer is reassured that the package 'supports the UK and Scottish [*sic*] National Curricula at Key Stages 2 and 3'. On one level, this provides further evidence of the narrowing definition of what counts as 'education'; although it also reflects the fact that the 'educational' dimensions of these packages are much less explicit than those of the other genres we have considered. This question of explicitness, and its implications for learning, is one we will return to below.

Learning with software

In this account, we have focused primarily on two dimensions of the design of these software packages (following Sims 1997). The first of these is to do with the amount and nature of the *control* that can be exercised by the user; while the second is to do with the nature of the *feedback* provided by the package itself. Identifying differences and variations in these dimensions enables us to characterize the *pedagogy* of these packages, at least at a fairly general level.

Nevertheless, how these dimensions relate – and how they *should* relate – will obviously vary according to the task at hand, and to the needs of the learner. As we have noted, discussions of educational software have tended to assume that increasing the amount of learner control is inherently desirable. From this perspective, the packages that are the most productive in terms of learning would be those we have categorized as 'educational games' (excluding those of the drill-and-practice variety). Perhaps paradoxically, it is these less overtly 'educational' texts that seem to provide the 'empowerment' or 'emancipation' that constructivists such as Robertson (1998) or Wellington (2001) are calling for. While we have some sympathy with this view, it is important to raise some caveats.

One of the issues raised at several points in our discussion is that of the *contextualization* of the skills or knowledge such packages are attempting to teach. One of the most obvious criticisms of the drill-and-practice packages is that they are attempting to teach 'skills' in isolation from the contexts in which they might be used. Likewise, one concern with the exploration and reference packages is that they teach 'facts' – or at least encourage users to accumulate them – without providing any broader context in which they might become relevant or meaningful. Both types of package appear to fetishize *performance* – that is, the mastery of particular techniques, or of factual recall – in its own right, and hence in a fundamentally decontextualized way.

By contrast, the educational games we have considered do seek to provide at least a simulated context in which performance is made to *matter*. It matters in the sense that it has consequences that are intrinsic to the situation rather than extrinsic (for example, in the form of test scores or – less powerfully – the 'stickers' or other rewards offered by the exploration packages). Solving the problem is (or should be) inherently motivating. In fact, this varies somewhat between the three game-like packages we have described, in that *Sim Town* (unlike the others) seems to be lacking an explicit goal beyond that of survival – and hence, we would suggest, is likely to prove less compelling over the longer term. Nevertheless, by comparison, the mode of engagement that users are likely to have with packages like *World Explorer* is much less engaged and committed: rather like *The Guinness Book of Records*, these packages invite the user merely to *browse* in an undifferentiated compendium of more or less interesting facts and figures. With the exception of the games elements in such packages, the software itself does not provide the user with a narrative motivation that might help to make it comprehensible or meaningful (Plowman 1996b).

We might distinguish here between the intrinsically motivated learner of *The Zoombinis* – who is presumed to be motivated by a wish to solve the problem at hand – and the extrinsically motivated learner of *Learning Ladder* – who is presumed to have internalized a wish to compete in terms of test scores. By contrast, the learner of the 'exploration' or reference packages is assumed to possess an inherent and somewhat generalized 'thirst for knowledge' that the package itself will somehow magically unlock. Learners who are not blessed with such innate psychological drives are likely to wander aimlessly, alighting temporarily on one fact after another, without ever resting long enough to fully internalize it. In this context, learning becomes akin to a game of *Trivial Pursuit* – although without the element of competition. For this reason, we suspect that such packages are likely to be abandoned quite quickly, unless children find them useful for a specific purpose.

On the basis of their research, Diana Laurillard and her colleagues argue that the rhetoric of 'discovery' or 'exploratory learning' in educational software is frequently misplaced (Laurillard 1995; Laurillard *et al.* 2000). They suggest that truly open-ended exploration is more appropriately facilitated by direct experience (such as field trips or experiments). Most learners, they argue, are not yet ready to be researchers, interrogating audio-visual databases and reference works:

Finding their way for the first time through [a] subject area, they cannot be expected to set appropriate goals, or plot a reasonable

path: they will under-specify the problem, be distracted by
irrelevancies, be unsure how to evaluate the information they find,
over-generalise from instances, remain unaware of incompleteness,
fail to recognise inconsistencies . . . there is every opportunity to
fail to meet the objective.

(Laurillard 1995: 185–6)

Ultimately, these packages do not provide sufficient support for learners:
much more is needed by way of guidance and feedback if learners are to
achieve meaningful goals.

Likewise, we would argue that the fundamental *educational* problem
with the game-like packages is precisely that their conceptual principles are
not made explicit by means of feedback to the user. The player can struggle
away endlessly with *The Zoombinis*, working wholly by trial and error,
without ever being forced to make the logic of their choices explicit.
Likewise, one can continue to build one's town in *Sim Town* and watch its
progress over many hours, without ever being forced to make explicit the
relationship between one's choices and the consequences to which they
lead. (Indeed, one suspects that the lack of an explicit goal might well give
rise to a certain anarchic destructiveness, on the grounds that it is simply
more interesting to watch one's town degenerate into chaos than to watch
it thrive harmoniously.) In this case, there is insufficient 'scaffolding' or
feedback to the learner, with the result that the fundamental conceptual
'lessons' of the activity may simply be lost. Here again, we suspect that
the appeal of such packages may be quite short-lived, unless children are
somehow made aware of the broader issues the game is addressing.

At least in principle, multimedia is particularly well suited to what
Laurillard (1995) calls '*guided* discovery learning'. In some respects, this
style of learning lies between the 'reactive' and the 'proactive' approaches
identified above. Here, the learner is not compelled to follow a single
narrative line originated by the teacher (as in the drill-and-practice
packages), or alternatively to wander or experiment with possibilities of
their own free will (as in the exploration and reference packages). 'Guided
discovery learning' involves collaboration and dialogue between teacher
(or, in this case, software) and learner. It depends upon the agreement of
a shared goal, and the supply of guidance and feedback from teacher to
student. In this approach, it is important that learners should be kept
aware of the goal of the activity, and given guidance about how to
achieve it; but they should also have the opportunity to devise their own
approach, and to deviate from the line suggested. This perspective therefore offers learners a considerable degree of autonomy, while also avoiding aimless browsing or experimentation. At present, however, very little
educational software appears to be suited to developing this approach. In
the absence of adequate scaffolding or feedback from the program itself,
the interaction with 'real' parents or peers becomes particularly important.

Conclusion

As we have seen, a great many claims have been made about the value of multimedia as a learning resource. 'Interactivity' is often seen to be key to this: it is assumed to motivate and engage the learner; to offer learners choice and control over their own learning; and to encourage the autonomy and even the 'emancipation' of learners. However, as we have shown in this chapter, interactivity takes many different forms and serves many different purposes. In many cases, it seems to amount to little more than a marketing promise, or a superficial ornament. Compared with the potential of these new forms of learning – and indeed, with the experience of many computer games – the interactivity afforded by most educational software must ultimately be seen as quite impoverished.

CHAPTER 8

DECONSTRUCTING DINOSAURS
Imagery, fact and fiction in
information books

Dinosaurs have been a recurring theme within children's culture for many decades. The first dinosaur movie (*The Lost World*) was released in 1925, and has been followed by a plethora of prehistoric texts and arte-facts in a wide range of media. In the last decade, there have been four big-budget US films about dinosaurs; while in 2000 the BBC aired its enormously successful *Walking with Dinosaurs* series. On visiting a major store like Toys R Us, or indeed an educational attraction like London's Natural History Museum, parents and children are likely to be confronted with an extensive range of dinosaur commodities: books, CD-ROMs, videotapes, computer games, soft toys, clothing, plastic models, key rings, construction kits, and so on.

In some ways dinosaurs are the ideal subject for edutainment. The study of dinosaurs (palaeontology) is a science, whose history and meth-odology are explained in most children's reference books. However, dinosaurs also have the appeal of fantasy creatures. Publishers create dramatic narratives by focusing on the mystery, ferocity and enormity of the dinosaurs; and the ongoing search for dinosaur fossils is itself presented as a kind of heroic adventure. Like TV natural history pro-grammes, dinosaur books and other texts seek to provide an accessible, exciting view of science. They enable children to build up an encyclo-paedic knowledge of the subject which they can brandish at adults and friends. As we shall argue, their appeal in this respect is similar to that of other children's 'crazes' such as Pokémon. However, parents are likely to regard the study of dinosaurs as a more legitimate form of learning than the study of fictional Japanese monsters. And this may be one of the main reasons for the continuing popularity of dinosaurs:

they appeal to both parents and children, albeit for somewhat different reasons.

In this chapter we look at how education and entertainment are combined in dinosaur books (and some software) produced by various UK and international publishers, including Dorling Kindersley, Usborne, Kingfisher, Aladdin/Watts and Ticktock. (A list of these books is given in the Appendix to this chapter.) We begin with a brief overview of how dinosaurs have been used in different media.

The dinosaur industry

The release of Steven Spielberg's *Jurassic Park* in 1993 probably represents the main point of origin of the contemporary enthusiasm for dinosaurs; although there had been films on this theme over the previous five years, including the animated *Land Before Time* in 1988 and a remake of *The Lost World* in 1992. Very much intended as a 'family film', *Jurassic Park* became one of the biggest grossing movies of all time and was duly followed by two sequels. In each case, there have been significant merchandising tie-ins, including books and software: in the case of *Jurassic Park 3*, for example, these included books published by Random House and Boxtree and computer games such as *Jurassic Park 3: Dino Defender* and *Danger Zone*.

One important characteristic of this phenomenon is that publishers and toy manufacturers can benefit from the success of the films without necessarily having to pay licensing fees. Because these films are based on realistic models of dinosaurs rather than on fabricated (and hence copyrighted) creatures like Pokémon or Disney characters, the merchandise is instantly recognizable, and does not have to be marketed as a *Jurassic Park* or *Walking with Dinosaurs* spin-off. Dinosaur commodities can also reach retail outlets which licensed characters such as Pokémon might not (such as the UK's Early Learning Centre, which prides itself on its avoidance of media-related merchandise). A child who has seen the films or the TV series and wishes to find out more would not necessarily have to be confined to 'official' books or websites – whereas the same could not be said of fictional creatures like Pokémon.

One indicator of the impact which *Jurassic Park* has had on the dinosaur industry generally is that the film is now mentioned in most nonfiction books on this theme: it has become part of the folklore of the subject. However, its success has not been easy to replicate. Disney's animated *Dinosaur* was released in 2000, and although the film did well at the box office it was not as commercially successful or as critically acclaimed as previous Disney films such as *Toy Story* or *The Lion King*. Nevertheless, there were some merchandising tie-ins, including a book published by Dorling Kindersley (DK) (discussed in some detail below), as well as software and a PlayStation game.

In print, dinosaurs have proven to be a versatile subject, appearing in children's non-fiction, fiction and even poetry. Within non-fiction, they feature in humorous paperbacks such as Scholastic's *The Knowledge* series and in glossy hardbacks published by companies like DK and Kingfisher. Their popularity in non-fiction publishing shows no signs of waning: several non-fiction publishers produced new titles on dinosaurs in 2001, including Franklin Watts, Kingfisher, Usborne and Oxford University Press. Big Fish (a new imprint of Collins and Brown) chose dinosaurs as a topic for one of its first non-fiction series, which would suggest that they serve as a relatively safe option for publishers, despite the level of competition. Dinosaurs seem particularly suited to the glossy hardback format, partly because their size, ferocity and strangeness make them visually appealing for the 8–12 age group. And dinosaurs are internationally recognizable – an important factor for publishers targeting overseas markets.

Dinosaur books published in the last few years reflect the increasing convergence between media. Several of the books currently on sale are based on films or TV series; and many include information on internet sites which relate to the topic. Usborne, for example, produces a series of internet-linked books which include recommended websites chosen to 'take you further into the subject in a fun and informative way' (*Dinosaurs* 2001). Rather than listing these websites in an index, they are interspersed throughout the book and the content of each website is briefly described. Meanwhile, most of the CD-ROMs which feature dinosaurs are spin-offs from films or TV series. Dorling Kindersley is one of the few companies selling software which is not film- or TV-related (although, as noted in Chapter 3, they have recently stopped producing CD-ROMs). Significantly, dinosaurs are featured both in games software such as *Disney Dinosaur* (for the PlayStation) and educational/reference software such as DK's *Children's Encyclopedia of Dinosaurs*.

Catching 'em all

How might we explain the continuing popularity of dinosaurs in children's culture? One of the most obvious reasons is their sheer versatility. Dinosaurs can be employed in a wide range of contexts for different target markets. As with Pokémon, there are dinosaur products for different age groups (soft toys, information books, computer games) and for both boys and girls. Given the traditionally fragmented nature of the children's market, this ability to combine potentially disparate audiences remains comparatively rare. As Susan Willis (1999: 195) has pointed out:

> It's clear that dinosaurs can be just about anything. They can be your worst oedipal nightmare or an insipid, infantilized TV host. They can be masculinized or feminized . . . Because dinosaurs can be almost anything, both in science and in culture, they lend

themselves to the child's imagination, which shuffles and re-sorts all the available bits of knowledge to construct a version of dinosaurs.

One particularly significant aspect of this versatility derives from the dinosaurs' ambiguous status, somewhere between fact and fantasy. Thus, while *Jurassic Park* and *Walking with Dinosaurs* claimed to create 'realistic' images of dinosaurs using state-of-the-art digital technology, there has also been a commercial boom in what Susan Willis (1999) calls 'domesticated' dinosaurs. Barney, star of the children's TV programme, is the ultimate domesticated dinosaur: he talks, laughs, sings, plays, gives advice and generally takes on the role of a benign teacher/parent figure. In physical appearance Barney is the antithesis of the scary dinosaur: he is bright purple, has only a vague suggestion of teeth, and his rounded belly and head give him a soft, cuddly appearance.

Images of dinosaurs in print texts are similarly diverse. In glossy hardback information books, there is often a considerable degree of realistic detail, both in the illustrations of the dinosaurs themselves, and in the surrounding landscape of lush vegetation and active volcanoes. By contrast, humorous paperbacks (such as *The Knowledge* series) use cartoons of anthropomorphized dinosaurs. Thus, for example, a cartoon from *Dead Dinosaurs* shows a herbivore sitting down to dinner and asking for some salad cream. Elsewhere dinosaurs are shown wearing clothes, using walking sticks, conducting orchestras, winning awards, talking to each other and addressing the reader. The humour in these cartoons is based on the anomalous idea of these mysterious prehistoric creatures behaving like humans.

Despite the tendency to anthropomorphize dinosaurs (which we discuss in more detail below), the element of mystery is clearly fundamental here. As one author points out, many dinosaurs 'were every bit as strange as the monsters in mythology or the imagined inhabitants of alien worlds' (*Big Book of Dinosaurs*: 6). Perhaps the greatest mystery is how they became extinct. Although the books we are considering focus on 'serious' theories of mass extinction, they also mention some of the 'bizarre' (but interesting) explanations such as space-borne plagues or alien hunters. The *Best-Ever Book of Dinosaurs* repeats the legend that a descendant of the plesiosaurs (a prehistoric marine reptile) survives in the form of the Loch Ness monster. Even the more plausible explanations of the disappearance of the dinosaurs (erupting volcanoes or comets) seem fantastic. The books are quite willing to acknowledge that there are still many gaps in our knowledge; and the element of mystery allows scope for the imagination. Unlike living creatures (whose species characteristics restrict the imagination) dinosaurs can – in Willis's words – be 'molded and shaped to embody a huge variety of cultural meanings and serve a range of personal needs' (Willis 1999).

Juxtaposed with these allusions to the mystery of the prehistoric world is an almost fetishistic preoccupation with 'the facts'. *The DK Guide to Dinosaurs*, for example, claims to be 'packed with mind-boggling dinosaur facts'. Similarly, most of the double-page spreads in Usborne's *Dinosaurs* have a separate section beginning with the word 'Fact'. *Devastating Dinosaurs* is part of the *Fact Attack* series; whilst the subtitle for Michael Benton's *Walking with Dinosaurs* is 'The Facts' (this book is based on the TV series and appears to be targeted primarily at adults rather than children). This theme is also picked up in the publishers' catalogues. For example, the advertising blurb for *The Kingfisher Illustrated Dinosaur Encyclopedia* promises to provide readers with the 'hard facts' and 'reconstructions based on the latest scientific discoveries' (Kingfisher catalogue 2001). Even in fiction it is not possible to escape the facts: *Rex* has links to an Internet site featuring 'Mariah's Fascinating Dinosaur Facts' whilst *Dinosaur: the Essential Guide* (which is discussed in more detail below) combines fact and fiction in a somewhat uneasy manner.

Thus, most of these books contain exhaustive amounts of detailed information on dinosaur measurements – not simply of entire dinosaurs but of their component parts (legs, claws, teeth and jaws are particular favourites). Dinosaurs are compared in these respects with other dinosaurs, and with contemporary animals like whales or elephants. *The DK Guide to Dinosaurs*, for example, has a 'Dinodata' section listing various 'records', including the biggest dinosaur, the biggest predator, the longest predator and the longest neck. And of course there are hundreds of dinosaurs which can be subdivided by group, family, time period, habitat, and so on. One such book (*The Big Book of Dinosaurs*) is effectively a dinosaur catalogue: 74 dinosaurs are given 'fact-filled profiles' under the following subheadings: meaning [of name], group, size, time period and where found, and general description.

In some ways this focus on 'the facts' seems to contradict the assertion (made in several of these books) that there are still many gaps in our knowledge of dinosaurs and that mistakes in interpreting evidence have been made (see below). Nevertheless, it clearly makes it possible for readers to build up an encyclopaedic knowledge of dinosaurs and their habitats; and this acquisitive element may be one of the reasons for their continuing popularity. In this respect too, dinosaurs have a lot in common with Pokémon. As Buckingham and Sefton-Green (in press) have pointed out, the activity of acquiring information is central to the appeal of Pokémon: the successful player or collector needs to build up a detailed taxonomy of the various species and their unique characteristics. Just as the dinosaurs belong to different families, Pokémon also belong to different categories (Water, Fire, Psychic, etc.); and there is a premium on gathering and applying accurate knowledge drawn from a range of media sources. Within the wider peer-group culture surrounding the phenomenon, knowledge of this kind clearly serves as a kind of power.

Yet despite these and other similarities, the differences between dinosaurs and Pokémon are also instructive. While both are centrally to do with acquiring information, critics of Pokémon typically suggest that the learning that is at stake here is educationally worthless: children, it is argued, are simply developing an encyclopaedic knowledge of trivia. By contrast, although dinosaurs have the appeal of fantasy creatures, they cannot be condemned by parents as the latest fad dreamed up in America or Japan. Children are able to acquire expert knowledge of dinosaurs with which they can dazzle family and friends (as they might do with Pokémon); but this is unlikely to pose a threat to their parents' conception of what constitutes educationally legitimate or valid information. Indeed, it may well appeal to their pedagogic aspirations for their child. As Willis (1999: 187) points out:

> I have encountered many young boys (and a few girls) who
> use their knowledge of dinosaur facts and figures as a means
> of demonstrating mastery in a particular subject equal to the
> sorts of masteries they see their fathers (and possibly mothers)
> brandishing, but in a field not likely to impinge on parental
> expertise (unless, of course, the parent is a palaeontologist or the
> sort who competes for knowledge no matter what). This is an
> important consideration, especially in professional families in
> which the acquisition of knowledge is valued as a stepping-stone
> to a good education and a secure future ... Knowledge about
> dinosaurs, particularly statistical information, enables children to
> brandish expertise without directly challenging parental authority.

Of course, the criticisms of Pokémon were not simply about its pedagogic value: there were also concerns about the merchandising and the allegedly 'addictive' nature of the trading card game. However, if children were to suddenly start buying and trading dinosaur cards, it is unlikely that this would meet with the same level of adult hostility. While Pokémon seemed almost designed to exclude parents, dinosaurs are much more accessible: most parents understand what they are and may even have been interested in them themselves at some point. Perhaps paradoxically, dinosaurs seem to present less of a threat to parental conceptions of education than the much 'cuter' monsters of Pokémon.

Striking the right tone

In her analysis of dinosaur texts, Susan Willis (1999: 184) describes how editors balance the 'wonderousness of rich illustrations' (featuring volcanoes, swamps and lush vegetation) with a concern for scientific pedagogy, as each image is meticulously labelled. A similar balancing act is evident in the dinosaur books being produced today, as publishers try to combine entertainment with science. These disjunctions in tone are occasionally apparent in the written text of these books. Thus, authors can move between a scientific discourse ('By studying the arrangement of bones in the skeleton and seeing the points of attachment for individual muscles, scientists have worked out what the fleshed-up Allosaurus would have looked like', p. 14) to something more informal and dramatic ('What was the biggest, strongest and fiercest meat-eating dinosaur that ever lived? Tyrannosaurus? Not any more!') (*Carnivores*, p. 31).

However, these disparities are often particularly apparent in the disjunction between the written text and the visual imagery. In the *Usborne Pocket Science* book, *Where Did Dinosaurs Go?*, for example, a sober pedagogic text is 'enlivened' with cartoons of anthromorphized dinosaurs sunbathing, in bed, and so on. In many other cases, the visual imagery of dinosaur books seems to tell a more dramatic story than the texts themselves. For example, several books acknowledge that *Tyrannosaurus rex* could have been a scavenger rather than a predator, but the images in these books seem to imply that it was a predator. It is usually shown pursuing or attacking *live* animals, or simply baring its teeth and looking ferocious – it is never shown in a non-confrontational way.

Front covers, in particular, may lead readers to expect a more dramatic text than they actually get. One of the most striking cover images in recently published books is that of a *T. rex* (with open jaws and sharp teeth) about to pounce on a hapless bird-like dinosaur (*The Best-Ever Book of Dinosaurs*). Inside there are other dramatic scenes, for example of dinosaurs drowning in a flash flood, complete with tangled bodies, wild eyes and gaping mouths. Yet whilst the visual imagery is quite striking, some sections of the text are reminiscent of a biology book. At one point dinosaurs are described under the headings 'circulation', 'respiration', 'digestion' and 'reproduction', whilst the dinosaur body is labelled using scientific terms such as 'trachea', 'vertebrae', 'pubis' and 'metatarsal'. The text in these sections is arranged into columns, in a manner that is again reminiscent of a school textbook.

Image and text

Broadly speaking, the balance between image and text in dinosaur books has changed significantly over the past few decades. The illustrations are larger, and occupy a greater proportion of the space; while the images themselves are more dramatic and sensational. These changes may well reflect a more general move towards the visual in children's and educational publishing. In order to explore these changes, we reviewed a range of books produced over the last thirty years. Here, we focus particularly on a comparison of two glossy hardback books: *The Best-Ever Book of Dinosaurs* (1998) and *The Amazing World of Dinosaurs* (1976). The first of these was published by Kingfisher, one of the main UK reference publishers, while the second was designed and produced by Grisewood and Dempsey, and published by Angus and Robertson. (Kingfisher started out as Grisewood and Dempsey, so the publisher is effectively the same.) The two books are aimed at a comparable age group (8+) and would have been sold through high-street shops.

Kress and van Leeuwen (1996: 34) have suggested that over the last fifty years visual communication has become more important in school textbooks, newspapers and other media: 'Language is moving from its former, unchallenged role as *the* medium of communication, to a role as *one* medium of communication'. Whilst this change is reflected in children's dinosaur books, the shift from written to visual communication is not as dramatic as might have been expected. Images played a central role in children's non-fiction, even 25 years ago. In the case of *The Amazing World of Dinosaurs*, the proportions of space allocated to text and image vary between sections: in some cases it is about half and half, but in the sections on 'carnivores' or 'the search for dinosaurs' it is closer to one-third text and two-thirds image. The amount of imagery is not entirely surprising, given that this book would have been sold in high-street shops and targeted at the home and library market. Publishers of these kinds of books may have been more prepared to entertain and engage their readers through images, compared with publishers of the school textbooks discussed by Kress and van Leeuwen (1996). Yet while the proportion of text to image has not changed dramatically, there is still more written information in the older book because the text is compressed into a smaller space and laid out more systematically.

In fact, the more significant changes are to do with the *organization* of the page and the relationships between text and image, rather than simply to do with the amount. In terms of written text, it is important to make a distinction between general introductions or outlines of a theme, and text which accompanies particular images (captions). (*Dinosaur*, in the *Eyewitness Guides* series, provides a good example of this distinction: the text on the top left of the first page of each double-page spread introduces the subject, whilst the various images each have their own captions, usually in smaller print than the main text.) In older books, the bulk of the text was in the form of a general introduction or outline, whereas in contemporary books a substantial part of the text is in captions attached to specific images. This appears to invite and encourage a different style of reading: it is easier to browse through contemporary books because image and text form their own self-contained units (see Chapter 6). For example, in some of the double page spreads in *The Best-Ever Book of Dinosaurs*, approximately half of the text is in captions. The text has effectively become a commentary on the images, whereas in older books the bulk of the text was independent of the images. Thus, in *The Amazing World of Dinosaurs* the general introduction or outline is much longer, whilst the captions form a much smaller proportion of the overall text. The text in each double-page spread is clearly designed to be read consecutively from beginning to end.

The two books also differ in terms of the way in which text and image are set out in relation to one another. There is a much clearer separation between text and image in *The Amazing World of Dinosaurs*: a typical page/double-page spread has columns of written text on one side and images on the other. Image and text are clearly confined to separate spaces on the page. The only time text strays into the image side of the page is if there is a caption relating specifically to that image. The layout here (particularly the use of justified columns of text) is reminiscent of a school textbook. Columns of text and text boxes have not disappeared entirely from contemporary books (as we have seen in Chapter 6), but they are much less frequently used.

By contrast, the separation between text and image is less rigid in *The Best-Ever Book of Dinosaurs*. Images often dominate the centre of the double-page spread and the written text is either arranged around the images or superimposed onto them. In many cases the text follows the contours of the picture. Thus, one picture from *The Best-Ever Book* shows a tree branching out in different directions, with the text arranged around this central image. The use of images which cut right across the page (both from left to right and from top to bottom) also results in a more fragmented text. By contrast, the images used in older books tend to be smaller, so that instead of one main image, there will be several small images. On one page of *The Amazing World of Dinosaurs*, for example, there are six small boxed images of palaeontologists at work. Some pictures cut across the double-page spread, but these are in the minority. The result is that the imagery of the older book does not dominate the page in the manner of contemporary books.

Meanwhile, the images themselves have become much more dramatic and sensational. This is particularly evident in front cover images, which are obviously a key factor in establishing sales appeal in shop displays. Front covers produced in the 1970s and early 1980s often showed herbivores, and used whole-body shots (for example, *The Children's Prehistory: Dinosaurs* or *Dinosaurs and Other Early Animals*). By contrast, contemporary books usually show carnivores, and the main focus is on the head and mouth. *The Best-Ever Book of Dinosaurs* reflects this trend. The front cover shows a *T. rex* looking off to the left; and when you follow the direction of its gaze on to the back cover, you discover its prey – a frightened bird-like dinosaur. In effect, the book cover begins to tell a story, which is left to the reader's imagination to finish. The focus on the front cover is on the head and the mouth of the *T. rex*: the head shot alone takes up about a quarter of the page and seems to be quite out of proportion with the rest of the body. The gaping mouth reveals sharp teeth (some broken), a long pointed tongue and the shadows at the back of the mouth. The front cover of *The Amazing World of Dinosaurs* also shows what appears to be a *T. rex*. Here, however, the head is comparatively small: it could easily fit into the gaping jaws of the dinosaur on the cover of *The Best-Ever Book*. The *T. rex* is looking straight ahead and in the background there is a duck-billed dinosaur, also looking straight ahead. There is no sense of conflict between the two dinosaurs or of an impending attack: these dinosaurs are simply posing for the 'camera'. And whereas the dinosaur in *The Best-Ever Book* is shown in a (supposedly) realistic habitat, the background in the older book shows five rows of different prehistoric animals. Only the outlines of these animals are shown: there are no realistic details. These smaller images seem to detract attention away from the *T. rex*, whereas on the front cover of *The Best-Ever Book* the *T. rex* is clearly the centre of attention.

Meanwhile, there are also some significant differences in the written text. In general, the language of the older books is lexically denser and syntactically more complex. The tone of *The Amazing World of Dinosaurs* also places a premium on the value of scholarly endeavour. Thus, the author comments that 'in the early days of fossil hunting, the task was approached in an amateur way rather than as a professionally scientific undertaking'. After relating two different theories on whether the stegosaurus's plates ran down its back or its side, he comments that 'It is this sort of continuing argument which makes palaeontology such an endlessly fascinating science'. As one publisher indicated, the tone nowadays is more 'chatty' and personally engaging. Nevertheless, both in the older books and in the more recent ones, the tone also depends upon the type of dinosaur being described. As we shall see in the following sections, there are some key distinctions made between different types of dinosaurs, which serve primarily to generate entertaining narratives.

The social life of dinosaurs

Barbara Crowther (1999) has argued that TV natural history documentaries are preoccupied with narratives of aggression and reproduction. Narratives which do not support 'the primacy of the patriarchal macrostory' (with its 'adversarial potential') remain largely untold: the less aggressive males and other 'substandard' individuals are virtually invisible (Crowther 1999: 53). She suggests that although these programmes are scientifically informative, their ultimate purpose is to entertain.

Dinosaur books are similarly selective: even though there were hundreds of different dinosaurs, a select few always seem to appear. Two of the main criteria for inclusion appear to be size and perceived ferocity. Most books and CD-ROMs play on the 'scary' image of the carnivorous dinosaurs. As we have noted, front covers set the scene by featuring close-ups of open-jawed carnivores (usually *T. rex*) staring out at the reader or looking off to the side in search of prey. Gruesome images are frequently matched by equally gruesome descriptions:

> Holes found in victims' bones indicate that this predator's curved fangs punched deeply into flesh and bone. Then they pulled back, wrenching out huge mouthfuls of meat. The jaw and neck of Tyrannosaurus were tremendously powerful. It could pick up victims and shake them violently apart to kill them, before feasting on the dismembered corpse.
>
> (*The DK Guide to Dinosaurs*: 31)

As in many fictional films about animals, these non-fiction texts create a dramatic narrative by focusing on the conflict between the herbivores and carnivores, with the former playing the role of good guy and the latter that of bad guy. Meat-eaters are variously described as 'monsters', 'savage carnivores' and even 'the scourge of the North American continent'; whilst the plant eaters are 'docile herbivores', 'victims', 'peaceful vegetarians' and 'gentle plant-eaters'. Some carnivores (like *T. rex*) are presented as having an almost demonic nature. The velociraptor is another bogeyman in the dinosaur world, though it is accredited with having a more cunning nature than *T. rex*. *The DK Guide to Dinosaurs* provides a particularly judgemental account of carnivorous dinosaurs:

> The flesh-eating dinosaurs – theropods – had to kill to survive. Lethal weapons equipped these animals for a life of violence: razor-sharp fangs, claws like grappling hooks, powerful jaws for tearing flesh, and muscular legs to stamp the life out of small victims. Many would have preyed on small fry – baby dinosaurs, lizards, or eggs. Others may have ganged together, using stealth and cunning to trap larger victims, and teamwork to overwhelm them. One of the most savage of these pack-hunters might have been the theropod Velociraptor.
>
> (p. 26)

The crime metaphor ('lethal weapons', 'life of violence', 'ganged together', 'victim') adds drama and reinforces the distinction between good and bad dinosaurs. The 'violence' of the theropods is made all the worse by their preying on 'small fry'.

As this implies, the texts tend to judge animals in terms of moral categories drawn from human values and behaviour. This kind of anthropomorphism is a common characteristic in media representations of the animal world. In the case of natural history documentaries, for example, Crowther argues that producers draw on conventional perceptions of gender differences in humans in order to interpret animal behaviours. According to her, these documentaries feature 'a constant flow of metaphors around mothering and fathering roles, grooming, disciplining, jealousy, jilted lovers, coyness and so on' (Crowther 1999: 45). In fictional films and games, humans can be cast as the good guys who take on the evil carnivorous dinosaurs, as in the *Jurassic Park* films. Writers of non-fiction are more constrained by the fact that dinosaurs have been extinct for over 65 million years, although in fact several of these books use images of children and dinosaurs together in order to illustrate size and/or ferocity. *The New Book of Dinosaurs*, for example, shows children standing next to dinosaurs in nine out of its 32 pages; while the front cover of *How Big Is a Dinosaur?* shows a dinosaur (with the usual gaping jaws and sharp teeth), looking down at two screaming children. The child reader may also be invited to imagine what dinosaurs would do to them if they had the chance:

> Imagine a monster with teeth the size of daggers peering at you through an upstairs window. Lunging in, it snatches you in its immense jaws and swallows you whole. In the Age of the Dinosaurs such creatures were no nightmare but terrible reality.
>
> (*The DK Guide to Dinosaurs*: 30)

The distinction between good herbivores and bad carnivores also seems to reflect a more general trend in children's media. Because they do not kill other animals for food, herbivores are generally good guys: think of the portrayal of rabbits, elephants and giraffes in children's media. However, we should not be too ready to present this as mere vegetarian propaganda. For example, a further distinction is frequently drawn between mammals and reptiles. Meat-eating mammals like lions and tigers can be presented in a favourable light (as in Disney's *Lion King*), but reptiles are almost uniformly devious and evil (particularly snakes). Further distinctions can be made between hunters and scavengers: scavengers such as vultures and hyenas are generally presented as the dregs of the animal world. 'Cuteness' can, however, be a saving grace: so although bears are carnivorous predators, they are commonly presented in children's picture books as lovable and cuddly.

Although they tend to be typecast as monsters, there is a degree of relish and perhaps even admiration in the representation of animals like *T. rex*. In *Carnivores*, for example, the author acknowledges that it is the 'huge and fierce' dinosaurs that have 'captured our imagination'. He goes on to point out that some dinosaurs were in fact quite small, but reassures readers that others 'really did live up to their reputation of being enormous fearsome beasts' (p. 14). This admiration is further illustrated by the author's reaction to the possibility that there may have been a dinosaur that was even stronger and fiercer than *T. rex*. On the one hand, there is excitement that something bigger and fiercer may have come along; but there is also a sense of regret that *T. rex* might be about to be displaced as the 'king'. Under the heading 'Comparing Kings' the author points out that:

Both Carcharodontosaurus and Gigantosaurus were longer than the previous record-holder Tyrannosaurus. However, as shown above only Tyrannosaurus is known from complete skeletons and there is still a lot we don't know about the other two. Even so, Tyrannosaurus seems to have been a much heavier animal and was higher at the hip, so we could still say that the biggest meat-eating dinosaur that is completely known is Tyrannosaurus. Still the king!

(p. 31)

As the above extract suggests, there is a preoccupation with size in books about dinosaurs. Indeed, just as the *T. rex* is guaranteed a mention, so too are the sauropods (particularly the brachiosaurus), largely because of their size. Pictures show these creatures towering over tree tops, whilst detailed measurements (such as height, weight and length) are given in the text. Their size is described with relish: 'The biggest of the lot – the long necked sauropods – were the heaviest, longest, and tallest land animals ever' (*The DK Guide to Dinosaurs*: 8). Yet while the *T. rex* is a monster, the brachiosaurus is generally described as a 'gentle giant'. In fact (as these books acknowledge), many dinosaurs were probably quite small; but information on the smaller dinosaurs tends to be limited – unless, of course, they are among the *smallest* known dinosaurs, particularly if they have an unpleasant nature like the 'crafty' Compsognathus (ibid.: 12).

In general, then, it would seem that the desire to dramatize the dinosaurs has several consequences. Dinosaurs are frequently anthropomorphized, and their characteristics and behaviour are presented in terms of human moral discourses. Their social world is represented as necessarily hierarchical; although those at the summit of the hierarchy are seen with a considerable amount of ambivalence. Clearly, ideological messages about human behaviour are far from being confined to fictional texts about animals.

Representing science

Nevertheless, the study of dinosaurs is also a science; and one of the most distinctive features of books about dinosaurs is their emphasis on the history and methodology of the discipline (palaeontology). Readers are told how the study of fossils began in the nineteenth century, and the books frequently contain anecdotes about some of the early pioneers and the most significant finds. Thus, several books contain an account of two Americans (Othniel Charles Marsh and Edward Drinker Cope) who competed with each other to find dinosaur fossils in the late nineteenth century. *The Best-Ever Book of Dinosaurs* even includes a photograph of these early 'bone hunters', several of whom are carrying rifles.

This gives the books a rather different emphasis from that of other comparable texts. In the case of natural history documentaries, for example, the naturalistic style of presentation makes it easy to forget how carefully constructed these packaged interpretations of nature are, and even that they are interpretations in the first place (Crowther 1999). By contrast, books on dinosaurs tend to acknowledge that what is presented is an interpretation, and to illustrate how these interpretations are constructed. All of the books analysed here include some information on methodology. In *The Best-Ever Book of Dinosaurs*, for example, six pages are given over to a description of how sites for excavation are identified, how fossils and bones are extracted, cleaned and moved, and how scientists reconstruct what dinosaurs might have looked like when they were alive. Another unusual feature of dinosaur books is their acknowledgement that there are still many gaps in our knowledge of the subject. Some of the more pedagogic texts present different theories rather than suggesting that there is a consensus within the discipline. In *The New Book of Dinosaurs*, for example, there are numerous references to palaeontologists disagreeing and having 'furious' debates about dinosaur biology. The books even describe some of the mistakes that have been made in interpreting evidence. There is a striking contrast here with the books about human history discussed in Chapter 6: interpretations and theories are seen to change over time, and the study of dinosaurs is presented as an ongoing process of discovery and debate, not simply an established body of knowledge.

These descriptions of methodology establish the scientific basis of the study of dinosaurs, but they also provide a dimension of narrative and entertainment. Palaeontologists are presented as adventurers (or at least as people with really interesting jobs), and the ongoing research has an element of cutting-edge discovery. *The New Book of Dinosaurs*, for example, opens with the following passages:

Dinosaurs dominate the science of the 1990s, much as they ruled the world millions of years ago. The pace of research on dinosaurs is greater than ever before and has been fuelled by some astonishing new discoveries, such as a dinosaur sitting on a nest of eggs ... Here you can read for the first time about the largest meat-eating dinosaurs that ever lived, the tracks of huge herds of migrating dinosaurs, nesting dinosaurs and the latest ideas about why they became extinct ... Modern technology has come to the aid of the palaeontologist. Today, the scientist can use the most powerful electron microscopes to reveal the tiniest details of remains, while high-powered drills and even explosives can expose fossils in even the toughest layers of rock. All of this has greatly expanded our understanding of these amazing animals that mysteriously disappeared about 65 million years ago.

(pp. 2–3)

This description gives the study of dinosaurs a sense of urgency, immediacy and contemporaneity. The most highly valued terms relate to size and magnitude ('greater', 'largest', 'huge', 'tiniest'), power ('dominate', 'ruled', 'most powerful', 'high-powered', 'toughest') and modernity ('new discoveries', 'new dinosaurs', 'read for the first time', 'greater than ever before', 'modern technology').

This is compounded by the heroic representation of the palaeontologists – again, a feature characteristic of fictional dinosaur narratives. Far from being seen as either mad professors or 'geeks', palaeontologists are given a rugged outdoor image. As is the case in the educational TV series described by Willis (1999), the palaeontologist is generally male, and is seen wearing jeans or khakis and a flannel shirt, clambering over an excavation site or posing next to a giant fossil trophy to illustrate its scale. Similarly, in *Walking with Dinosaurs* (an adult book), Michael Benton conjures up the image of 'the traditional "field season", when professors and curators jump into their jeeps or Land-Rovers and set off into the wilds' (p. 8). Palaeontologists are described as adventurers ('fossil hunters') who are on a difficult quest over difficult terrain:

> Palaeontologists (fossil hunters) will leave no stone unturned and no corner of the world unexplored in their quest for new dinosaur discoveries. Recent expeditions have taken them to some of the least hospitable places on the planet, including the Sahara Desert, Alaska and Mongolia.
>
> (*New Book of Dinosaurs*: 3)

In *The DK Guide to Dinosaurs* the palaeontologist's work is compared to that of a police detective. Under the heading 'dinodetectives', the author writes:

> Just as the police hunt for clues at the scene of a crime to solve a mystery, so palaeontologists hunt for clues in rocks millions of years old to reveal secrets about the dinosaurs and how they lived.
>
> (p. 56)

Meanwhile, in *The Best Ever Book of Dinosaurs*, palaeontologist Paul Sereno is photographed in what looks like a study or office: there are book-lined shelves behind him, and on the desk at which he sits there is an open book and part of a skeleton. In contrast to this indoor setting, Sereno himself is dressed as one might expect palaeontologists on excavation sites to dress, in jeans, an open-necked shirt and a sleeveless jacket such as that worn by Indiana Jones. He is also young, tanned and good-looking. This photograph is unusual in that the palaeontologist is simply posing for the camera – almost every other photo in this and other books shows palaeontologists in an active role.

Descriptions of the work of palaeontologists in the laboratory or museum focus on making moulds, creating dinosaur models, working out how they moved, and so on – all of which may fit in with another boyish fantasy of putting things together and figuring out how they work. *The DK Guide to Dinosaurs* has one of the most detailed descriptions of this process, including pictures of people creating the moulds, whilst others (wearing hard hats) work on huge platforms in order to create displays of the larger dinosaurs. Several software packages take this a stage further by enabling the user to re-create dinosaurs: for example, DK's *3D Dinosaur Hunter* allows you to 'piece together fossilised bones in the excavation pit'.

As if to contrast with this emphasis on scientific method, some of these books also look at how dinosaurs have become part of popular culture. Most mention *Jurassic Park*, and some discuss whether the creation of dinosaurs from DNA (as in the film) could be possible. Nevertheless, these sections may serve as a means of reinforcing the author's serious pedagogic intentions. In *The Best-Ever Book of Dinosaurs*, for example, there is a picture of the Flintstones' pet dinosaur, Dino, with Fred Flintstone on his back. However, in case there is any doubt, readers are reassured by the author that Dino was 'scientifically inaccurate but fun'.

Dinosaur: The Essential Guide

Several of the tensions and uncertainties we have discussed here come together in our final case study. *Dinosaur: The Essential Guide* was published by DK in 2000 as a tie-in with the Walt Disney film. The book and film tell the story of an iguanodon (Aladar) who is brought up by a group of lemurs after his mother is killed by carnotaurs. When a comet hits the island on which they live, Aladar and the lemurs are forced to seek refuge on the mainland. They join a herd of dinosaurs on a hazardous trek to the nesting grounds. *En route* there are conflicts both within the herd and between the herd and the predatory carnotaurs. In the end they reach the nesting grounds, Aladar is confirmed as the hero, he finds a mate and they have their own baby dinosaur. The story of exile and return is reminiscent of a number of Disney films, including *The Lion King*, *Bambi* and *The Jungle Book*. The moral of the story, as encapsulated in the book, is that 'with courage, hope and loyalty' you can 'triumph over the greatest obstacles'.

Books based on children's films are commonplace, but *Dinosaur* is unusual in that it combines fiction and non-fiction. As well as elaborating on the film's story, the publisher has added factual information on dinosaurs and their habitats. For example, one double-page spread describes a scene from the film where a pteranodon picks up a dinosaur egg and drops it onto a tree on Lemur Island. On the second page there is a boxed section which provides the reader with general information about pteranodons, such as their wing span and life expectancy. This pattern is repeated throughout the book. At some points, however, the juxtaposition of fact and fiction becomes decidedly awkward. For example, at the beginning of the book dinosaurs and other animals are labelled to indicate their physical features (e.g. different bones, muscles and wings), although later in the book labels are used to show a lemur's 'expressive hands', 'big softie heart', 'shoulders stooped with age' and so on. Thus, a device normally used in non-fiction, particularly biology, is extended to fiction. Another confusing element is that both the film story and the factual information about dinosaurs are narrated in the present tense, making it more difficult to distinguish between what is real and what has been made up. This rather ambivalent status is accentuated by the lack of scientific accuracy – such as the fact that lemurs obviously did not exist in the age of the dinosaurs.

Like most DK publications, *Dinosaur: The Essential Guide* is a glossy, large-format hardback book. The book is divided into double-page spreads with, on average, at least half of the spread taken up by pictures. The text is divided into paragraphs, boxes, bullet points and captions, and is interspersed between the various pictures. A similar format is used for DK non-fiction titles. In series such as the *Eyewitness Guides* each picture and caption forms its own unit of information, so that it is not necessary to read the main text in order to make sense of the illustrations. As Meek (1996) has pointed out, the written text in these kinds of illustrated topic books is 'a kind of adjunct' to the pictures. The fact that photographs and captions form their own self-contained units makes these books ideal for browsing. Applying this approach to fiction is rather problematic, however. The narrative text of *Dinosaur: The Essential Guide* is so fragmented that it is difficult to piece together. In addition, the story is not told in a chronological order. The double-page spreads describe each character and their reactions to different events – but these will only make sense for readers who have already seen the film.

Dinosaur also contains many examples of how animals are anthropomorphized. The central conflict of the story is between the plant-eating and meat-eating dinosaurs. Some of the plant-eaters fight amongst themselves also, but in general they (and their friends the lemurs) are the good guys, in both the film and the book. While iguanodons are described as 'peaceful plant-eaters', raptors are 'truly evil' and carnotaurs are 'huge, vicious, flesh-eaters'. The latter even have bad breath. The producers create an opposition between the 'savagery' of the mainland where the dinosaurs live, and Lemur Island, a mysterious and peaceful place occupied by 'a colony of quick and intelligent mammals'. As in so many other animal texts, the mammals and plant-eaters represent good and the meat-eating reptiles represent evil.

As with all Disney films, there is a moral to the story, but this moral is articulated in far greater detail in the book than in the film. For example, the mother figure is idealized in the film, but even more so in the book. There are three mothers in the story: the first dies trying to protect her nest, the second (a lemur) saves the young dinosaur, and in the final scene of the book the two main characters have their own baby dinosaur. In the book these individual actions are linked into wider discourses of gender and motherhood. So, for example, we are told that the female lemur rescued the young Aladar because 'her maternal instinct is to hold it and give it protection'. There are numerous references to 'mother love', 'maternal instinct' and even 'maternal hands'. Elsewhere in the book, female characters rescue orphans or act as midwives. The males, on the other hand, are valued for their strength and courage: Aladar had a 'strong, masculine hand', while Zini's courage 'makes him the girls' idol'. Some of the female characters are also courageous, but males tend to be the main heroes in the story. By the end of the book, Aladar has 'fulfilled his destiny, as a leader and a father'. Elsewhere, the monogamous relationships of the lemurs are brought to our attention: not only do they 'stay with their chosen mates for life' but they 'remain faithful'. Overall, the moral message of the film is less overt than that of the book: the greater explicitness allowed by the written text seems to permit a heavy-handed moralism that doggedly links the actions of the characters to wider assumptions concerning gender, procreation and monogamy. Here again, there is an ideological 'hidden curriculum' not very far beneath the surface.

Conclusion

This chapter has brought together several of the broader themes addressed in this part of the book. While we have focused to some degree on the content of these texts, our primary focus has been on their verbal and visual 'rhetorics' and on the ways in which they position their readers. In particular, we have focused on the ways in which elements of 'entertainment' (such as fiction and narrative) have been combined with elements of 'education' (such as factual information and exposition). It has not been our intention to suggest that this combination is inherently impossible – or indeed that it inevitably represents a form of 'dumbing down'. 'Education' and 'entertainment' are by no means opposed or incompatible. Nevertheless, the combination of the two may be problematic, particularly when devices from popular entertainment are used primarily to 'sugar the pill' of learning. We will return to these broader issues in our conclusion. Before doing so, however, we need to look at how the kinds of materials we have been discussing are actually used by parents and children in the home.

Appendix: Books discussed

Amazing World of Dinosaurs, The (1976) London: Angus and Robertson.
Best-Ever Book of Dinosaurs, The (1998) Kingfisher: London.
Big Book of Dinosaurs, The (2001) Philadelphia: Running Press.
Carnivores (2001) Tunbridge Wells: Ticktock Publishing.
Children's Prehistory: Dinosaurs, The (1977) London: Usborne.
Dead Dinosaurs (2000) Scholastic: London. (*The Knowledge* series.)
Devastating Dinosaurs (1999) London: MacMillan Children's Books. (*Fact Attack* series).
Dinosaur (1989) London: Dorling Kindersley. (*Eyewitness Guides* series.)
Dinosaur: The Essential Guide (2000) London: Dorling Kindersley.
Dinosaurs (2001) London: Usborne. (*Internet-Linked Discovery* series.)
Dinosaurs and Other Early Animals (1979) London: Latimer House.
DK Guide to Dinosaurs, The (2000) London: Dorling Kindersley.
How Big Is a Dinosaur? (1999) London: BBC Worldwide. (Based on the *Walking with Dinosaurs* TV series.)
New Book of Dinosaurs, The (1997) London: Aladdin/Watts.
Rex (2001) Frome, Somerset: Chicken House.
Walking with Dinosaurs: The Facts (2000) London: BBC Worldwide.
Where Did Dinosaurs Go? (2001) London: Usborne. (*Usborne Pocket Science* series.)

PART **THREE**

CHAPTER 9

'I'M NOT A TEACHER, I'M A PARENT'

Education, entertainment and parenting

In the preceding sections of this book, we have considered some of the ways in which teaching and learning are defined within educational media. The materials we have examined all construct pedagogic *positions* for learners – and in many instances, for parental mediators as well. They rest on implicit assumptions about learners' motivations, interests and desires; and, as such, they inevitably attempt to encourage learners to conform to those assumptions. In this sense, they could be seen as more or less powerful or coercive.

Nevertheless, these positions are not necessarily coherent or consistent. For instance, there may be contradictions between the overt appeals that are made within the marketing and packaging of materials and the actual form and content of the materials themselves. The pleasure (or 'fun') that is so frequently proclaimed here often seems to serve merely as a kind of reward or superficial ornament. Different forms of 'education' and 'entertainment' embody different assumptions about what counts as knowledge, and about how learners might learn; and the combination of these elements is often awkward and uneasy. These tensions are reflected in the somewhat uncertain ways in which these materials address and attempt to engage their readers.

Of course, whether learners actually occupy the positions they are offered is another matter. Learners are not simply passive objects of educational strategies: they do not necessarily consent to the designs that educational texts have upon them. In order to understand the complexity of this process, therefore, we also need to look at the consumers of these texts – that is, at the parents and children who buy and read them. As we shall indicate, the ways in which educational texts are used and interpreted depend upon family circumstances, and upon the negotiations that go on between parents and children in the home. In particular, they reflect families' overall orientations towards education, and how they see their role in relation to formal educational institutions such as schools. In this chapter, we consider these more general orientations and practices; in the next, we focus more specifically on how parents and children use and evaluate the kinds of educational resources with which we are concerned.

Methodology

The data we use in these chapters are drawn from a survey and a series of qualitative interviews conducted in London in 2000 and 2001. It is important to consider the methodology and the location of the study in some detail, not least because of their relevance to our broader themes.

We began by distributing an eight-page questionnaire to parents of children aged between 5 and 13 (school years 1–9) in four schools (two primary, two secondary). The schools were carefully selected to provide populations that were representative of the national average in terms of socio-economic status, as indicated by the proportions of children receiving free school meals. We offered an incentive (a prize draw) in order to encourage a good response; and of approximately 2000 questionnaires distributed, 789 were returned (around 40 per cent).

Despite this relatively good rate of return, our respondents were not representative, either of the general population or of the schools themselves. The proportion of respondents (or partners) working in non-manual occupations was significantly higher than the national average (74 per cent as against 56 per cent); as was the proportion with a degree or postgraduate professional qualification (37 per cent as against 20 per cent). The proportions of single-parent families and unemployed parents were also lower than average. This skew in our sample had predictable implications in terms of our findings on specific areas of interest. For instance, no fewer than 85 per cent of parents reported that they had a home PC, and nearly one-third of these had more than one. At the time, national surveys tended to put this figure at around 40 per cent (e.g. Office for National Statistics 2000), although it was undoubtedly rising rapidly. While there were significant variations in terms of occupation and employment status (see Chapter 10), PC ownership within our sample was consistently well above the national average, right across the socio-economic spectrum.

In essence, then, our sample was a self-selecting one. Our questionnaire was more likely to be returned by parents who were already positively disposed towards schooling or education in general; and these parents tended to be more middle-class. Of course, there is considerable room for debate about how socio-economic status is assessed: our initial measure (free school meals) is not identical with our eventual measures (occupation, employment status, level of education), and labels like 'middle-class' are undoubtedly crude. Nevertheless, the more enthusiastic response to our survey on the part of middle-class parents might easily have been predicted from research on parental involvement in schools, outlined in Chapter 2.

We asked parents to indicate on our questionnaire whether they were willing to be interviewed (a further level of self-selection); and here again, we provided financial incentives to encourage participation. We selected 20 families, who were interviewed in their homes approximately six to nine months after completing the questionnaire. The majority of the children in these interviews were aged between 8 and 11. (It is important to note here that, despite our clearly expressed wish to interview the whole family, fathers consistently managed to absent themselves from our interviews, even when they were physically present in the house at the time. Astonishingly, only three fathers of a possible total of 16 saw fit to be involved in any way (cf. David *et al.* 1993).)

Of course, we were most likely to be interested in families whose responses suggested that they were heavy or at least moderate users of educational media; and while we did attempt to achieve some balance here in terms of social class and family composition, we did not expect or intend that this qualitative sample would be demographically representative. Even the families who were financially worst off could generally be described as keen users of such material; and indeed, some of them were more enthusiastic than the more middle-class families whom we interviewed (see below). At the same time, we noted on comparing questionnaire and interview responses that some parents were inclined to exaggerate their use of such material, for example by overestimating the number of information books or CD-ROMs that had been bought for their children in the preceding year.

As this implies, research of this kind is likely to run into problems of 'social desirability'. Parents – and perhaps to a lesser extent children – are likely to provide the kinds of answers they believe will present them in a positive light. We have encountered this phenomenon in previous research on children and television (e.g. Buckingham 1993: Chapter 5; 1996: Chapter 9); although in that research, parents were occasionally prepared to admit that their children did not always obey the 'viewing rules' they attempted to lay down. In the context of research about education, however, the risk of 'losing face' appears to be somewhat greater. 'Responsible' parents are, by definition, those who fulfil their allotted educational role; and to admit that you are incapable of doing so – or even worse, that you could not care less about it – is almost inconceivable.

Thus, we frequently came away from interviews feeling that we had been offered the 'official version' of family life rather than the gritty reality. The means by which we had contacted our families (and the fact that we came from the Institute of Education) effectively positioned us as some kind of educational police. Parents and children had to be on their best behaviour, for fear that we might take them in for further questioning. It proved quite hard to penetrate this form of impression management, and to encourage parents to discuss the conflicts that might have occurred in this area, or their own uncertainties and anxieties. In some instances, we even arrived to find that educational materials had been gathered together and put on display for our benefit, thus indicating their status as 'symbolic goods' – as tangible proof of the fulfilment of 'good parenting'.

Location

These tendencies were to some extent compounded by our choice of location. Parental views of education are obviously likely to depend upon the nature of local 'education markets' (Gewirtz et al. 1995). As we noted in Chapter 1, the publication of league tables of schools' examination results, combined with the rhetoric of 'parental choice', means that there is now considerable competition for places at the 'best' schools. In the part of West London where our families lived, there was a range of secondary schools, including private schools, selective and non-selective state schools and denominational schools. As we shall see, many of the parents of primary age children were already experiencing considerable anxiety about their children's forthcoming transfer to secondary school (even when this was several years away). According to one of our parents, the nearest selective (grammar) school was oversubscribed by approximately 20:1. Another parent said that she had moved her son to a private preparatory school at age 9 partly in order to avoid the 'massive bottleneck' that arose at age 11.

Meanwhile, this area was also characterized by stark divisions between rich and poor. In one neighbourhood in particular, the railway line seemed to mark a clear division between owner-occupied dwellings (small but expensive terraced houses) and public housing (a large and somewhat dilapidated council estate). On one occasion, we were even advised by one of our interviewees not to walk through the estate as we left, reinforcing our sense that this was seen as 'the other side of the tracks'.

In London, the interaction of these two factors is reflected in the housing market: estate agents advertise properties as being within the catchment area of 'good' schools, and there is a definite (though as yet unresearched) correlation between property prices and school results or reputations. As Gewirtz et al. (1995) suggest, this represents a form of 'selection by mortgage', which in turn contributes to a growing polarization between schools in social class terms. Far from being a free market, it is one that is clearly rigged in favour of those who have the ability to buy. While this is most acute at secondary level, it increasingly applies at primary level as well: one of our parents described how families were moving house in order to be in the catchment area for the 'right' primary school.

These tendencies are almost certainly more acute in parts of London than they are elsewhere in the UK (the ratio of children attending private schools in London is significantly higher than the national average, for example). As such, in choosing to interview these parents about their use of educational materials in the home, we were inevitably touching on what (for some at least) was very sensitive territory.

Education and entertainment in the home

In this chapter and the next, our concern is mainly with how parents and children perceive the *meanings* of education in the home, and how they account for what actually happens. We will therefore be drawing primarily on our qualitative data, although we will briefly refer to some findings from our survey in order to provide a broader picture.

One aim of our survey was to identify patterns of media access and use. We found that almost all our sample had a television and a video recorder (99 per cent and 97 per cent respectively). Beyond this, however, it was possible to detect some significant differences in terms of social class, age and gender. Within the terms of our sample, the following were among the most worthy of note:

- Home computers and Internet access were more likely to be found in families where one or both parents worked in non-manual occupations; and where one or both parents had a degree or postgraduate qualification. They were significantly less likely to be found in single-parent families and in families where parents were not employed.
- By contrast, ownership of computer games consoles was significantly higher in households where one or more parents worked in manual occupations.
- Boys were more likely than girls to have access to media (computers, TVs, video recorders, games consoles) in their bedrooms, although these differences were not as large as differences due to age. Children whose parents worked in manual occupations were more likely to have video recorders, TVs and (to a lesser extent) computers in their bedrooms.
- Households with non-working parents, and single-parent households, were less likely to buy educational software, to use educational websites, or to buy information books.

- The above patterns were largely reflected in patterns of use, as identified by a simple tally of children's leisure activities. Major differences emerged here in terms of gender: boys were more likely to play computer games than girls, whereas girls were more inclined to read and listen to music.

Despite the skew in our sample, these findings are broadly in line with recent surveys, particularly the *Young People, New Media* study conducted in the UK a few years ago (Livingstone and Bovill 1999). Some of these differences might be attributed to preferences or tastes. For example, boys and girls prefer different activities, even where they can potentially have access to the same things. Thus, there was little difference between boys' and girls' access to computers; but boys were significantly more likely to play computer games. However, others may be attributed to financial resources: non-working parents and single parents are likely to be prevented from giving their children access to particular activities because they lack the means to do so, rather than simply through choice. Nevertheless, social class operates in a complex way here. At least where the parents are employed, middle-class parents seem to prioritize the (potentially) 'educational' medium of the PC above the 'entertainment' medium of the games console, whereas working-class parents do the opposite; although working-class children are more likely than middle-class children to have access to all media (including computers) in the relatively unsupervised space of the bedroom, as compared with elsewhere in the house.

Similar findings emerged from our interviews. In most cases, we were able to interview parents and children separately and then together. We began our interviews with the children by reviewing the questionnaire responses relating to their leisure interests. The discussion here tended to confirm the findings of our survey. For example, boys in general appeared to have greater access to media technology than girls, particularly in their bedrooms. They were significantly more interested than girls in computer games and sports; and while they were less interested in reading than girls, they were inclined to favour non-fiction, whereas girls generally preferred fiction. Despite these differences, watching television clearly emerged as all the children's major leisure-time pursuit (cf. Livingstone and Bovill 1999).

Our aim in starting in this way was partly to encourage the children to relax; but it was nevertheless striking how the tone became much more sober and less enthusiastic when we moved on to discuss educational matters. Indeed, when we asked them to talk about their TV viewing, many children responded by laughing or smiling, as though TV were somehow non-educational by definition, and thus perhaps an inappropriate topic in this context. In a few cases, parents were openly dismissive of TV viewing: when we were talking about preferred programmes, one spoke of 'tripey cartoons and football' and encouraged her son to nominate 'something that's a bit more educational'. Other parents spoke of their attempts to encourage their children to engage in activities other than TV viewing. Several children also mentioned that the demands of homework and private tuition placed constraints on their leisure time (see below). In general, both parents and children appeared to be very clear about where the lines between education and entertainment were to be drawn.

Orienting towards education

For the reasons identified above, nearly all the parents we interviewed could be described as having a very positive attitude towards education in general. These were not the disaffected parents to whom the government and schools feel they must reach out (see Chapter 2). Nevertheless, there were some important differences here. At the risk of being unduly schematic, it is possible to identify three broad orientations that recur across our sample.

We will label the first category as *aspiring*. These were parents living on modest means, but with a highly motivated approach to education in the home. Often in manual or unskilled occupations themselves, they were looking to education as a means of ensuring upward mobility on the part of their children. These parents were particularly keen on homework. Dina Lang, for example, was a single parent who worked as a nursery nurse. She lived in a modest rented maisonette with her daughter Julia (aged 8). She had recently been unemployed and (according to her) was unable to afford a television licence or a home computer. Yet she was one of the most persistently enthusiastic parents, and appeared to spend a considerable amount of her disposable income on books and study aids for Julia, as well as using the public library. Dina was keen to present Julia as a bright, well-motivated child, who was already well ahead of her contemporaries.

The second category consisted of the *anxious* parents. They had greater amounts of disposable income, and were generally home owners. They may have had limited education themselves, but seemed to have experienced upward mobility in their own lifetimes; and having achieved middle-class status, were anxious that their own children should hold on to it. These parents invested in educational resources and home tutors, and were considering private education. They too believed their children should be set more homework. Val Watkins, for example, was a full-time homemaker, who lived with her husband (now retired) and her daughter Ruth (aged 8) in a relatively small owner-occupied house in a gentrified neighbourhood. Their living room was overflowing with toys and books. Ruth's parents had become concerned that she was falling behind in class, and now – like several of her classmates – she was attending a private tutor for maths and English. She was also regularly bought information books to support her school work. Her spoken accent was significantly more middle-class than her mother's.

In the third category were the *comfortable* parents. These parents were middle-class professionals, mostly graduates, and were the most obviously affluent. They seemed confident that their children would succeed, and that they would be able to support them in this. They were fairly relaxed about homework, and about providing sufficient resources in the form of computers, books and software. The Blatchfords, for instance, lived in a large, well-appointed house in a very desirable area. They had transferred their son John (now aged 9) to a private preparatory school, although they claimed that this was simply in order to ensure that he would get into the 'right' school at age 11. They had a very extensive collection of information books and CD-ROMs; and while they were involved in assisting with homework, there was little overt sense of 'pushing'. They professed to have quite traditional views on discipline, and the children appeared to follow highly ordered lives.

Of course, these are ideal types, and we interviewed many parents who would not fit easily into any one of these categories. Without the time or resources to observe their lives in greater detail, it is also hard to know whether these differences were merely a matter of self-presentation. Nevertheless, our brief sketches are intended to suggest that parents' different orientations towards education are the result of a complex combination of factors. Differences in access to resources, family composition, philosophies of child-rearing and the child's actual experiences of schooling are all significant. However, it is clear that social class plays a pre-eminent role in this respect. As we argued in Chapter 2, social class functions here more as a matter of *trajectory* than of *position*: it is not just a matter of where you stand now, but of where you have come from and where you think you (or your children) might be going. Parents' levels of aspiration, anxiety or comfort around the issue of education therefore partly reflect how they interpret their own personal histories, and how they foresee their children's futures.

Buying teaching

One area in which many of these aspirations and anxieties were most apparent was in the discussion of private tutoring. Anecdotal evidence would suggest that the use of private tutors to provide additional coaching for secondary school entrance examinations has significantly increased in recent years: leading agencies have reported an annual rise in enquiries of more than 50 per cent (see Moorhead 2001). However, the full extent of this phenomenon is hard to gauge, not least because it is an unregulated market; there is no requirement that tutors should be qualified, and no system of inspection. One parent, Lucy Jensen, described her situation as follows:

> The competition to get into [the local selective grammar school] is horrendous. I mean, like 1500 girls sit the exam and they have 80 places. So if you want any chance whatever of getting in, you have to do this coaching. . . . [The tutors] obviously saw that there was a, you know, a niche in the market, parents who wanted their children to have a chance to get into grammar school, and they do these test papers. They have one for homework and they do one during the actual class. And they take cash in a brown paper envelope and I think they must be doing very nicely, thank you.

According to Lucy, the tutors concerned also tested the children before they were accepted for their classes, and would refuse to take on children who were unlikely to pass. Other parents confirmed that there was competition to gain admission to the 'right' tutorial classes.

The existence of selective and independent (private) schools – and the parents' apparent lack of faith in the local state comprehensives – was the key factor here. By comparison, their children's performance in government tests (SATs) was barely a concern for parents: one of them described such tests as 'an internal school thing', while another saw them merely as the government's way of 'testing teachers' – although very few even mentioned them. While some parents were critical of the quality of the primary schools (particularly in terms of the lack of homework), most seemed quite satisfied. However, the anxiety about secondary transfer began to set in at a fairly early age; and (as in the case of the Blatchfords above) those parents who could afford it were pre-empting this by moving their children to private preparatory schools (or so-called 'pre-prep' schools) at the age of 8, or even earlier.

As Gewirtz et al. (1995) suggest, middle-class parents' discussion of secondary school choice is often characterized by coded (but not directly stated) concerns to do with ethnicity and social class. Thus, one aspiring parent described the local comprehensive as 'a school of epic proportion' where there was too much 'noise and disruption in the classroom'; and cited this as the major reason for seeking private tutoring. Apparently the tutor she had chosen had told her that 'every independent school these days expects the child at the age of 11, when they're going in, to have an academic standard of a 14-year-old'. Even where parents were committed (or resigned) to the local comprehensive, they saw private tutoring as a way of ensuring that their child would be placed in a 'higher stream' on entry.

This sense of growing competitiveness was explicitly noted by several parents. One of our 'anxious' parents, Val Watkins, for example, was concerned that her daughter Ruth was 'falling behind' in primary school, but had then been surprised to discover that many of her classmates had private tutors:

> Huge amounts of them have tutors, and I think we caught on to that quite late in the day really. Seems to be quite common these days.

Another parent, Rachel Lynch, commented on the contagious nature of home tutoring in more detail:

> You know, suddenly, you usually say 'I'm not going to go the tutor route, if they're falling behind, I'll give them a bit of extra help'. And then you hear that two or three people in the class have got a tutor, and then a couple of parents say 'well, maybe we should do that, just to make sure they keep in the upper group'. And then suddenly, it's like tutors everywhere and then you discover that people that you thought were like minds to you, they've actually had their children tutored for the last two years, you know.

According to Rachel, the rise of home tutoring was symptomatic of a general rise in anxiety and competitiveness, which was manifesting itself at a younger and younger age:

> [In state schools] those who can afford it will send their children to private school or to a prep school once they hit junior level. And all through the infants, they're going 'No, no, no, we support the school, we're going to keep them.' And then a few people will say 'well actually, we're thinking about sending our child to [a private school]'. And then you kind of say 'well, maybe we should be doing that'. And then suddenly there's this mass exodus and it pulls the school level down, which is a shame because I think if everybody held steady it'd be fine. But there is this thing that 'well, they're doing that for their child, so maybe we should be doing it, you know, maybe we're not doing enough as parents ourselves'. So there's peer pressure amongst children for the right kind of kit to wear and toys to have but there's pressure on parents about, you know, quite how much you're putting in to your child's education. Or how you're being seen to do it.

As one of our 'comfortable' parents, Rachel presented herself as critical of – or at least comparatively distanced from – these concerns; and she claimed that she was currently holding out against the tide of parents seeking private tutors. Yet even where parents had resorted to private tutors, several of them appeared to regret or even resent the fact. Several expressed concern that the overall level of competition was much higher than it had been for them as children, and that it was affecting children at an ever younger age. But even where parents were ambivalent about the benefits of selective schools, it seemed to be hard for them to resist the emerging sense of educational panic. As Lucy Jensen put it:

> I think perhaps parents get too wound up about, you know, where their child's going to go to secondary school. And I can feel myself getting a bit sort of washed along in the flow of worry and stress and tension – which is one reason that I wish the grammar school didn't exist, and that Sarah would simply go to the local comprehensive school.

Predictably, several of the children too were resentful of additional tutoring, although principally because they saw it as eroding their leisure time. In most cases, the tutor also set homework: in the case of Ruth Watkins, for example, this amounted to an extra 20 minutes per night. In a couple of instances, this additional demand was a source of friction between parents and children.

Homework pressures

As we noted in Chapter 2, government policy has placed a growing emphasis on the importance of homework – despite the fact that (at least at primary school level) there is little evidence that it contributes to raising standards of achievement. Children in the UK already spend more time in school than their European counterparts, and there are moves to extend the school day by instituting more formal homework provision. In our survey, 47 per cent of children between 8 and 11 and 50 per cent between 12 and 14 were reported to have between one and three hours of homework per week; while 20 per cent of 8–11-year-olds and 40 per cent of 12–14-year-olds had between four and seven hours. (Parents also claimed that girls were spending more time on homework than boys.) Eighty-eight per cent of parents indicated that they sometimes or always helped with homework, although this declined as children got older. Middle-class parents were more likely to say they always helped their children with homework than working-class parents.

We raised the issue of homework in our interviews both with children and with parents (separately and then together). Unsurprisingly, most children who expressed a view said they had enough or too much homework. None expressed more than mild enthusiasm for homework, and most presented it as a boring, if necessary, chore. Here again, there was resentment at the erosion of their leisure time. Ian Stevenson (aged 10), for example, agreed that homework was 'a good thing to do', but he also said that 'it wastes a lot of time that we have at home – so that basically all the time we have is to eat and then probably read a book and go to bed'.

Several parents argued that their children were set more homework than they themselves had been set when they were the same age. Many said that they could not remember doing homework in primary school; although it was seen by some as a necessary preparation for secondary school, where the homework demands were described as 'a shock' and even a 'bombardment'. As Mrs Kennedy put it:

> [In secondary school] it's just there every day and, you know, it's like you can't have other out-of-school activities because, you know, you've always got this looming, you know. When you're working full-time and then you've got that, and then you've got to take them there, pick them up here, you know, and you just think 'Oh no, we're going home and he's got to do the homework, and there's going to be a big argument and he's tired.'

Parents generally accepted that it was their responsibility to ensure that homework was completed on time; but in some instances, children's skill in avoiding it until the last minute had generated conflicts. Val Watkins, for example, described the 'resentful scramble' to catch up on homework as her daughter Ruth prepared for her private tutorial class; while Alison Stevenson accused her son of 'forgetting homework on purpose'. She found this an additional pressure on her as a working single parent:

> I do feel guilty about being a working parent. I was off for a year . . . and we both thoroughly enjoyed the year. Number one, Ian liked it because I was able to pick him up from school and it wasn't a hassle. He had a lot of time to do the homework. Whereas now we've got half an hour before tea because I'm cooking tea for you as well. So, you know, let's do it now. Or at the weekends we do it in between shopping, housework, whereas when I did have the time it was a lot easier and happier for both of us. . . . He knows that I feel guilty. I wish I had more time to spend with him and do the homework because I think that he would achieve a lot more. But I can't, unfortunately.

Nevertheless, there were some variations in parents' view of the value and necessity of homework. In general, most parents said they felt the amount of homework set was about right. However, some of the 'aspirational' parents in particular felt there should be more. Dina Lang, for example, complained about having to ask for homework, and was supplementing it with study aids because her daughter was 'bored' and 'needs to do more'. 'Anxious' parents like Val Watkins expressed similar concerns: the teacher's apparent failure to mark her daughter's homework had been a factor in her decision to engage a private tutor.

By contrast, some of the 'comfortable' parents were more inclined to play down the necessity of homework, particularly for younger children, stressing the need for 'balance' in children's lives. As we have seen above, Rachel Lynch was keen to distance herself from parents whom she described as 'pushy' in this respect:

> I think it's a bit pressured sometimes. I just think at 4 and 5, they don't need homework. I think it's quite a middle-class school and quite pushy middle-class parents, I mean who like it to be seen to be, you know, their children are doing well. I'm sure [homework] is done more for the parents than it is for the children. You know, I'm not sure they get that much from it. . . . I think the children would do just as well without it.

However, some of the 'comfortable' parents had made comparisons with acquaintances whose children were attending private schools, where more homework was set. Mrs Waldron had been one of a number of parents who had put pressure on the school when they decided the maths homework was 'too easy'; and she described herself a 'committed' parent who would prevent the teachers from 'slipping' in this respect. Rachel Lynch described a similar phenomenon, where she suspected parents had been comparing their own children with those from a local private school:

> It's a supposition, but parents were then going to [the primary school] and saying 'well, they're doing this at this school, and this at this school, maybe we should be doing it, maybe our children aren't getting the right . . .'. Well I'm sure it was done for that, because if you ever speak to parents who are teachers, they don't see the need for it, and I don't see the need for it. But I think I did notice at some meetings, you know, parents were saying 'well, the children don't seem to be getting much homework'. And I was thinking 'well that's a good thing, isn't it?' You know, I don't particularly want to spend my evenings supervising them either. But there was obviously a pressure and the school's responded to it. It keeps parents happy, keeps the kids at school, there you go.

This kind of parental pressure for homework represents a clear example of the kind of 'class action' described by Reay (1998) and others. Here, informal networks of self-consciously 'committed' middle-class parents act collectively to demand and secure greater access to school resources for their own children.

In this context, teachers may feel they are setting homework more for the benefit of parents than of students themselves. As 11-year-old Peter Kennedy put it, teachers sometimes 'can't think of anything to give us, so they give us something that we don't even need to know'. This account was confirmed by one of our parents, Anne McGarvie, who was also a teacher herself:

> There is pressure on you as a teacher to set it, and I found myself setting ludicrous homework just for the sake of it. And looking at it from the other angle, it sometimes feels like parents want homework because it is keeping [their children] occupied, as opposed to it fulfilling a particularly useful learning function.

As this implies, homework may have symbolic and disciplinary functions that supersede its potential in terms of learning. There is a cycle of escalating expectations here, as schools attempt to look good for parents, and parents strive to compete with each other. As Alison Stevenson suggested, it is the children who may be the ultimate victims of this process:

> I do find it a bit disheartening that the schools are under that pressure, which in turn puts the parents under the pressure. And more importantly, it's the child that's under pressure as well. Whereas to me, you learn more if you're happy. You learn more if you don't feel that you've got to, to achieve something.

Helping out

As might be expected, there were several parents in our sample who felt enthusiastic about their role as educators. For some, this was more than simply a matter of fulfilling an abstract responsibility. This was most clearly expressed in relation to family outings. Mrs Smith, for example, talked about the pleasure of taking her children to museums, not merely in order to make school work more interesting for them, but also to discover things for herself. She said to her daughter: 'I can't wait till you do a bit more science and we can go to the Science Museum'. Mr and Mrs Waldron were also enthusiastic visitors to educational attractions, particularly those (like the Roman site at Fishbourne) that had a participatory dimension.

A couple of parents seemed equally positive about their involvement in homework. Mrs Walker, for example, said that she found it 'stimulating' in comparison with her job, which she described as 'fairly mundane'. Others seemed to take an almost vicarious pride in their children's achievement. However, while it was generally agreed that it was 'good' for parents to help with homework, few parents appeared to feel very engaged or interested in the content. Some, like Mrs Meade, resented the imposition on their own leisure time:

> The other day, I said to her [daughter] 'I'm 39 years old and I don't do geography homework!' Sometimes it does annoy me to some extent, you know, because I had hoped that I'd sort of gone

past that stage in life. . . . Gone are the days when the children seemed to do the homework and that was it. There does seem to be quite a lot of involvement now with parents and I don't, I don't mind it all the time but sometimes there is too much, I think.

There was also a sense among some disadvantaged but 'aspirational' parents that they felt ill-equipped to help their children with homework. Several claimed to find particular types of homework – most notably maths – quite difficult; and this obviously increased as their children got older. Mrs Turner, for example, felt that some parents were disadvantaged in this respect:

It is a bit of a disadvantage, I think, for parents that find it very hard or can't do it, you know. They're a bit, it's too much expected of them, and [if] they can't do it, their child's going to fall behind. . . . I think for some parents perhaps it's a bit overwhelming. They find it's not, they can't cope or they feel embarrassed that they don't know, which is, you know, they shouldn't be really.

These problems were accentuated in some cases where parents complained of poor communication between the home and the school, or of a lack of guidance on how to support their children. Alison Stevenson, for example, was under pressure of time as a single working parent (see above), but she also found it hard to cope with her son's learning difficulties:

I just find it terribly frustrating that he doesn't understand the [homework] instructions that he's written down. . . . If I could afford it, I would have private tuition for him because he does benefit from the one-to-one. Because I haven't got the patience. I'm not a teacher, I'm a parent.

This kind of stress was also apparent in the case of Mrs Klenowski, who worked as a classroom assistant in a primary school. She too said that she became impatient with her own children, even though she was known for being patient with the children she had to deal with at school. She could not understand why they appeared to have problems with homework, and even said that she had thrown things at the wall in her frustration. As with the Stevensons, there were additional pressures here, though more to do with space (there was only a small kitchen table to work at) rather than time. It was striking that both parents voiced the desire to employ a personal tutor, although neither was in a position to afford one. Mrs Klenowski even said that this would have enabled her to get back to 'just being a mother' – suggesting, as does Alison Stevenson, a wish to make a clear distinction between the role of a parent and the role of a teacher.

Mrs Harper was in a similar position, as a single parent of four children, one of whom had severe learning difficulties. Although she felt the situation was now under control, she described a period in which she had been spending her evenings juggling the conflicting homework demands of her children, and would end up doing most of it for them. Despite their difficulties, however, all these parents were very positive about the importance of homework: the more relaxed or even critical attitude of some of the 'comfortable' parents did not seem to be an option for them. This may have been partly to do with the potential value of homework in 'keeping children occupied' (as Anne McGarvie put it above), but it also reflected the generally aspirational orientation of these parents.

Conclusion

In the following chapter, we will look more specifically at parents' and children's uses of educational resources, both in the context of homework and more broadly. Parents' overall orientations towards learning and education of the kind we have considered here are bound to influence the kinds of educational materials they buy for their children, and the ways in which they are used. In this respect, there are some significant differences within our sample, which are partly related to social class.

In general, however, the impression communicated by the majority of our parents was one of increasing stress and pressure. Education seemed to be perceived as an area of intense and growing competition; and while this was most acutely experienced in relation to the transfer to secondary schools, it seemed to be felt at an ever younger age. Some of the parents whom we interviewed – particularly the more affluent parents whom we have described as 'comfortable' – seemed able to resist (and in some cases, to criticize) this pressure. Nevertheless, most appeared distinctly vulnerable to it. Their educational role as parents was not, by and large, seen as a source of pleasure or family togetherness, but as one of conflict, inadequacy and guilt.

In this context, investing in educational resources – both in hardware such as computers and in books and software – would seem to provide at least a potential means of dealing with that pressure. It offers parents a way of satisfying themselves that they have fulfilled their pedagogic responsibilities – or at least, it may do so for those who are able to afford it. In this respect, it would be fitting to close this chapter with the judgement of Anne McGarvie, one of the few parents who seemed able to criticize this pressure – while simultaneously recognizing that she too remained victim to it. Significantly, she was one of the few parents who worked in education herself, and yet she was especially critical of what she called parents' 'panic buying' of educational materials:

You're encouraged to believe that if you don't [buy these materials] your child will not be up there, not be a contender, not have the head start that they require. I remember when our kids were babies we were always sent this stuff that promised you a sort of complete learning package – do you remember those things? – *Postman Pat* – and you bought from book clubs. The whole thing is all part of the same idea that makes you believe that you are not doing enough. And obviously middle-class parents are extremely susceptible to thinking that they are not doing enough, particularly if they are very busy. And that is the same business, I think, as the homework. I am too busy, but at least if they are doing their homework and not watching the television and not playing on a PlayStation game, then I can feel a little bit relieved that they are properly occupying their time. This is all part of the anxiety, the moral panic, that I object to.

CHAPTER 10

CONSUMING LEARNING

Using and reading educational media

In recent years, children and parents have increasingly been targeted as 'educational consumers'. From the moment children are born, parents are subjected to a whole range of commercial appeals, many of which seek to invoke their 'better nature' – their sense of what they *should* be doing in order to qualify as Good Parents. These appeals are apparent in the marketing of a whole range of commodities, from baby care products to educational toys to home computers. While concerns with education are by no means the only feature of these appeals, they are among the most significant, particularly as children grow older. As several of the quotations in the previous chapter make clear, parents' role in relation to education is often heavily invested with a sense of guilt and inadequacy. Particularly for parents who lead pressured lives, one solution is to throw money at the problem: paying for educational goods and services offers the promise of educational advantage which they may feel unable to secure on their own behalf or in their own time. For those who have fewer economic resources, this option is less available, and to pursue it may require some difficult choices. Meanwhile, the moral imperatives embodied in government policy on education may make it even harder to resist this pressure. If parents feel they are incapable of becoming the conscientious pedagogues imagined by government initiatives (such as those described in Chapter 2), a little 'panic buying' may help to assuage their anxieties.

Media companies have certainly acknowledged the power of these educational appeals. Nevertheless, their success in capitalizing on them is far from guaranteed. As we indicated in Chapters 3 and 4, these are insecure times for both publishers and retailers. Economic and technological changes have unsettled the relatively secure and predictable world of children's educational publishing. This instability, combined with the narrowing agendas of government policy, appears to be resulting in a growing conservatism, both in terms of the range of material on offer and in terms of the formulaic character of educational texts themselves. Meanwhile, the changing balance and composition of the retail sector has also exacerbated long-standing problems in ensuring that goods actually reach consumers, and in a form that they are interested in buying. While some sectors of the market appear to be booming – particularly the sales of study aids – most are looking rather less than healthy.

These conclusions are largely confirmed by the research with families reported in this chapter. While purchasing educational materials was still important for many of our parents, it was largely dominated by the need to support specific school work. Particularly in the case of CD-ROMs, but also to some extent in the case of books, they found it hard to discover what was available in the first place. Predictably, the children were primarily interested in the 'entertainment' elements of these materials: 'education' was frequently associated with being 'boring'. Parents were more ambivalent on this point; although most accepted that their children were unlikely to find a more didactic approach to education particularly engaging, and would often leave materials unread or unused for this reason.

Significantly, we found that 'new' digital media were gradually replacing 'older' media, even though this was a development that several parents seemed to regret. In this chapter, therefore, we consider educational uses of 'old' and 'new' media in turn, outlining families' different practices and orientations in relation to them. As we shall argue, the technological shifts that are currently gathering pace here have significant implications for educational policy; yet the problems with current initiatives to support home learning are writ large in some of the parents' responses to the government's Learning Journey initiative, with which our chapter concludes.

Buying books

The large majority of respondents to our survey (90 per cent) said that books had been bought for their child in the last year. Purchasing of books was statistically related to age – books were bought for 98 per cent of the nursery/primary age children, compared with 87 per cent of the secondary children – and to social class – 95 per cent of the non-manual households bought books, compared with 83 per cent of manual households. (For the reasons identified in Chapter 9, these figures are probably much higher than those for the general population.) Children in all age groups were more likely to have been bought fiction books than non-fiction, although the proportion of boys who were bought non-fiction was slightly higher than the proportion of girls. Technological changes also appear to be playing a role here. Unlike girls, boys generally prefer non-fiction to fiction; but our interviews suggest that they may be increasingly inclined to use computers instead of books to find information. Meanwhile, younger children are less likely to have access to the Internet and may be more likely to read non-fiction as a result.

In general, however, even our more assiduous parents did not seem to buy information books on a regular basis. Computers (and in some cases home tutors) were their main item of educational expenditure. Non-fiction books seemed to be more of an optional extra, or were bought as gifts on special occasions (particularly the glossy hardbacks). In some instances, purchases were motivated by a trip to a museum or other educational site, but the majority of parents were 'reactive rather than proactive', as one mother put it:

> We've been quite voracious readers of the things you pick up if
> you go somewhere, like you know Carnarvon Castle. We went
> on holiday there a couple of years ago and we bought this
> book . . . He voraciously went through this Carnarvon Castle book
> and he had every fact and that's actually being motivated by
> having been there, not by 'Oh, let's just go into Waterstone's
> and buy a book about Carnarvon Castle.' And I think we went
> to Guernsey and we went round a castle and the same thing
> happened. We were inspired, if that's not too strong a word,
> we were inspired by actually seeing it and then getting the facts
> afterwards. So we're very reactive, not proactive it seems.

Aside from this, the majority of non-fiction books were bought either to support specific school work (study or revision aids, or topic books) or because children had an interest in particular book series (generally inexpensive paperback series of the *Horrible Histories* variety). Relatively few parents reported visiting bookshops on a regular basis: the more assiduous book buyers were more likely to buy from book clubs, school book fairs, mail order catalogues or from publishers' representatives (notably Dorling Kindersley, who organize home selling in the style of Tupperware parties) – all of which offer discounted prices.

Nevertheless, there were some differences between parents, which partly reflected their different orientations towards education. Dina Lang, one of the 'aspiring' parents identified in the previous chapter, was one of the most enthusiastic book buyers, despite being financially less well off than most of the other parents. Significantly, she did not have a television or a home computer, claiming that this was on the grounds of cost – although there may have been an element of choice here too. Most of her books were bought in discount or remainder shops. She saw reading non-fiction as a means of satisfying her daughter's curiosity, and also helping her stay one step ahead of her class mates:

> And she [her daughter] always asks, 'Why this? Why that? Why this? Why that?' ... So it's like she can read about them beforehand and sometimes when they do it at school she goes 'Oh, yes, I've read about it.' And she can take [books] to school and can show them.

The Waldrons were very different from Dina Lang in terms of qualifications and income, but they too bought books on a regular basis. They had an extensive collection of educational books and CD-ROMs, several bought through a Dorling Kindersley (DK) representative. They also bought study aids for their seven-year-old son and his younger sister: according to Mrs Waldron, 'we do bits of these, like a page every now and again when I can tie him down, strap him down'. Despite the apparent compulsion, their son Adam did not seem to object to the study aids, especially if there was a reward (a gold star) at the end of the exercise. Mrs Waldron had bought these materials on her own initiative to extend school work, rather than on the school's recommendation; and indeed, she expressed some concern that the work her son was given in school was 'too easy'. At the same time, she felt uncertain about helping with homework in some areas, and saw buying books as a way of compensating for this:

> I have this big thing that I just know very little about the history of, the history of anything really. So I bought this book which I thought would be quite useful. I also bought a huge DK one which is for me really, but it's just a brilliant reference book if he [her son] comes back and asks about anything ... The history thing is partly me wanting to find out about history because he came back asking questions about when something happened and I didn't know and we didn't have any real reference book. It's just not my strong point.

In general, the more enthusiastic book buyers in our sample were parents with younger children. Older children (particularly boys) seemed to be moving on to the Internet, or – if they did not have access to the Internet – to CD-ROMs to find out information. Some parents who might otherwise have been regular book buyers were also deterred by the price of glossy hardbacks. Nevertheless, most children tended to have a few encyclopaedias or other information books (like *The Guinness Book of Records*) that they would 'dip into' on an irregular basis as a way of passing the time when there was nothing better to do. Peter Kennedy, for example, reported that: 'Sometimes when I'm up in bed and I'm a bit bored, when the news is on, I'll go and look in my encyclopaedia, sometimes I'll just have a look.' These are books for browsing or consulting for specific queries rather than reading consistently, and so probably have a long shelf life. By comparison, the cheap paperback series like *Horrible Histories* or *The Knowledge* were viewed by several parents and children as 'collectables' (albeit of a more ephemeral nature), which would be read regardless of topic.

Reading information books

In order to explore parents' and children's views of these different styles of information books, we asked them to read two contrasting texts. Nine families were sent *The Rotten Romans* (one of Scholastic's *Horrible Histories* series) and *Ancient Rome* (one of DK's *Eyewitness Guides*); and six were sent *Dead Dinosaurs* (from Scholastic's *The Knowledge* series) and *Dinosaur* (another *Eyewitness Guide*). In each case, therefore, the families were given a glossy, large-format text with colour illustrations, and an inexpensive, humorous paperback. These books were discussed in Chapters 6 and 8.

The children's preferences here were fairly clear. Eight out of the nine children who were sent books on Roman history said that they preferred the *Rotten Romans*. Most had already read one or more titles from the *Horrible Histories* series. They enjoyed the humour, the cartoons and the 'gory' stories. Only one child said that he preferred the DK book. He was one of the youngest in the interview group (7 years old) and his mother felt that the *Rotten Romans* was a little beyond his reading ability at that stage: he preferred the immediacy of the pictures in the DK book. Most children said they liked the glossy pictures in the DK book; but several said that it seemed boring in comparison with the *Rotten Romans* and – as we shall see below – that it did not contain enough 'information'. In the case of the dinosaur books, opinion was more divided. When asked to choose, three of the five said they preferred the DK book, which may reflect the importance of visual images in the appeal of dinosaurs, described in Chapter 8.

The majority of parents also liked the *Rotten Romans*, and a few even preferred this book to the more 'serious' *Ancient Rome*. Some argued that the artefacts and information in the DK book were not placed in historical context, and that they preferred the narrative style of the *Rotten Romans*. One mother (who had previously bought several DK books) felt that the DK style was too predictable: 'it's a formula, they do get a bit samey'. However, most parents were impressed with the 'beautiful' photography of the *Eyewitness Guides* and the fact that these books were easy to browse: some said that they reminded them of trips to museums or historic sites. Indeed, some parents seemed to view the DK book as a valued object in itself: as one parent put it, such a book was 'a treasured item that you'd have in your bookcase for the foreseeable future'. A few parents felt that these two types of books complemented each other, and said they would find it hard to choose between them. Ultimately, however, they would be inclined to buy whichever book they thought their child would read, which in most cases meant the cheaper paperback.

Interestingly, one set of parents (the Blatchfords) actively disliked the *Horrible Histories*, and said they would actively discourage their son from buying such a book. This was partly to do with what they saw as the 'clear, straightforward' style of the DK book: 'you know, you can pick this up and find out specific facts, it's beautifully laid out, nice illustrations and I just feel it's easier to work with'. However, their main objection to the *Horrible Histories* was the tone and style of the book, rather than its pedagogic value. As parents who described themselves as 'keen on behaviour and manners', they took particular exception to jokes at the expense of teachers (see Chapter 6):

> There was one bit in here which, as I mentioned, my father's a retired teacher, but there was a thing about 'How to Trick your Teacher' and it's really – things to suggest to say to your teacher and it was something like, 'Please Sir/Miss/Gorilla Features' and if my father, who I think was still allowed to use the cane, that would be several swipes of the cane for the 'Gorilla Features'. Well that might be how you get the kids interested in this day and age but, again, coming from a more traditionalist standpoint, I just think that's complete rubbish. Even remotely encouraging that sort of thing as a joke I think is . . . it's a joke, it is educational I can see but not in a way that I'd ideally like to see or, how I believe, kids should be educated.

Clearly, these elements of the *Horrible Histories* – which we would see as only mildly subversive – do appear to represent a challenge for a minority of parents, even if there were children who positively appreciated them. Nevertheless, the majority of children – and some parents – thought that the paperback series were informative and educational, perhaps even more so than the more serious DK texts. Ian Stevenson (aged 10) complained that there was not enough written text in the *Eyewitness* book. As his mother explained:

> He finds that there's too much picture and he doesn't get enough information from it. He says, 'Well it doesn't tell me much about that. Can you tell me about it?' And I don't know anything about the Rotten Romans. So that's the reason that he shies away from those [*Eyewitness Guides*]. There are a lot of pictures but not a lot of detail in the explanation – it is very simplified.

Even the Blatchfords acknowledged that there were 'a lot of very good facts' in *Rotten Romans* and that it was 'well researched'. There was also a sense that the *Horrible Histories* brought history to life in a way that the *Eyewitness Guides* did not. One parent pointed out that the DK books did not elaborate or explain: they simply stated the facts, or presented arte-facts in a decontextualized way. By contrast, the *Horrible Histories* gained from a more personal approach:

> It is the way it's presented; it's the way it's written. You know, if you're reading the diary of somebody who was fighting the Romans, or was a Roman legionnaire or whatever, you know, as it was for him, I think it's a much more powerful way of learning about it, how people lived in those times. To me that's essentially what history is all about – it's not really about learning dates, it's about learning how people felt and reacted to the situation that they were in at that time. And if you can understand that then I think you're far more likely to remember all the sort of, you know, the dates and the battles.

Likewise, Sarah Jensen (aged 12) argued that the objects in the DK book were not placed in a broader historical context:

> It's just talking about this artefact, just that artefact. So instead of saying like 'Hair clips were made of gold', [it says] '*This* hair clip is made of gold' so you don't really know if it's just that or the whole thing.

By contrast, the *Horrible Histories* were seen to be telling children what they wanted to know: as one girl put it, the book 'tells you all the funny facts and the things that you would rather want to know'. The anecdotes and gory details gave children a form of knowledge that they could use to impress (or occasionally outrage) others, including parents. One mother told us:

> From time to time she comes out with these little snippets of facts and I sort of look at her open-mouthed and say, 'What? That can't be true.' So she goes off and looks it up, 'Yes, yes, it is.'

Ultimately, these popular paperback series were seen by both parents and children as a successful combination of education and entertain-ment. One eight-year-old girl summed this up as follows:

> It is not just kind of cartoons, there is information as well and it is funny . . . and there are funny cartoons. And if you are just a person who likes to study you can do that and not just read the cartoons. So if you want to read cartoons you can read cartoons. If you want to study when you have studied all through the book you can have some fun and look at the cartoons.

Parents' response was almost pragmatic: several said they felt that books like the *Horrible Histories* were more educational simply because children were willing to read them, whereas they were less inclined to read a complete *Eyewitness Guide*. Indeed – as we have implied in earlier chapters

– these different types of books are clearly designed to be 'read' in different ways. Several children described how they would read *The Rotten Romans* and *Dead Dinosaurs* as they would a story book – starting at the beginning and reading entire chapters. Once the book had been read in this way, and once they were familiar with the format, they might browse through looking for 'interesting bits'. By contrast, the *Eyewitness* books were browsed rather than read consecutively: some children said that they would read the introductory text on the double-page spread, but others just read the captions attached to the images that attracted them.

Buying computers

As we noted in Chapter 9, owners of home computers were proportionately more highly represented in our survey than in the population as a whole. Nevertheless, even within the terms of our sample, there were some significant differences that reflect current national trends. Thus, computer ownership and Internet access were highest amongst families where one or both parents worked in non-manual occupations, and in two-parent families (cf. Office for National Statistics 2000). Computer ownership was also linked to education: respondents with a degree or postgraduate qualification were most likely to have a computer, whereas those with GCSEs/O levels and equivalent qualifications were the least likely.

The vast majority of respondents in our survey said that their child used the computer. Less than 3 per cent (20 children) did not, and most of these were in the younger age group (7 or under). In common with Livingstone and Bovill (1999), we found that boys were more likely than girls to have access to computers in their bedrooms, although the gender differences in our sample were not as great as in their study. Age was more strongly associated with access to media in the bedroom: the proportion of children with computers was almost twice as high among 12–14-year-olds as it was among 3–7-year-olds.

Amongst our interview sample, all but one family had a home computer. A few families had bought their first computer over five years ago, and had either upgraded or bought new computers since that time. Only one had no computer, although two had second-hand computers which could not play new CD-ROMs and were without Internet access. While economic considerations seemed to be a major determinant both in whether a family owned a computer and in the quality of the computer, money was not the only factor. Parents' attitudes to computers and other media also played a role.

In almost all cases, education was cited one of the reasons for buying the computer. Other reasons included work, computer games, and generally 'keeping up with the rest of the world'. Yet although most families had bought a computer at least partly to support their children's learning, there were mixed feelings about whether it was being used in the manner originally intended. Some parents found that their children were only willing to use the computer for games; while others were concerned because their children were more interested in using educational software rather than books. Among our interview sample, we can identify at least three distinct types of computer users.

The *enthusiasts* believed strongly in the educational potential of computers. Mr Heshmat, for example, bought his son his first computer when he was aged 5. This computer is in his bedroom and he is the only one who uses it. Mr Heshmat felt that the computer had lived up to their expectations in educational terms, and that computers make learning easier and more enjoyable:

> To begin with, it's the ease with which you can get information. You put a CD-ROM in there; it can contain the equivalent to about 10–15 books easily. And it's just a question of pressing a button so it comes and the noises they make and things like that, it makes it more interesting for the children. They put in a game where you answer questions, a door opens – it's, you're learning as you play kind of thing, you know. That makes it a lot more interesting for the child to actually see what is happening and learning without realizing he's learning, you know. Whereas books you open it, you start reading, all you see is words and pages, some children they love it, some children don't but I've yet to see anybody saying, 'I hate finding these things out on the computer.' You know. And I think . . . the other big part it plays is every child loves television so that monitor becomes another television where the child has got some control over it. It's not what they put in and they feed us and we just watch it.

Some enthusiasts seemed to know little about computers, but were nevertheless very keen that their children should learn early. These parents seemed to feel that although it was too late to learn about computers themselves, they did not want their children to 'miss out'. Mrs Klenowski, one of our 'aspiring' parents, had bought a home computer mainly for educational purposes, and had one of the largest collections of educational software amongst the interview group. Her youngest son had been bought his first educational CD-ROM when he was only 4. Mrs Klenowski felt that he was learning not just from the content of the CD-ROM but also by developing 'mouse control'. Personally, however, she said that she knew very little about computers and even felt intimidated by them; and she also confessed that her children used the computer largely for games, and rarely used the educational packages. Yet despite her ignorance about computers, she remained absolutely convinced that her children needed to have them at home.

At the opposite end of the spectrum were the *resisters*. The Lynches, for example, seemed to have reluctantly given in to the need for a home computer. Despite being one of the most affluent families in the group, they had only bought their computer in the last few years. They were determined to have only one computer in the house, and that their children would never have a TV or computer in their bedrooms. They said they had bought their computer for a number of reasons, including education, work and the desire to 'keep up with the twenty-first century'. Mrs Lynch spoke of their purchase with resignation rather than enthusiasm ('And it's the way it's going to go, isn't it?'). She also expressed a degree of resentment that marketers were 'blackmailing' parents into buying computers by appealing to anxieties about their children's education:

> Actually I kind of resent that sort of advertising . . . It annoys me
> – especially before Christmas – it's, you know, you have some
> 16- or 14-year-old saying 'and for only £1,800, I've got my own
> computer' and I thought, 'Well, lucky for you.' You know, actually
> it does annoy me that there is this pressure that each child should
> have their own computer in their own room – they're not cheap.
> I know they're cheap compared to what they used to be. But
> I . . . resent that the parents feel that they're inadequate as parents
> or not providing their children with the best educational start if
> they don't have their own computer . . . It's an additional tool –
> it shouldn't be the main focus and it worries me, it annoys me
> rather than worries me, that it's being pushed as *the* main thing
> and if your child doesn't have this they're going to fail their A
> levels, you know. A lot of people are worried – they want to give
> their children the best start in life and this thing about jobs, you
> know, good education, so it's an easy pressure point to push. You
> know, 'If you do this, your child will stand a better chance; and
> if you don't, others will get ahead and your child will be left
> behind'. And it's an easy button to push really. And as software is
> changing all the time, it can be a very expensive thing to get into.

Mrs Lynch also felt that computers and other media should be kept in a family space, to avoid a situation where each child is 'beavering away' on a computer in their own room. There was also the danger that children might end up in chat rooms or doing 'stuff they shouldn't be doing'. As we shall see below, other computer 'resisters' were concerned about their children's declining use of books, and were holding out against the pressure to invest in new and better equipment for that reason.

The majority of parents could be described as *followers*, who were somewhere between the two positions outlined above. Although they had some reservations about computers, they also accepted the idea that they were a valuable aid to learning. These parents seemed to feel that computers were something that everyone had, and therefore they had to get one too. Mrs Kennedy, was typical of this group:

> I suppose it's just everyone's getting a PC, you've just got to go along with it, haven't you? You've got to get in, you know. And I think, yes, probably with the Internet it was really for, you know, looking up information for Peter with his homework.

For this parent, having a computer also compensated for the fact that she did not have sufficient time to help with homework. As a working single parent, she was unable to take her son to the library in the evenings, and the Internet served as a useful substitute: 'you can look up anything on it'.

However, some parents in this group were not entirely convinced that the computer was being put to good use in terms of education. As one mother, Mrs Blatchford, pointed out:

> I think we certainly realized it would be an educational tool.
> Whether we've used it particularly well as one is another point.

Even if they were not using it for strictly 'educational' purposes, Mrs Blatchford felt that it was useful for her children to become familiar with how a computer works. Given that she herself knew very little about computers, this was an important first step:

> The mere fact that John is confident to go into the computer, knows his way around it, these days seems to me to be a very good step in the right direction, because I was about 38 when I [first] used one.

Buying software

While most parents in the interview group were broadly satisfied that computers had educational potential, surprisingly few of them seemed to buy educational software. This was partly confirmed by our survey. Just under half of the parents who had a computer with a CD-ROM drive said that educational CDs had been bought for their child in the past year. A slightly higher proportion of boys had been bought CD-ROMs than girls. There were also significant differences here in terms of family composition and employment: over half of children (52 per cent) living in two-parent families but only one-third of children in single parent families were bought educational CD-ROMs; and approximately a half of one- or two-income families bought software, whereas only a quarter of non-working households did so.

The other striking finding here was the relatively narrow range of titles that had been purchased. The large majority of titles bought for primary age children were numeracy and literacy 'drill-and-practice' packages (see Chapter 7); whereas by far the most popular title for secondary age children was the *Encarta* encyclopaedia – a title that is usually 'bundled' with the purchase of the computer itself.

As mentioned in Chapter 4, the market for educational software has been slowing down over the last few years. While this is partly due to competition from the Internet, it is also a consequence of the limited number of retail outlets through which software is sold. While specialist computer hardware shops may be intimidating for mothers and younger children, mainstream high-street outlets tend to stock a limited range of titles. Customers are generally unable to try out the software before purchase, and the retail price is often expensive. All these factors contribute to parents' reluctance to buy new software.

This was certainly confirmed by our interviews. Although most families had the capability to use CD-ROMs, most parents did not buy educational software on a regular basis and some had stopped buying software altogether. Much of the software which was in use had either been provided with the computer or had been purchased at a discounted price. Several parents said that they would only buy software if it was discounted, for example through clubs, school fairs or from DK representatives. Some said that they found specialist shops like PC World offputting: as one mother told us, PC World is 'just not a shop where you would want to go to' – it was 'always too busy', it was not easy to browse, there were not enough staff, and the staff 'don't give you the information you want'. Here again, the home-selling approach adopted by DK's 'Family Network' system seems to have an advantage, in that representatives offer advice and give customers the opportunity to try a sample disk.

The high retail price of software was also a key consideration. As one parent pointed out:

> it's a gamble when you spend that sort of money [£25] and you don't know whether it is going to be good or not.

Another parent said:

> it seems to me you could buy a whole load of stuff which is relatively expensive and could be a complete waste of time.

Parents who had in the past bought software which proved to be disappointing were less inclined to make repeat purchases. When parents did buy software, it was often because someone had recommended it or their child had seen the software at a friend's house or at school. In general, schools do not offer advice on software, although a few parents reported that school fairs give them a rare opportunity to browse through educational titles. Very few had seen reviews of educational software, and while some felt that there might be information 'out there', they simply were not aware of where to find it.

Some parents reported that they did not buy software because they had had difficulties in loading it onto their computers. In a few cases this was because the computer was too old to run recently produced CD-ROMs, but difficulties arose even with relatively new computers. Problems which have no apparent cause can be particularly frustrating, as one mother pointed out:

> It worked for a couple of times and then I had to go back to the manufacturers just to try and get it sorted out and they still couldn't sort it out. And that just drove me to despair really because I just thought 'this is crazy' because it's not as though we've got an old computer . . . Computers are great as far as I'm concerned but once it goes wrong I just want it to be somebody else's problem, because they just drive me mad.

Judging software

These obstacles aside, there were mixed views about the value of educational software. Some parents had stopped buying such material on the grounds that their children simply refused to use it. Several children reported that so-called 'fun learning' software was boring and repetitive. In some cases the learning involved seemed to be very superficial: one child commented that they had 'really boring stuff' which involved activities like 'shoot the aeroplane which has the right number of 16 take away 4 divided by 3'. Another child was equally disparaging of software which was too easy, involving simple and repetitive exercises like 'two plus two is four, four plus four is eight' – and he was equally unimpressed when bunny rabbits appeared on screen as a reward for completing these exercises. Several parents had similar complaints. Commenting on the *Carmen Sandiego* programs, for example, one parent pointed out that 'the format is so repetitive – once you have done about two or three of these you feel you wouldn't really go back'. As several parents pointed out, this lack of sustainability also had economic dimensions: given that software is so expensive, they expect children to use it beyond the first week.

In other cases, parents and children were unsure of how to actually use the software and eventually lost interest:

> Well you're supposed to collect all the bones to make up a dinosaur and then watch them come to life and I made the children try several times and they sort of investigated and came across various dinosaurs so it was quite interesting from an information point of view for a while. But we never actually worked out how to pick up these bones and then construct the dinosaur so they lost interest and so did I.

On the other hand, it was argued that software which was designed specifically to support key stages of the curriculum was too limited and repetitive. According to Alison Stevenson, this was contrary to the purpose of educational software, which she believed was to make learning 'fun':

> I don't think it's fun for children . . . It's like being at school. And I don't think the idea of a computer is to be at school. To me the idea of a computer is to have fun while you are learning. Because let's face it, it's easier to learn if you're enjoying something.

However, some parents had found that the 'entertainment' elements of the software had undermined its educational intentions. In the case of the DK *Explorer* packages, for example, children had been able to find short-cuts to collecting points for their 'certificates' without having to engage with any of the information; while in 'drill-and-practice' packages like *Maths Blaster*, they were inclined to select levels that they found easier, in order to stand a better chance of gaining a good score.

Nevertheless, most families could point to at least one piece of software which they had found useful. When asked about their favourite educational software, some children selected an encyclopaedia (like *Encarta*) because it was useful for homework or for their own general interest. Children also chose software which they perceived to be 'interactive' or which had a game-like format. Interestingly, in the light of our argument in Chapter 7, a few children chose simulations like *Theme Park* or *The Sims* as their favourite educational packages. These were seen as skilled games which required practical thinking and forward planning. As one child pointed out, he learned how 'to look after money' and plan ahead, and his mother agreed that he was 'definitely learning' from this software. However, another parent was less sure about the educational benefits of *The Sims*:

> My husband and I were both getting a bit twitchy, you know, about her spending *so* long [playing *The Sims*] but she persuaded us, well she tried to persuade us, that it was educational and we thought, well perhaps it's a little bit educational, it's a bit better than just watching soaps on the telly . . . I would have thought they're perhaps 10 or 20 per cent educational, the rest I think is just fun.

CD-ROMs were also seen by some to be particularly useful if a child is not interested in books but is too young to use the Internet, or does not have access to the Internet. Younger children, in particular, found them easier to use than the Internet. As in the above quotation, parents also felt that playing 'educational' games was preferable to watching TV or playing computer games – even if there was an ongoing debate here about what might count as 'educational'.

Using CD-ROMs

Four families were each sent two CD-ROMs. One CD was chosen for its 'fun learning' or game-like format (*Maths Blaster*, *Play and Learn with Skipper and Skeeto*, *Age of Empires*) while the other took a more straight-forwardly didactic approach to education (*DK Learning Ladder*, *DK History of the World*). Several of these packages are discussed in Chapter 7.

There were mixed reactions to the software. Some children and parents found the 'entertainment' aspects of the CD-ROMs 'gimmicky' and patronizing, whilst others thought that they were fun and helped children to learn. For example, one ten-year-old found the 'serious' learning part of *DK Learning Ladder* dull and difficult to follow, but really liked the 'talking pencil' character who introduces it. By contrast, a 12-year-old praised the educational content, but found the talking pencil irritating and patronizing. The same child also asserted that *Play and Learn with Skipper and Skeeto* was boring and annoying:

> They say these pointless comments which get annoying and plus you're on a time limit and so you've got this Skipper and Skeeto [characters] going 'Oh, my gosh it's a man-eating plant.' And they go, 'Oh, my goodness me.' And they keep going on and your time is going down and down and then you actually want to get on with the game but all the time they're just talking . . . He's like 'Be careful Skipper.' And you have to move out of the way and 'Oh, that was a close one.' And you think, 'Shut up!'

The difference in reaction here may have been partly due to the age of the children, but it illustrates a key problem for the designers of edutainment software, who are frequently obliged to target the widest possible market. For example, the packaging for *Play and Learn with Skipper and Skeeto* suggests that it is aimed at children aged between 6 and 14, although it is bound to be difficult to appeal to such disparate age groups.

One problem which several children had with the software (regardless of whether they liked it or not) was figuring out how to actually play or navigate their way around. In the case of *Maths Blaster*, this (rather than the maths questions) seemed to be the main challenge – as one ten-year-old put it:

> I got really, ahh, I just spent like one day trying to figure that – it's a really fun game, when I understood it, it was great, it was so fun.

Likewise, although our 12-year-old found *Play and Learn with Skipper and Skeeto* slow and childish in some respects, she never managed to finish the game because there were very few instructions:

I just don't understand how a child is supposed to know what to do.

Parents were also divided in their views, although this seemed to depend mainly on whether or not their child had enjoyed the software. Some enthusiasts, like Mr Heshmat, were confirmed in their view that computers made education more fun:

A little bit of fun makes it a lot easier. It's like trying to swallow a bitter pill, you drink a bit of orange juice with it, you don't taste it, it goes down.

More sceptical parents such as Mrs Turner thought that there were too many 'gimmicks', but conceded that children might enjoy this, even though her own daughter did not:

I find them frustrating and, you know . . . and the visual bits that you have on it are just a gimmick to me, they're not – it's all very nice, I'm sure they grab children's attention. I mean children are different, you know, they're different from how we were because their expectations are different; they're used to all that. So they sort of almost need that attraction to something. To me a book is just for getting information out of and I don't need a little whirly globe or a voice talking, I just find it a bit distracting, you know. It's just the ease of finding the information, I would find that very frustrating. I mean you [daughter] did, didn't you? And you know about using the computer, so there's no hope for people that don't sort of understand, you know.

These comments suggest that the 'balance' between education and entertainment depends upon the point of view of the user. While some users may find the 'entertainment' and 'fun' provided by educational software engaging, there are others who find it merely patronizing and irritating. Most parents also recognize that packaging can be misleading in this respect. Some parents may be dissuaded by the packaging of 'fun learning' software, because to them it does not look sufficiently educational. One of these parents, for example, said that she would not have bought *Maths Blaster* if she had seen it in a shop because it did not look like an 'educational' CD-ROM; although after seeing her daughter use the software she had changed her mind.

New media, old media

The majority of children who had the option said that they would prefer to use new media (either the Internet or CD-ROMs) rather than books for finding information. When they were given homework which involved some research, their first instinct was check on the computer, rather than use a book. This was particularly the case for older children. Tony Harper (aged 13), for example, had used books and visited the library on a regular basis before the family installed a network connection on their computer. He described his initial reaction to the Internet with the enthusiasm of a convert:

> And I mean, I was brought up with books for quite a while and then when I reached about 10 or 11 or 12 years old, I just got on to the Internet and I was thinking 'Wow, what's this? Something on the computer.' . . . You can find anything you want. It's really, it's like TV, books and everything put together in one. Because you can watch TV on the computer when you're on the Internet. You can listen to people speaking on there. I don't know – you've just got a lot of things.

Now he almost never uses books for research unless it is a 'real emergency'. He explained why he preferred the Internet:

> [With books] you have to like flick through so many pages and then you've got to look and look down and . . . it's just so slow. And when you're on the Internet it's so fast, you just type up something, like Henry VIII, and it will just come up with a million websites and it will say Henry VIII, how many wives did he have, the names of his wives and the information.

These comments were echoed by other children: the Internet in particular was seen as faster and easier to use than books, and as giving access to seemingly limitless amounts of information. Looking something up on the computer was not only more effective, but also more interesting and engaging, than looking it up in a book. In this respect, our interviews provide further evidence of how the market for non-fiction books is being undermined by new media.

However, some parents felt that their children were becoming too dependent on computers for finding information. They were concerned that computers might displace books or that their children would grow up without an appreciation of books. This had led to a struggle over the use of new versus old media in some households. Mrs Lloyd, for example, had refused to buy a new computer with Internet access, despite pressure from her two sons, both of whom are in secondary school. According to her, the children generally used *Encarta* for their homework, and she was concerned that if they had Internet access at home, they would never use books again. There was also a sense that printing information off the computer was almost a form of cheating – as if computers made things too easy, and were therefore incompatible with real learning. Mrs Lloyd did not even approve of her sons typing their homework, as she thought they needed to practise their handwriting.

Similar – although less extreme – objections were voiced by several of our 'resistant' parents. For these book lovers, the form in which the information was conveyed was of central importance – unlike the computer enthusiasts, for whom it did not matter either way. Alison Stevenson, for example, had an almost nostalgic view of books: she said she had loved reading when she was a child and could not understand why her son did not feel the same way about fiction books. She blamed other media (particularly television and video) for this situation:

> I liked reading when I was a child and I think he's missing out on a lot in the aspect that he doesn't read story books. But then again, I would say blame the television. And, as you can see, we've got quite a lot of videos about. I blame that as well. When I was a child it was black and white to begin with. Then we had the first colour television so that made it more exciting. However, the programmes that were aimed at children were really basic and you didn't have a film on a Saturday and you didn't have a film on a Sunday. You didn't have video machines, so you didn't have a video, so you probably read more . . . You got enjoyment out of [a programme] because you'd read about it first of all and then you saw it. Whereas now you see it before you read it and I think that's where society's gone wrong and I think that's where we've gone wrong, in the aspect that it is too available. And it is easier to watch something than it is to sit down and read.

For these 'resistant' parents, technological progress is seen to lead directly to social and cultural decline. Part of the explanation, of course, is that the majority of parents do not feel as comfortable with computers as their children do. While the homes in our sample were quite well equipped, only a minority of parents seemed entirely secure in their own computer skills. However, there may be a gender dimension here too – and it may not be a coincidence that the parent who was the greatest enthusiast in this respect, Mr Heshmat, was one of the few fathers whom we were able to interview. Furthermore, several of the mothers mentioned that their partners knew more about computers that they did themselves.

Here we find an awkward paradox. On the one hand, it appears that mothers are still primarily responsible for their children's learning in the home (cf. David *et al.* 1993); yet, on the other, mothers are also less likely to feel comfortable or competent with computer technology – or indeed, may be more likely to resist or reject it. While the 'gender gap' in relation to technology may be rapidly disappearing among younger people, it seems likely to persist in the older generation – particularly where mothers have few opportunities to use technology in the workplace. As education becomes increasingly 'technologized', it may well become harder for mothers to support their children's learning.

A role for government?

The technological changes we have identified in this chapter have significant implications for educational policy. Despite the growing influence of commercial forces, the government clearly does have a significant role to play in overcoming divisions between the 'education rich' and the 'education poor'. New technology poses new challenges here, in terms not just of inequalities of social class but also of gender. In this context, the Learning Journey initiative, discussed in Chapter 2, provides an illuminating case study of the limitations and possibilities of government intervention. We therefore conclude this chapter with a brief discussion of how the parents in our interview sample responded to the DfES materials.

Parents whose children were in the 7–11 age group were sent some of the topic leaflets from the Learning Journey initiative, in some cases relating to the subject matter of the books we had provided (e.g. ancient Rome). Predictably, it was the 'aspiring' parents who were most approving of the initiative, and said that they would try the activities suggested in the leaflets. Dina Lang, for example, wanted to get hold of more of these leaflets, although she did concede that it would be difficult to find time for the activities because she worked full-time. Another mother, Mrs Meade, was even more enthusiastic:

> I think they're great. I mean I often remember Edward doing projects and me thinking, you know, I wish I could do more with him and get more involved. I think it's an excellent idea. I quite enjoyed reading it myself. And I think sometimes you feel that your child is in school and you're not really part of what they're doing and you would like to do that, to make some learning at home relevant to what they're doing at school and this is a good sort of communication between the school, the parent and the child.

However, these parents were exceptional. Although most parents seemed to think that the Learning Journey initiative was a good idea in principle, they said they were unlikely to try the activities with their children. There were a number of reasons for this. One of the main constraints was the lack of time, particularly for working parents. In addition, many parents argued that the activities would feel alien or uncomfortable. The ancient Rome leaflet that we sent out, for example, suggested that parents should dress up in togas made of old sheets, or make sweet wine cakes with their children. Several parents clearly found such suggestions laughable. As one pointed out, these activities were 'too forced':

> I personally am just not the sort of mother that's going to sit down and make sweet wine cakes with my children.

Others felt incompetent to help – another parent said:

> we're not really terribly good on the cutting and sticking, arty-crafty things.

Her husband (one of the few fathers whom we interviewed) added that because he came from a 'macho all-male background', the idea of dressing up in togas and making cakes seemed a bit 'girly' to him. Mrs Kennedy was particularly scathing in her criticism:

> You know, sweet wine cakes, you know, I'd never, ever say to Peter, 'Ooh, you're learning about Romans, let's go in the kitchen and make some cakes.' That just wouldn't happen. You know, the practical side of it, we just wouldn't do it. Playing games and making cakes and all that sort of thing – no ... And it wouldn't help him in any way, shape or form with his Roman work at school, I shouldn't think. They'd be better off sending the kids off to a few days away somewhere and go and have a look at some proper Roman remains and mosaics somewhere, you know, than doing this sort of thing.

The fact that the leaflets were produced by the DfES seemed to make some parents even more inclined to dismiss them. Mrs Kennedy said that the leaflets were

> exactly what I would have imagined the government to produce [because] they are so out of touch.

Mrs Jensen (who worked as a classroom assistant) also seemed to feel some resentment about this:

> Because I mean half of me perhaps reading that book thought, 'Well, okay why have they sent me this?' you know, 'It's up to the school to teach the children, why do I need to know?' But then the other half of me, the teacher's assistant, went 'Ahh, yes.' ... I think parents have got so much to teach children from their own selves, to sort of pick up a leaflet and 'Right, what can I teach my child this evening?' I find it a bit sort of forced and unnatural somehow. I mean what I feel sort of passionate and enthusiastic about, I'm going to communicate to them anyway and I, you know, I sort of almost feel slightly resentful about that.

Her daughter also had reservations:

> But if mum was really like making me learn extra about the stuff I was doing at school, like really in-depth I would probably scream. Because sometimes it's just annoying at school when you like go there for like six hours every day and most of the time it's just people drumming facts into you. And it would be annoying to have that at home.

Anne McGarvie (a teacher) was critical of the government's education policies more generally. Although she felt that the Learning Journey initiative was a good idea in principle,

> the trouble is, it comes as part of a stifling load of initiatives towards this kind of new puritanism, every hour of every day has to be pointfully kind of filled.

She went on to say:

> I just get fed up with the way the government kind of endlessly directs us how to spend our time, in case we might be doing something like thinking along irregular lines. I do. I don't like to be a po-faced parent because I think it would really turn my kids off because they have [parents who are teachers] at home. If we were continually saying 'let's go to the British Museum and have an improving day', I think they would not want to come.

Even the parents who were more approving of the initiative in principle were inclined to view it as something that was more appropriate for *other* people. This 'otherness' was defined in terms of both class and ethnicity. Anne McGarvie felt that as a self-declared 'middle-class parent', her rejection of the leaflets might not be typical, and that other parents might welcome the advice. Meanwhile, Mrs Watkins argued that the initiative was 'an excellent idea', even though she could not envisage doing any of the activities herself:

> In a school like Ruth's where you have got a fair amount of children whose parents have probably come to this country and don't necessarily speak English or know the culture we thought, well I thought that would be very helpful, so they knew what their children were learning and they might not necessarily have the background on the Romans if you have come from India or wherever.

Of course, the likelihood of these materials ever reaching the 'other' parents who were deemed to be in need of them was fairly slight. Dina Lang, for example, was one of the few who expressed the wish to find out more, but she did not have access to the Internet, and so would have been unable to obtain the leaflets in the first place.

Despite the majority of parents' acceptance of the principles behind the initiative, then, nearly all those whom we interviewed were inclined to draw the line at this point. For the reasons we have identified, the parents in our sample were almost certainly more enthusiastic about their role in home learning than the population in general. Yet even they seemed to perceive this kind of initiative as unrealistic and unnatural – and, in some cases, as downright intrusive. They felt that their educational responsibilities as parents would be more effectively met in less formal, didactic ways. Here again, they did not want to be turned into teachers.

CHAPTER 11

CONCLUSION

The research described in this book took place against a background of growing interest in the potential of learning in the home. On the one hand, there has been a range of government initiatives and publications emphasizing the value of homework and parental involvement in education as means of raising standards of achievement and addressing social exclusion. On the other, commercial corporations are now increasingly regarding the home as a significant new market for educational goods and services – of which the media we have been discussing here are merely one example. These developments have led to a blurring of boundaries between the home and the school, between parents and teachers, between the public and the private, and between education and entertainment.

While our focus of interest has been fairly specific, therefore, the phenomena we have been describing are indicative of much wider developments. Thus, the changes in the publishing and retailing of educational texts identified in Part One of the book reflect more general changes within the contemporary media and cultural industries. The combination of 'education' and 'entertainment' analysed in Part Two can also be seen as symptomatic of broader developments in other areas of the media, such as television and the Internet. Finally, our discussion of parents' orientations towards home learning, and of children's uses of educational texts, is indicative of more general tendencies in educational policy and practice. While we have separated these three aspects for the purposes of analysis, we have also sought to illustrate the connections and relationships between them. In this brief conclusion, we provide a summary of the areas we have covered, and identify some of the broader issues for debate.

Production and marketing

After years of relative stability, children's educational publishing is now entering a period of rapid change. It has been significantly affected by developments in government policy on education, by technological innovations and by the broader restructuring and globalization of the cultural industries. However, this is a diverse field, which contains several subsectors. In the case of book publishing, for example, one should distinguish between hardback reference books, paperback non-fiction, early learning texts and study guides. These different sectors have been affected in different ways by recent changes: sales of early learning texts and study guides, for example, are booming, largely as a result of the extension of national testing; while the market in reference texts is faltering, partly because of competition from the Internet. The fate of software publishing is even less certain, not only because of the advent of the Internet, but also because of longer-term problems with retailing for the home market.

As a whole, the industry has come to be dominated by a small number of large multinational companies. In several areas – such as reference books and software – international markets are increasingly influencing the selection and presentation of content. Now that most publishers are part of multimedia conglomerates, they are able to exploit copyrights (such as licensed characters), and develop content, across a range of media. Nevertheless, their main response to growing competition has been to minimize potential risk. Thus, in the case of both reference works and more popular non-fiction texts, series publishing has become the norm; while in other areas – such as early learning – publishers' priorities are now largely determined by government policy. The major boom in educational publishing in recent years has been in the field of study guides and revision aids; while specifying the relationship to national tests has become an almost indispensable aspect of marketing to parents.

Retailing has also seen a significant concentration of ownership in recent years. This, combined with the deregulation of the industry, has shifted the balance of power from publishers to retailers. Meanwhile, there has been a rise in non-traditional outlets such as supermarkets, which have helped to create and develop particular areas of the market, such as early learning texts. Retailers are also looking for new ways to attract the children's market, via multi-product merchandising and attempts to turn shopping into a 'leisure experience'. However, the retailing of educational materials – particularly of software – remains problematic, not least because of the limited financial returns it can offer.

In general, therefore, the production and distribution of children's educational materials has increasingly come to be governed by commercial imperatives. As in other areas, market forces exercise a broadly conservative influence on the provision of educational goods and services; and this is largely being reinforced by the centralizing tendencies of government policy. While there have undoubtedly been some significant areas of new development, these have largely arisen in response to the growing anxiety about national testing. In the competitive environment we have described, publishers tend to play safe, relying on tried and tested formulae; while the growing concentration within retailing is also resulting in a reduction in the diversity of products available to the consumer. In the current climate of educational policy, what counts as learning has become ever more narrowly defined; and sheer commercial logic dictates that publishers will be bound to follow this tendency – and thereby to reinforce it.

Nevertheless, this is also a market in which children's sovereignty as consumers is increasingly acknowledged – and so parental (and indeed governmental) notions of what counts as learning cannot reign unchallenged. In attempting to engage with the changing enthusiasms of children, educational publishers have been obliged to rethink the relationships between 'education' and 'entertainment'; and while some of these changes have been superficial, others have been rather more profound.

Texts

One of the reasons why this is such a complex and difficult market is precisely that it has to target both parents and children. Publishers know – and our research confirms – that children are generally not interested in materials that adopt a traditional, didactic approach; and they are particularly resistant to reading or using such materials in their leisure time. While it is mostly parents who actually buy (or pay for) the materials, they see little point in doing so if their children are unlikely to use them. As a result, there is growing pressure on publishers to appeal directly to children, by providing material that is 'entertaining' as well as 'educational'.

The case studies contained in Part Two of the book illustrate some of the different ways in which learning is now being constructed, packaged and sold to parents and children. In examining the various forms of education and entertainment that are emerging in children's information books, magazines and CD-ROMs, we considered a range of textual characteristics: the balance between narrative and exposition in written text; the ways in which texts address and attempt to engage readers; the relationship between written text and images; the role of page layout and design; and the various forms of 'interactivity' that are on offer.

The early learning magazines analysed in Chapter 5 provide a symptomatic example of these new forms of 'edutainment'. Mostly based on popular television series or characters, they form part of the integrated marketing that characterizes contemporary children's media. These magazines sell entertainment to children, but they also sell education to parents. They seek to redefine everyday domestic and play activities as forms of educational 'work', and thereby encourage parents to take on the roles of teachers. In doing so, they tend to reinforce relatively narrow definitions of what counts as legitimate learning, and contribute to a more general 'curricularization' of family life. Yet while parents are the purchasers of these texts, they are not the primary readers; and as such, the magazines must also attempt to engage children directly, by offering pleasures that go beyond the purely pedagogical.

While these magazines are a relatively recent development, the market in information books is much better established. It is currently dominated by two main genres: inexpensive paperback series and glossy hardback reference texts. In the case of the history books analysed in Chapter 6, we found that the former adopt a much more irreverent approach to presenting information. They use a more personal, informal style, and rely on narrative more than exposition. These books emphasize entertainment (in the form of humour and 'gory details') rather than education, but they also avoid the more traditional, authoritarian approach to history that characterizes the reference books. Nevertheless, the informality and 'child-centred' approach of the popular series is ultimately rhetorical: its primary function is to flatter the child reader into a kind of complicity with the author, rather than promoting more general questioning or critique.

The dinosaur books analysed in Chapter 8 seek to entertain and engage the reader in a rather different way, relying more on spectacular images and tending to represent dinosaurs in terms of human moral codes and social stereotypes. Comparing equivalent texts produced over the past 25 years, we found that images have come to dominate the design, and that the separation between image and text has become increasingly blurred. However, the combination of image and text – and of education and entertainment – in these books is sometimes awkward and contradictory.

Meanwhile, 'interactivity' has become a key term in the marketing of educational goods and services, not least in the educational software analysed in Chapter 7. Broadly speaking, however, we found that interactivity in these packages serves mainly as a kind of superficial ornament. The 'drill-and-practice' packages that currently dominate the market offer very limited control and feedback to the user; and while the reference packages allow greater control (at least in the form of browsing), the feedback remains quite limited. In fact, the most developed – and in our view, most intellectually demanding – forms of interactivity can be found in the packages that most resemble games.

In general, our analysis of these texts refutes the idea that combining entertainment with education necessarily results in a kind of 'dumbing down'. The more entertaining materials we have considered clearly do make learning accessible to children who might otherwise be reluctant to engage in it. More significantly, our analysis suggests that the more entertainment-oriented texts (the *CiTV Telly Tots* magazine, the *Horrible Histories* books, the computer game packages) are in some respects the least educationally 'authoritarian', in the sense that they allow greater control for the learner and permit a wider range of learning outcomes. In many instances, however, this approach is relatively superficial. The apparently anti-authoritarian populism of the *Horrible Histories*, for example, is far from genuinely challenging; while the 'interactivity' and 'fun' so frequently proclaimed in the marketing of educational software are often little more than window-dressing – and our interviews suggest that children often recognize them as such.

Consumption and use

To what extent might these developments contribute to a narrowing of the 'education gap' between rich and poor? Our survey confirms that such a gap is far from disappearing. Although our sample was dominated by 'enthusiastic' parents, we found that middle-class families were more likely to have access to educational resources (multimedia computers, Internet connections, information books and software) than working-class families. Families with less disposable income – notably single-parent families, and families where the parents were unemployed – were particularly disadvantaged in this respect. However, the relationship between social class (or indeed disposable income) and families' orientations towards education is not straightforward: it is as much to do with future aspirations as with past experience.

While some parents were enthusiastic about their role as educators, this was largely to do with shared family activities or outings rather than specific support for school work. Many insisted that they did not wish to be regarded as teachers; and in several cases, they described their role in terms of their children's schooling with feelings of inadequacy and guilt. Several parents felt they were being pressured to pay for home tutors for their children, largely as a result of increasing competition at the point of transfer to secondary schools. Many were doing so against their wishes, but that the level of competition was intensifying and becoming impossible to avoid. Others noted that children were being set increasing amounts of homework; and some argued that this was unnecessary. Supporting homework posed particular difficulties for single parents and for working parents.

Parents' purchases of educational materials reflected their general orientations towards education. For some, even those who were on limited means, buying books and other resources was a tangible indication of their educational aspirations for their children; while for others, it was described as a form of 'panic buying' that might help (however temporarily) to allay feelings of guilt and insecurity. In general, however, the children were primarily interested in the 'entertainment' aspects of these materials: 'education' was frequently associated with being 'boring'.

Nearly all the parents cited education as one reason for purchasing a home computer, although there was a considerable degree of scepticism as to whether computers had fulfilled their educational promise. Few parents bought software on a regular basis, and only a narrow range of titles was in use. The 'fun' element of educational software was often seen as patronizing and superficial. In some families, there was an ongoing struggle between 'new' and 'old' media. Several mothers expressed a personal preference for books, while fathers tended to be seen as experts on computers. However, mothers are still primarily responsible for their children's learning in the home; and as computers become more important in education, there is a danger of a new 'education gap' emerging – in this case, between mothers and their children.

However, the extent to which such gaps or inequalities might be addressed through direct government intervention may be limited. As our analysis of the government's Learning Journey initiative suggests, relying on state provision in this field may prove even less palatable than leaving it to market forces. In general, the parents in our sample resisted the 'curricularization' of family life that these materials so strongly promote. While they welcomed the attempt to provide information about what their children were doing in school, they rejected the approach to home learning as unrealistic and almost puritanical. More independent and realistic – and less authoritarian – sources of advice and support are clearly needed.

Indeed, commercial publishers and retailers can justifiably claim to have bridged at least some of the gaps that the government has failed to do. For example, supermarkets and more popular high-street retailers appear to have been quite effective in attracting consumers who would be unlikely even to enter specialist bookshops – and who might also be least likely to respond to government initiatives in this field. However, as our survey and our interviews with parents show, such materials are predominantly being purchased by parents who are already positively disposed towards education; and there is some room for debate about whether even these parents are getting what they pay for.

Towards a broader view of learning

We began this book with a series of optimistic platitudes. 'The parent is the child's first teacher.' 'Children are learning all the time.' Yet however clichéd they may seem, these statements still ring true. Parents clearly do teach their children, even if they do not wish to be seen as teachers. The family is undoubtedly a significant – perhaps the *most* significant – location for children's learning. And yet much of the difficulty here stems from the question of what we choose to count as learning in the first place. Much of the learning and teaching that goes on in homes and families is not recognized by schools; and much of the cultural capital that children bring into the classroom is ignored or devalued by teachers. This is not to blame teachers, however. The past two decades have seen a steady narrowing in policy-makers' definitions of education. The dominance of national testing in particular has had an extremely reductive influence, not just on the range of educational materials available in the marketplace, but also on what is seen as a legitimate or recognizable form of education in the home. It is time to develop a broader view of the ways in which parents and children might learn together.

REFERENCES

Ahmed, K. (2000) It's not junk mail, it's the latest teaching aid, *Observer*, 10 September.

Aldrich, F., Rogers, Y. and Scaife, M. (1998) Getting to grips with 'interactivity': helping teachers assess the educational value of CD-Roms, *British Journal of Educational Technology*, 29(4): 321–32.

Alexander, T. (1997) *Family Learning*. London: Demos.

Anning, A. (1998) Appropriateness or effectiveness in the early childhood curriculum in the UK: some research evidence, *International Journal of Early Years Education*, 6(3): 299–314.

Back to School Bookseller (2000) An all round view, *Back to School Bookseller*, 16 June: 19–21.

Bartolome, A.R. (1992) Interactive levels and cognitive styles, *Learning Resources Journal*, 8(3): 63–9.

Bernstein, B. (1977) *Class, Codes and Control, Volume 3: Towards a Theory of Educational Transmissions*. London: Routledge.

Bernstein, B. (1990) *Class, Codes and Control, Volume 4: The Structuring of Pedagogic Discourse*. London: Routledge.

Bernstein, B. (1996) *Pedagogy, Symbolic Control and Identity*. London: Taylor & Francis.

Blair, T. (1997) *New Britain: My Vision of a Young Country*. Boulder, CO: Westview.

Blunkett, D. (2000) Partners in time, *The Guardian*, 12 September.

Book Marketing Limited (2000) *Books and the Consumer*. London: Book Marketing Limited.

The Bookseller (2000a) Parragon creates Bright Sparks, *The Bookseller*, 27 October: 8.

The Bookseller (2000b) The force deserts DK, *The Bookseller*, 28 January: 28.

The Bookseller (2000c) Book trade needs brands, *The Bookseller*, 12 May 2000: 18.

The Bookseller (2000d) Parents under pressure, *The Bookseller*, 8 September 2000: 4.

Bookseller Publications (2001) *theBookseller.com Bulletin*, 26 February.

Bourdieu, P. and Passeron, J.C. (1977) *Reproduction in Education, Society and Culture*. London: Sage Publications.

Bridges, D. and McLaughlin, T. (1994) *Education and the Market Place*. London: Falmer.

Brown, A. (1993) Participation, dialogue and the reproduction of social inequalities, in R. Merttens and G. Vass (eds) *Partnerships in Maths: Parents and Schools: The IMPACT Project*. London: Falmer.

Brown, A. (2000) Positioning, pedagogy and parental participation in school mathematics, *Social Epistemology* 14(1): 21–31.

Brown, A. and Dowling, P. (1992) 'Who's been restructuring *my* primary socialisation?' The impact of school mathematics on domestic space, in R. Merttens and J. Vass (eds) *Ruling the Margins: Problematising Parental Involvement*, Submitted conference papers. London: University of North London/ Impact project.

Buckingham, D. (1993) *Children Talking Television: The Making of Television Literacy*. Basingstoke: Falmer.

Buckingham, D. (1995) On the impossibility of children's television: the case of Timmy Mallett, in C. Bazalgette and D. Buckingham (eds) *In Front of the Children*. London: British Film Institute.

Buckingham, D. (1996) *Moving Images: Understanding Children's Emotional Responses to Television*. Manchester: Manchester University Press.

Buckingham, D. (1997) Schooling goes to market: some lessons from the Channel One controversy, *International Journal of Media and Communication Studies* 1. http://www.aber.ac.uk/~jmcwww/1997/channel1.html

Buckingham, D. (2000a) Been there, dome that, *English and Media Magazine*, 42: 4–11.

Buckingham, D. (2000b) *After the Death of Childhood: Growing Up in the Age of Electronic Media*. Cambridge: Polity.

Buckingham, D. (2002a) The electronic generation? Children and new media, in L. Lievrouw and S. Livingstone (eds) *Handbook of New Media*. London: Sage.

Buckingham, D. (2002b) Child-centred television? *Teletubbies* and the educational imperative, in D. Buckingham (ed.) *Small Screens: Television for Children*. Leicester: Leicester University Press.

Buckingham, D. and Sefton-Green, J. (in press) Gotta catch 'em all: structure, agency and pedagogy in children's media culture, *Media, Culture and Society*.

Buckingham, D., Davies, H., Jones, K. and Kelley, P. (1999) *Children's Television in Britain: History, Discourse and Policy*. London: British Film Institute.

Buckingham, D., Scanlon, M. and Sefton-Green, J. (2001) Selling the digital dream: marketing educational technology to teachers and parents, in A. Loveless and V. Ellis (eds) *Subject to Change: Literacy and Digital Technology*. London: Routledge.

Burke, P. (1991a) Overture: the new history, its past and its future, in P. Burke (ed.) *New Perspectives on Historical Writing*. Cambridge: Polity.

Burke, P. (1991b) History of events and the revival of narrative, in P. Burke (ed.) *New Perspectives on Historical Writing*. Cambridge: Polity.

Cairns, J. and Inglis, B. (1989) A content analysis of ten popular history textbooks for primary schools with particular emphasis on the role of women, *Educational Review*, 41(3): 221–6.

Campaign for Learning (2000) *A Manifesto for Family Learning*. London: Southgate.

Cawson, A., Haddon, L. and Miles, I. (1995) *The Shape of Things to Consume: Delivering Information Technology into the Home*. Aldershot: Avebury.

Central Advisory Council for Education (1967) *Children and Their Primary Schools*. London: HMSO.

Children's Bookseller, The (1998) Reader's Digest co-ventures, *The Children's Bookseller*, March: 29.

Children's Bookseller, The (1999) Preparing for now, *The Children's Bookseller*, March: 18–20.

Clee, N. (2000) Prospecting at Brighton, *The Bookseller*, 26 May: 32–4.

Cooper, H. (1989) *Homework*. White Plains, NY: Longman.

Cowan, R. and Hallam, S. (1999) *What Do We Know About Homework?* Viewpoint no. 9. London: Institute of Education.

Crawford, K. (1995) A history of the Right: the battle for control of National Curriculum history 1989–1994, *British Journal of Educational Studies*, 43(4): 433–56.

Crowther, B. (1999) The birds and the bees: narratives of sexuality in television natural history programmes, in D. Epstein and J.T. Sears (eds) *A Dangerous Knowing: Sexuality, Pedagogy and Popular Culture*. London: Cassell.

Cuban, L. (1986) *Teachers and Machines*. New York: Teachers College Press.

David, M., Edwards, R., Hughes, M. and Ribbens, J. (1993) *Mothers and Education: Inside Out: Exploring Family – Education Policy and Experience*. London: Routledge.

David, R.G. (2000) Imagining the past: the use of archive pictures in secondary school history textbooks, *The Curriculum Journal*, 11(2): 225–46.

Del Vecchio, G. (1997) *Creating Ever-Cool: A Marketer's Guide to a Kid's Heart*. Gretna, LA: Pelican.

Department for Education and Employment (1997) *Excellence in Schools*, Cm. 3681. London: HMSO.

Department for Education and Employment (1998a) *Extending Opportunity: A National Framework for Study Support*. London: DfEE.

Department for Education and Employment (1998b) *The Learning Age: a Renaissance for a New Britain*, Cm. 3790. London: DfEE.

Department for Education and Employment (1998c) *Meeting the Childcare Challenge*. London: DfEE.

Department for Education and Employment (2000) Parents get a bigger say in education. Press notice, September.

Douglas, J. (1967) *The Home and the School*. St Albans: Panther.

Duke, N.K. and Kays, J. (1998) 'Can I say "once upon a time?"': Kindergarten children developing knowledge of information book language, *Early Childhood Quarterly*, 13: 295–318.

Duxbury, S. (1987) Childcare ideologies and resistance: the manipulative strategies of pre-school children, in A. Pollard (ed.) *Children and their Primary Schools*. Basingstoke: Falmer.

Edwards, R. (1997) *Changing Places: Flexibility, Lifelong Learning and a Learning Society*. London: Routledge.

Elkind, D. (1981) *The Hurried Child: Growing up Too Fast Too Soon*. Reading, MA: Addison Wesley.

Ellsworth, E. (1997) *Teaching Positions: Difference, Pedagogy and the Power of Address*. New York: Teachers College Press.

Foster, S.J. (1998) Politics, parallels and perennial curriculum questions: the battle over school history in England and the United States, *The Curriculum Journal*, 9(2): 153–64.

Furlong, A. and Cartmel, F. (1997) *Young People and Social Change: Individualization and Risk in Late Modernity*. Buckingham: Open University Press.

Gewirtz, S., Ball, S. and Bowe, R. (1995) *Markets, Choice and Equity in Education*. Buckingham: Open University Press.

Giacquinta, J., Bauer, J. and Levin, J. (1993) *Beyond Technology's Promise*. Cambridge: Cambridge University Press.

Hallam, S. and Cowan, R. (1998) Is homework important for increasing educational attainment? Unpublished paper, Institute of Education, University of London.

Halsey, A.H., Heath, A.F. and Ridge, J.M. (1980) *Origins and Destinations: Family, Class, and Education in Modern Britain*. Oxford: Clarendon Press.

Harris, S. (1999) Secondary school students' use of computers at home, *British Journal of Educational Technology*, 30(4): 331–9.

Heath, S.B. (1983) *Ways with Words: Language, Life and Work in Communities and Classrooms*. Cambridge: Cambridge University Press.

Hilton, M. (ed.) (1996) *Potent Fictions*. London: Routledge.

Home, A. (1995) The public television view, *Metro Education*, Special World Summit Edition, 5: 21–9.

Home Office (1998) *Supporting Families: A Consultation Document*. London: HMSO.

Horn, C. (1997a) Balancing the books, *The Children's Bookseller*, September: 14–16.

Horn, C. (1997b) Leisure shopping for kids, *The Children's Bookseller*, September: 18–20.

Horn, C. (1998a) Sending the piggies to market, *The Children's Bookseller*, March: 8–10.

Horn, C. (1998b) The commitment to sell, *The Children's Bookseller*, September: 22–3.

Horn, C. (2000) Hodder makes the most of new opportunities, *The Bookseller*, 21 January: 35.

Huggins, M. (1996) An analysis of the rationales for learning history given by children and teachers at Key Stage 2, *The Curriculum Journal*, 7(3): 307–21.

Jones, K. and Hatcher, R. (eds) (1996) *Education after the Conservatives: The Response to the New Agenda of Reform*. Stoke-on-Trent: Trentham Books.

Jowett, S. (1990) Working with parents: a study of policy and practice, *Early Child Development and Care*, 58: 45–50.

Kean, D. (2000) Waterstone's clash with indies, *The Bookseller*, 3 November: 6.

Kenway, J. and Bullen, E. (2001) *Consuming Children: Education – Entertainment – Advertising*. Buckingham: Open University Press.

Kinder, M. (1991) *Playing with Power in Movies, Television and Video Games: From Muppet Babies to Teenage Mutant Ninja Turtles*. Berkeley: University of California Press.

Kline, S. (1993) *Out of the Garden: Toys and Children's Culture in the Age of TV Marketing*. London: Verso.

Kralovec, E. and Buell, J. (2000) *The End of Homework: How Homework Disrupts Families, Overburdens Children, and Limits Learning*. Boston: Beacon Press.

Kress, G. and van Leeuwen, T. (1996) *Reading Images: The Grammar of Visual Design*. London: Routledge.

Lareau, A. (1989) *Home Advantage: Social Class and Parental Involvement in Element-ary Education.* London: Falmer.

Laurillard, D. (1987) Computers and emancipation of students: giving control to the learner, *Instructional Science,* 16(1): 3–18.

Laurillard, D. (1995) Multimedia and the changing experience of the learner, *British Journal of Educational Technology,* 26(3): 179–89.

Laurillard, D., Stratfold, M., Luckin, R., Plowman, L. and Taylor, J. (2000) Affordances for learning in a non-linear narrative medium, *Journal of Interactive Media in Education,* 2: 1–17.

Lee, P., Dickinson, A. and Ashby, R. (1996) Children making sense of history, *Education 3–13,* 24(1): 13–19.

Livingstone, S. and Bovill, M. (1999) *Young People, New Media.* London: London School of Economics and Political Science.

Luke, C. (1989) *Pedagogy, Printing and Protestantism: The Discourse on Childhood.* Albany, NY: SUNY Press.

MacLure, M. and Elliott, J. (1992) Packaging the primary curriculum: textbooks and the English National Curriculum, *Curriculum Journal,* 4(1): 91–107.

Maw, J. (1991) Ethnocentrism, history textbooks and teaching strategies: present-ing the USSR, *Research Papers in Education,* 6(3): 153–69.

McAleavy, T. (1998) The use of sources in school history 1910–1998: a critical perspective, *Teaching History,* 91: 10–16.

McCabe, D. (1997) Children's bookselling comes of age, *The Children's Bookseller,* March: 12–14.

McPartland, M. (1998) The use of narrative in geography teaching, *The Curric-ulum Journal,* 9(3): 341–55.

Meek, M. (1996) *Information and Book Learning.* Stroud: Thimble Press.

Merttens, R. and Vass, G. (eds) (1992) *Ruling the Margins: Problematising Parental Involvement* Submitted conference papers, University of North London/Impact project.

Millard, E. (1997) *Differently Literate: Boys, Girls and the Schooling of Literacy.* London: Falmer.

Millard, E. and Marsh, J. (2001) Sending Minnie the Minx home: comics and reading choices, *Cambridge Journal of Education,* 31(1): 25–38.

Moorhead, J. (2001) Tutor age, *Guardian Education,* 7 August.

Mortimore, P. and Whitty, G. (1997) *Can School Improvement Overcome the Effects of Disadvantage?* London: Institute of Education.

National Center for Education Statistics (2000) *The Condition of Education 2000.* Washington, DC: US Government Printing Office.

Nichols, B. (1981) *Ideology and the Image.* Bloomington: Indiana University Press.

Nixon, H. (1998) Fun and games are serious business, in J. Sefton-Green (ed.) *Digital Diversions: Youth Culture in the Age of Multimedia.* London: UCL Press.

Office for Standards in Education (2000) *Family Learning: A Survey of Current Practice.* London: Ofsted.

Office for National Statistics (2000) *Family Spending: A Report on the 1999–2000 Family Expenditure Survey.* London: Stationery Office.

Olson, D.R. (1980) On the language and authority of textbooks, *Journal of Com-munication,* 30: 186–96.

Osler, A. (1994) Still hidden from history? The representation of women in re-cently published history textbooks, *Oxford Review of Education,* 20(2): 219–35.

Papadakis, M.C. (2001) *The Application and Implications of Information Technologies in the Home: Where Are the Data and What Do They Say?* Arlington, VA: National Science Foundation.

Papert, S. (1996) *The Connected Family.* Atlanta: Longstreet Press.

Plowden, B. (1987) Plowden twenty years on, *Oxford Review of Education*, 13(1): 119–25.

Plowman, L. (1996a) Designing interactive multimedia for schools, *Information Design Journal*, 8(3): 258–66.

Plowman, L. (1996b) Narrative, interactivity and the secret world of multimedia, *English and Media Magazine*, 35: 44–8.

Qualifications and Curriculum Authority (2000) *Curriculum Guidance for the Foundation Stage.* London: QCA.

Reay, D. (1998) *Class Work: Mothers' Involvement in Their Children's Primary Schooling.* London: UCL Press.

Rickett, J. (2000) Mere pawns in the game? *The Bookseller*, 25 February: 26–8.

Robertson, J. (1998) Paradise lost: children, multimedia and the myth of interactivity, *Journal of Computer Assisted Learning*, 14: 31–9.

Rose, J. (1984) *The Case of Peter Pan: Or The Impossibility of Children's Fiction.* London: Macmillan.

Sanderson, C. (1999) A studious business, *Back to School Bookseller*, 18 June: 14–15.

Schlesinger, K. (1999) *Book Retailing in Britain.* London: Bookseller Publications.

Sefton-Green, J. and Parker, D. (1999) *Edit-Play: How Children Use Edutainment Software to Tell Stories.* London: British Film Institute.

Seiter, E. (1993) *Sold Separately: Parents and Children in Consumer Culture.* New Brunswick, NJ: Rutgers University Press.

Sharp, J. (1991) History from below, in P. Burke (ed.) *New Perspectives on Historical Writing.* Cambridge: Polity.

Sims, R. (1997) Interactivity: a forgotten art?, *Computers in Human Behavior*, 13(2): 157–80.

Smith, R.S. (1995) Young children's interpretations of gender from visual text and narrative, *Linguistics and Education*, 7: 303–25.

Sylvester, D. (1994) Change and continuity in history teaching 1900–93, in H. Bourdillon (ed.) *Teaching History.* London: Routledge.

Tizard, B. and Hughes, M. (1984) *Young Children Learning.* London: Fontana.

Tizard, B., Blatchford, P., Burke, J., Farquhar, C. and Plewis, I. (1988) *Young Children at School in the Inner City.* London: Lawrence Erlbaum.

Toomey, D.M. (1989) How home–school relations policies can increase educational inequality, *Australian Journal of Education*, 37(3): 284–98.

Urwin, C. (1985) Constructing motherhood: the persuasion of normal development, in C. Steedman, C. Urwin and V. Walkerdine (eds) *Language, Gender and Childhood.* London: Routledge & Kegan Paul.

van de Kopple, W.J. and Crismore, A. (1990) Readers' reactions to hedges in a science textbook, *Linguistics and Education*, 2: 303–22.

Wade, B. and Moore, M. (2000) *Baby Power: Give Your Child Real Learning Power.* London: Egmont.

Walkerdine, V. and Lucey, H. (1989) *Democracy in the Kitchen.* London: Virago.

Weinberger, J. (1996) *Literacy Goes to School: The Parents' Role in Young Children's Literacy Learning.* London: Paul Chapman.

Wellington, J. (2001) Exploring the secret garden: the growing importance of ICT in the home, *British Journal of Educational Technology*, 32(2): 233–44.

Wells, G. (1987) *The Meaning Makers: Children Learning Language and Using Language to Learn*. London: Hodder and Stoughton.

Wernick, A. (1991) *Promotional Culture: Advertising, Ideology and Personal Expression*. London: Sage.

Weston, P. (1999) *Homework: Learning from Practice*. London: Ofsted.

Wignell, P. (1994) Genre across the curriculum, *Linguistics and Education*, 6: 355–72.

Willis, S. (1999) Imagining dinosaurs, in B. Lyon Clark and M.R. Higonnett (eds) *Girls, Boys, Books, Toys: Gender in Children's Literature*. Baltimore, MD: Johns Hopkins University Press.

Wolfendale, S. (1983) *Parental Participation in Children's Development and Education*. New York: Gordon and Breach.

INDEX